The
ENCYCLOPEDIA
of FLOWERS

Text and photography by Derek Fell

JG
PRESS

A FRIEDMAN GROUP BOOK

© 1995 by Michael Friedman Publishing Group, Inc.

Published in the USA 1995 by JG Press
Distributed by World Publications, Inc.

The JG Press imprint is a trademark of
JG Press, Inc.
455 Somerset Avenue
NorthDighton, MA 02764

ISBN 1-57215-096-3

THE ENCYCLOPEDIA OF FLOWERS
was prepared and produced by
Michael Friedman Publishing Group, Inc.
15 West 26th Street
New York, New York 10010

Editor: Elizabeth Viscott Sullivan
Art Director: Jeff Batzli
Designer: Susan E. Livingston
Photography Director: Christopher C. Bain

Typeset by Classic Type, Inc.
Color separations by Colourmatch Graphic Equipment
Printed in China by Leefung-Asco Printers Ltd.

For Carolyn

Acknowledgments

I owe a great debt of gratitude to the many property owners who allowed me to photograph their gardens; unfortunately, they are too numerous to single out. For help in compiling this volume, I must also thank Carolyn Heath, to whom this book is dedicated, not only for her warm friendship and cheerful support, but also for cross-checking my first draft manuscript. Also, thanks to Peggy Fisher, for her help in researching many of the entries, and to Kathy Nelson, my administrative assistant, and Wendy Fields, my grounds supervisor at Cedaridge Farm, who were invaluable in helping me meet deadlines by efficiently typing my scribbled notes and organizing my picture selections.

Introduction

According to biographer Emile Ludwig, the final miracle wrought by Napoleon was a beautiful flower garden—created during his last years of exile on the remote, windswept island of St. Helena—to relieve boredom and raise the spirits of his staff. He had always been fond of gardens, finding in them both privacy and inspiration to fuel his ambitions. His empress, Josephine, established one of the most important collections of roses in the world at the couple's romantic home, Malmaison, near Paris. Even the British Navy had orders not to impound shipments of plants destined for her garden if apprehended on the high seas.

Sir Joseph Banks, a wealthy sponsor of Captain James Cook's voyages of exploration—the greatest voyages of discovery ever conducted on the face of the earth—was fired with enthusiasm for the trips as a result of his passion for botany and the prospect of finding many new plants for the Royal Garden of Kew. Indeed, the three voyages of circumnavigation did yield many botanical treasures and started a passion for plant exploration among the British that extended to all areas of the world, including the great wildflower concentrations of the mist-shrouded Himalaya mountains, the valleys of northwest Africa and Namaqualand, the plains of Texas, and the California hills.

The great Rothschild banking family also had a love of flowers; they created some of the world's most beautiful gardens in England and France. With these new plant discoveries, British aristocracy even financed the hybridizing of vast collections of rhododendrons, camellias, and magnolias. Similarly, in the United States, the Du Pont family (who were of French descent) created some equally fantastic flower gardens, particularly the extensive woodland and meadow garden of Winterthur in Delaware and the sumptuous display garden of Longwood in Pennsylvania, where Pierre S. Du Pont, former chairman of General Motors as well as of the Du Pont Company, established what has been described as a "horticultural Disneyland," with numerous theme gardens and almost seven acres (2.8ha) of plants under glass.

Flower gardens have not only provided visual pleasure and relief from stress in an increasingly machine-oriented world, they have inspired prominent artists and photographers. The French Impressionist painter Claude Monet and his lifelong friend Pierre-Auguste Renoir both established beautiful flower gardens, which they immortalized in their paintings. Monet established an elaborate flower garden north of Paris, where he used flowers in great monochromatic sweeps like daubs of paint on a canvas. This style of garden is known as *Clos Normand* (Normandy garden) and consists mostly of annuals, perennials, and flowering bulbs similar to the English cottage garden style popularized by English painter/photographer Gertrude Jekyll and prolific Victorian garden writer William Robinson. Both Jekyll and Robinson wrote popular garden books that rejected the highly formal type of flower gardening known as carpet-bedding, where large uniform plantings of mostly flowering annuals were established in garish color combinations inside geometric beds.

Monet also established an elaborate water garden as his pictorial ideal. This garden was actually an interpretation of the stroll gardens depicted in Japanese woodcuts and scroll paintings. Monet planted the surface of a pond with islands of colorful perennial water lilies, while a path around the perimeter of the pond threaded through beds of peonies, iris, and daylilies and over an arched footbridge overhung with a canopy of fragrant white and blue wisteria. Languid weeping willows draped their leaves into the water, and dense clumps of hardy bamboo provided exquisite backgrounds to the flower beds. All of this can be seen today in a superb restoration of the nine-acre (3.6ha) garden, thanks to contributions made mostly by North American art patrons.

Renoir, on the other hand, favored a more natural garden. He encouraged native wildflowers (especially poppies and lavender) to flower throughout an old olive orchard he purchased near Nice on the Côte d'Azur, within sight of the Mediterranean. He even admonished his gardeners for mowing too often, as he liked indigenous oat grasses to form decorative clumps, their beautiful flower plumes glowing golden when lit from the back by the sun. Renoir's nine-acre garden, *Les Collettes*, is also open to the public.

In North America, off the coast of Maine, on Appledore Island in the Isles of Shoals, Impressionist painter Childe Hassam immortalized the tiny but intensively planted cutting garden of author Celia Thaxter by painting the garden each summer. He also illustrated her exquisite memoir about the garden, *An Island Garden*. Although the cottage Thaxter lived in is no longer there, each summer the restored garden attracts hundreds of visitors who willingly pay a $25.00 entrance fee and take an $11.00 ferry ride to have a glimpse of the fifteen-by-fifty-foot (4.6-by-15.2m) plot that inspired such beautiful paintings, lyrical poetry, and vivid writing.

My own garden, Cedaridge Farm, is a photography garden, a twenty-four-acre (9.7ha) property where I create planting schemes for the sole purpose of making beautiful photographic compositions. Taking inspiration from planting ideas gleaned from my travels worldwide, I grow masses of cutting flowers to make indoor floral arrangements. I also grow a large assortment of everlasting flowers to make long-lasting wreaths and other dried arrangements.

I highly value fragrance and take special care to grow tall stands of sweet peas and huge pendant, honey-scented trumpets of the spectacular hybrid datura 'Charles Grimaldi'. Too tender to remain outdoors after frost, this repeat-flowering woody plant is grown in clay pots and

My cutting garden at Cedaridge Farm features black-eyed Susans (*Rudbeckia fulgida*), shown here in the foreground, and mixed annuals.

spends the winter indoors. Billowing old-fashioned lilacs and shrubby antique roses also pervade the air with their haunting fragrances.

Furthermore, each plant at Cedaridge is evaluated ruthlessly to determine whether it is worth the space in the garden. The earliest flowers to bloom are white nodding snowdrops, dwarf blue iris, iridescent yellow aconites, and freckled Lenten roses in white and pink. But the best early display is from a choice collection of daffodils planted in bold drifts at the edges of the property; these are followed by brilliant displays of tulips, with a heavy emphasis on wild species and 'Fosteriana' hybrids flaunting huge, shimmering, water lily–like blossoms. Spanish bluebells—lavishly planted in shady beds—complement heart-leaf hostas and frilly ferns.

Among my favorite perennials are tall, stately hollyhocks, particularly in mahogany shades, and various kinds of iris, mostly in blue and purple, especially the German, Siberian, and Japanese varieties. I have also planted bold clumps of poppies, particularly the gigantic oriental varieties, and daylilies in a rainbow of colors, some with flowers the size of Christmas amaryllis. There

are also six vivid colors of beebalm in the mixed perennial borders, plus a large assortment of daisylike members of the family Compositae. These include oxeye daisies, wonderful companions to Siberian iris, and the brilliant yellow, floriferous, sterile hybrid rudbeckia 'Goldsturm' and its near relative, the purple coneflower (together, the rudbeckia and coneflower are flamboyant summer companions). Spirelike foxgloves reseed themselves in every shady bed with such profusion that there is hardly a month from late spring to autumn frost when they are not in bloom. Almost a trademark of the garden is *Sedum spectabile,* but not the long-lasting sterile hybrid 'Autumn Joy' favored by so many perennial experts. I prefer the old-fashioned lighter pink variety, despite its briefer flowering period.

For shrubs, I favor berry-bearers, since they are decorative in bloom and, when laden with fruit clusters, attract songbirds. Large plantings of annual zinnias and marigolds help to attract butterflies. The large-flowered, hardy trumpet vine, 'Madame Galen', (hybridized by French nurserymen by crossing the hardy North American species *Campsis radicans* with the tender Chinese species, *C. grandiflora*) flowers all summer, attracting hummingbirds. Along the banks of a small pond and narrow stream, cardinal flowers not only attract hummingbirds, but also the look-alike hummingbird moth.

Autumn at Cedaridge produces an incredibly beautiful leaf display. In fact, many flowering shrubs such as fothergillas, amelanchiers, calycanthus, and Stewartstonian azaleas are chosen deliberately for their bonus of good autumn leaf coloring. In this season, mass plantings of chrysanthemums compete successfully, even with the vibrant foliage display of bright orange sugar maples and crimson Japanese maples. The gorgeous cushion-type chrysanthemums diminish only at the onset of freezing cold weather in November, when the rich red and gold carpet of leaves finally shrivels to parchment brown. At this time the leaf litter is collected into immense piles for decomposing into leaf mold. The mold is used to mulch flower beds for weed control and moisture retention, and to add humus to the soil as a conditioner.

The garden is groomed over winter. I continue to plant flowering bulbs until Christmas, when the ground finally freezes solid. I also prune trees and shrubs constantly, whether to create a shapely appearance or to rejuvenate the plants. I prune dense rosebushes and forsythia hedges to keep their sweeping limbs clear of the ground so that mulch and fertilizer (usually in the form of well-decomposed animal manure) can be piled around the plant stems.

At this time of dormancy, I do much planning indoors. I study seed and nursery catalogs and order new plants and seeds by mail. I consider each garden area individually; for example, for the cutting garden, I order many varieties from a cut-flower specialist; for the walled vegetable garden, I consult a vegetable seed catalog. I also buy bulbs from bulb specialists (although I always order new daffodil additions from a company that deals almost exclusively in daffodils). Garden magazines are a good place to find such specialist sources.

Winter is not only a time for reflection and advance planning. It is also a time to walk out onto the bare frosty ground or snow-covered landscape and decide where new beds and structures should be placed so that at the first sign of a spring thaw, tools can be sharpened and that humble product of nature, soil, turned over to start a new surge of gardening enthusiasm.

Of course, it is not within everyone's means to have a garden as lavish as Monet's or as ethereal as Renoir's, but almost everyone can fill their world with flowers by growing them on windowsills and patios or seeking out public gardens.

A DRIFT OF DAFFODILS BLOOMING THROUGH THE LAWN IN MONET'S GARDEN IS MADE POSSIBLE BY PEELING BACK THE TURF IN AUTUMN, PLANTING THE BULBS INTO AN ISLAND OF GOOD SOIL, THEN ROLLING BACK THE TURF.

This book is an encyclopedia of easy-to-grow flowering plants that seem to create consistently the most spectacular floral displays in relatively small gardens. Some may be familiar, others unusual, but all command attention whether you desire flowers for cutting, fragrance, or pure ornament. This volume is not a mass of varieties too numerous to digest, but a careful selection of flowers guaranteed to please, illustrated by realistic color pictures, many of them from my own gardens at Cedaridge Farm, that show exactly how the plants grow.

How Flowering Plants Are Classified

This book features flowering plants noted for garden display. Most are herbaceous plants, that is, annuals, perennials, and flowering bulbs with soft stems. A few are woody plants, which comprise trees and shrubs that develop a durable cell structure called wood. The trees and shrubs featured are mostly precocious-flowering (bloom at an early age); some, such as forsythia and amelanchiers, will flower the first year after planting a year-old rooted cutting. The best flower gardens feature both herbaceous plants and woody plants. Even a cutting garden grown primarily to provide flowers to create indoor arrangements will benefit from selected woody plants such as lilacs and hydrangeas.

(In describing the physical appearance of flowers, the terms single, double, and semidouble are used. Single flowers, such as daisies, have one layer of petals. Double flowers, such as pom-pom dahlias, have multiple layers, often causing them to look ball-shaped. Semidouble flowers have two layers of petals, as do many poppies.)

The easiest-to-grow flower garden will depend largely on annuals, which complete their life cycles in one year, that is, within a single growing season. Annuals sprout from seeds, grow leaves, flower, set new seeds, and die all in the space of a few months. Because their lives are so short relative to other plants, their flowers tend to be extremely colorful. Many annuals, such as marigolds and spider flowers, also have the ability to flower continuously all season—from spring until autumn frost.

A large number of annuals, such as calendulas and zinnias, can be grown from seeds sown directly into the garden. The seeds are large and easy to handle, and the plants bloom within a matter of weeks from outdoor sowing. Another group of annuals has tiny seeds and prefers to be started early from seeds sown indoors. Transplants are put out into the garden when they are large enough to be handled. Pansies and impatiens belong to this group that needs up to ten weeks to develop flowering-size transplants.

Some annuals, like poppies and cornflowers, are hardy, meaning they tolerate mild frost. Others, such as wax begonias and coleus, are tender and are killed by frost. The listings in the encyclopedia section of this book will tell you whether an annual is hardy or tender.

Annuals look best planted in a mass to create colorful beds and borders. Many annuals also look sensational when grouped in containers such as tubs and window boxes. You may also wish to mix annuals with perennials, as annuals maintain continuous color in the garden, while perennials come in and out of bloom according to their season.

Perennials generally take two years or more to flower. They live on indefinitely from year to year by means of vigorous root systems that remain dormant in the soil during freezing weather. Most perennials flower during a particular time of year, and the flowering display generally is not as long-lasting as that of many annuals.

Perennials do not normally produce such an intense floral display as annuals, but many, such as garden lilies and peonies, have a more sophisticated beauty. These flowers hold their heads above the level of many annuals and also provide textural interest with their leaf shapes and coloring.

Biennials are like perennials in that they take two years to bloom and grow only leaves the first year. But, unlike perennials, which may live on for many more years, biennials die after the second year. Sweet William and foxglove are good examples of biennials; these flowers set enormous amounts of seed, however, which frequently self-sows to ensure repeat flowering once a planting has been established. In this book, most biennials are grouped with annuals; the reason for this is that if biennials are sown early indoors, they usually will flower the first year.

Flowering bulbs are another special group of perennials with the ability to live on for many years. Flowering bulbs are plants that develop a swollen underground bulbous structure, sometimes known as a tuber, rhizome, or corm, depending on the bulb's composition. This structure is a storage organ containing enough food to allow the plant to survive long periods of cold or drought as well as to flower each year in a particular season. Some of the most common spring-flowering bulbs include daffodils and tulips; summer-flowering, dahlias and gladiolus; autumn-flowering, colchicums and sternbergias.

Like perennials, bulbs can be classified as hardy or tender. Some tender bulbs, like dahlias and gladiolus, will survive freezing winters in sheltered locations, especially if planted at twice the recommended depth. Extremely tender bulbs, such as amaryllis, clivias, and agapanthus, can be overwintered indoors in pots and then put outdoors in spring to bloom on decks, terraces, and patios after the danger of frost has passed.

Trees and shrubs grow more slowly than other plants because they require more time to develop their longer-lasting woody cell structure. However, many trees, such as the saucer magnolia and the flowering dogwood, and many shrubs, such as azaleas and wisteria, can produce an astonishing floral display. The main advantage of trees over herbaceous plants is their ability to carry color high into the sky, where they tower well above most annuals, perennials, and flowering bulbs. There is no botanical difference between a tree and a shrub, but gardeners tend to think of a shrub as any woody plant that stays under fifteen feet (4.6m) high and produces multiple stems. Trees, however, are capable of growing to more than fifteen feet and form one main trunk.

AN AVALANCHE OF ANNUAL POPPIES COVERS THE
SLOPES OF A MOUNTAIN IN MOROCCO.

Trees and shrubs can be classified as deciduous or evergreen. Deciduous trees and shrubs drop their leaves in winter and go dormant, and some of them offer the bonus of spectacular russet leaf colors in autumn. Evergreens are classified as being either broadleaf (hollies and rhododendrons) or needle (conifers). However, since conifers do not produce spectacular flowering displays, it's best to rely on broadleaf evergreen trees and shrubs for dramatic floral effects.

Pruning is very important to the flowering performance of trees and shrubs. It is imperative to thin out dense, tangled branches so that light and air can penetrate to the center of the plants. Occasionally, shrubs such as lilacs and forsythia will benefit from drastic pruning whereby the entire plant is cut back almost to the ground so that new growth can sprout from the old stumps.

Botanical Nomenclature

The plants in this encyclopedia are listed by botanical name because not all plants have familiar common names; some have several common names, and a few have the same or similar common names.

Despite the use of botanical names for identification, the descriptions are not given in botanical terminology; therefore, inflorescence is described as a flower cluster or a spike depending on its form. A pubescent leaf is described as downy, velvety, or hairy, depending on its texture.

In the scientific community, botanical names are assigned by taxonomists who work at botanical gardens or universities. Taxonomists follow the *International Code of Botanical Nomenclature* and, unfortunately, they keep changing botanical names. The familiar Madagascar periwinkle, for example, used to have the charming

botanical name of *Vinca rosea*, but taxonomists recently changed it to *Catharanthus roseus*. Similarly, the familiar sweet alyssum's botanical designation was changed from *Alyssum maritimum* to *Lobularia maritima*. Where confusion may occur, the listings in the encyclopedia will feature both the old and new botanical names.

Most plants have botanical names comprising two Latin words. The first word identifies the genus, a general group of closely related plants. The second word identifies the species, that is, a specific type within the genus. Thus *Cercis canadensis* identifies a redbud tree *(Cercis)* native to North America, while *Cercis chinensis* identifies a redbud native to China.

However, if a variation in a genus occurs in the wild species, a third word is added to the plant's name. For example, a white form of the redbud is known as *Cercis canadensis alba*; this is a natural variety because the variation occurred in the wild. However, when a variety occurs as a result of professional plant breeding or garden cultivation, the plant is called a cultivar (short for "cultivated variety"). It follows then that a bronze-leaf form of redbud developed professionally would receive the cultivar name 'Forest Pansy'.

When two species within a genus are crossed to produce a hybrid, the rules of nomenclature say that the species names of neither parent can be favored. A new Latin designation is given and an × is inserted between the genus name and the second name to denote that the plant is a hybrid. Thus, *Amelanchier × grandiflora* describes a hybrid between *Amelanchier laevis* and *Amelanchier canadensis*—two wild species native to North America.

Botanical names are always given in Latin. Usually, the name will either describe certain characteristics of the plant or honor the country where it originated or the person who first introduced it into cultivation. Thus, *Poncirus trifoliata* describes a citruslike plant that has leaves *(folia)* arranged in threes *(tri-)*. *Primula japonica* describes a primrose native to Japan, and *Pieris forrestii* identifies a particular type of andromeda discovered by the British plant explorer George Forrest.

It used to be that when botanical names honored a country or person they were capitalized, but in recent years the preferred style is to capitalize only the genus and cultivar names. The modern tendency is also to make no distinction between variety names and cultivar names. Thus, *Cercis canadensis alba* is often written *Cercis canadensis 'Alba'*, and the term "variety" is used to describe both natural varieties and cultivars.

Common names are given wherever a common name is known. Sometimes a common name in Europe (Judas tree) is different from a common name in North America (redbud), so both names are listed.

•

The following encyclopedia is divided into five main categories: annuals, perennials, bulbs, shrubs, and small trees. Literally thousands of plants were considered, but the criteria for inclusion was the plant's ready availability and its flowering effect. Hardy, easy-to-care-for varieties were also given precedence over tender or challenging ones.

Annuals

Ageratum houstonianum

Common Name:	Ageratum, flossflower
Flowers:	Native to Mexico. Flossy lavender, pink, blue, or white clusters.
Leaves:	Broad, oval, pointed, fuzzy, dark green.
Habit:	4″–12″ (10–31cm) tall. Compact, mounded.
Culture:	Prefers full sun in well-drained, humus-rich, moist soil. Tolerates light shade. Needs good air circulation. Propagate by seeds started indoors six to eight weeks before outdoor planting.
Season of Bloom:	All summer to frost.
Hardiness:	Tender annual killed by frost.
Uses:	Excellent for edging beds and borders.

An easy-care everblooming plant. Though most often grown as a low bedding plant, new tall triploid hybrid varieties—such as 'Blue Horizon'—are colorful as tall backgrounds and superb for cutting.

Alcea rosea

Common Name:	Hollyhock
Flowers:	Native to China. Single, double, and semi-double flowers borne on giant, robust spikes. Colors include white, red, rose, pink, and yellow.
Leaves:	Mostly three-lobed, hairy, serrated, medium green.
Habit:	4′–6′ (1.2–1.8m) tall. Upright, spirelike.
Culture:	Prefers full sun in well-drained, sandy or loam soil. Plants may need staking. Propagate by seeds or cuttings.
Season of Bloom:	Mid- to late summer.
Hardiness:	Hardy annual that tolerates heavy frost.
Uses:	Old-fashioned favorite. Dramatic accent plant. Place along walls, fences, and back of gardens.

Though many hollyhocks are true perennials, some are best grown as annuals, such as the 'Majorette' and 'Pinafore' varieties, which grow dwarf bushy plants and attractive semidouble flowers. 'Summer Carnival' is an award-winning tall hollyhock that will bloom the first year from seed, especially if the seed is started early indoors so that eight-week-old transplants can be transferred to the garden.

Amaranthus
caudatus

**Common
Name:**   Love-lies-bleeding

Flowers: Native to India. Cascading tassels of red
flowers stream fountainlike away from their
branches. Flowers are long-lasting and spruce
up fresh and dried bouquets.

Leaves: On erect spikes. Vibrant shades of carmine-
tinted green at the leaf base change to an
almost fluorescent red towards the leaf tip.

Habit: 36″–48″ (91–122cm) tall. Upright, branching.

Culture: Prefers full sun in well-drained, sandy or loam
soil. Easy to grow even in poor soil. Propagate
by seeds, direct-sown. Amaranths also
transplant easily.

**Season
of Bloom:**   June to frost.

Hardiness: Tender annual killed by frost.

Uses: Grown primarily for its showy floral strands,
which need to contrast with other late
summer-flowering plants, such as dahlias.
Abundant displays tend to overwhelm
surrounding plantings. Use as an accent in
mixed beds and borders.

A closely related species—*A. tricolor*—is widely grown
for its extremely colorful crown of arching leaves.
Commonly called Joseph's-coat, some varieties of
A. tricolor display red, yellow, and green coloring
all in the same leaf.

Antirrhinum
majus

**Common
Name:**   Common snapdragon

Flowers: Native to the Mediterranean region. Vertical
spikes surrounded by tubular florets, some
with closed throats ("dragon's mouth"), others
with open ("butterfly-flowered"). Colors
include white, yellow, orange, red, pink,
and bicolors.

Leaves: Narrow, lancelike, smooth, dark green.

Habit: Three sizes: smaller dwarf spreading varieties,
6″–9″ (15–23cm); intermediate, 18″–24″ (46–
61cm); and tall, 36″–48″ (91–122cm).

Culture: Prefers full sun or light shade in well-drained,
sandy or loam soil. Propagate by seeds started
indoors six to eight weeks before outdoor
planting.

**Season
of Bloom:**   Cool weather of late spring and again in late
summer.

Hardiness: Reasonably hardy annual that tolerates mild
frost.

Uses: Intermediates are the most popular garden
variety. Use the small ones for low plantings or
in front of borders. The tall varieties make
excellent cut flowers.

Though old-fashioned snapdragons such as the 'Topper'
and 'Rocket' have what is known as a "dragon's mouth,"
newer varieties (such as 'Madame Butterfly' hybrids)
have open throats, which tend to produce a more
spectacular floral display.

Arctotis stoechadifolia

Common Name:	African daisy
Flowers:	Native to South Africa. Daisylike flowers perched on a long stem that is prized in flower arrangements. However, the flowers do close their blossoms at night and on cloudy days. Colors include white, yellow, orange, pink, red, and bicolors.
Leaves:	Toothed, narrow, bright green.
Habit:	12″–24″ (31–61cm) tall. Upright, clump-forming.
Culture:	Easy to grow. Prefers cool nights and full sun during the day. Needs well-drained, fertile, sandy or loam soil. Propagate by seeds; best sown where plants are to bloom.
Season of Bloom:	June to frost.
Hardiness:	Tender annual killed by frost.
Uses:	Excellent for coastal gardens. Ideal for mixed beds and borders.

Flowers resemble the famous gerbera daisy, an expensive cut flower that is much more difficult to grow.

Begonia semperflorens

Common Name:	Wax begonia
Flowers:	Native to the Andes. Extremely free-flowering. Single or double four-petaled flowers in clusters of white, pink, or red that are always in bloom.
Leaves:	Round, glossy, waxy, from green to bronze, depending on the variety.
Habit:	Mostly 8″–12″ (20–31cm) tall. Compact, mounded. Taller varieties have a bushy appearance.
Culture:	Prefers partial shade in well-drained, moist, humus-rich soil. Newer varieties do well in full sun or partial shade and develop best foliage and flowers in full sun. Fertilize regularly. Propagate by seeds started ten weeks before outdoor planting or by cuttings.
Season of Bloom:	All summer.
Hardiness:	Tender annual killed by frost.
Uses:	Excellent for massing in beds and borders. Frequently used in containers and hanging baskets.

In selecting varieties, choose only hybrids since they are not only more vigorous and free-flowering but grow well in full sun. Standard varieties demand cool shade to flower well. Seeds are highly susceptible to damping-off disease, so it's almost always best to grow wax begonias from ready-grown transplants.

Bellis
perennis

Common Name:	English daisy
Flowers:	Native to Europe. Multiple, colorful, single or double daisy flowers are borne on short stalks arising from a rosette. Colors include white, pink, rose, and red.
Leaves:	Oval, hairy, serrated, green; form a rosette.
Habit:	6″–8″ (15–20cm) tall. Low, mounded.
Culture:	Easy to grow. Prefers full sun to light shade in well-drained, moist, humus-rich soil. Propagate by seeds or division.
Season of Bloom:	Spring. Enjoys cool weather.
Hardiness:	Hardy biennial that tolerates mild frost; generally grown as an annual.
Uses:	Suitable for massing in mixed beds and borders. Makes a good underplanting for bulbs.

Though strictly biennials, growing foliage the first year and flowering the second season, English daisies are treated as annuals. Seed is best sown in late summer and the plants held over winter in cold frames for planting out into permanent flowering positions in early spring. 'Goliath Mixed' has flowers up to 3″ (7.5cm) across.

Borago
officinalis

Common Name:	Borage, talewort
Flowers:	Native to the Mediterranean region. Lovely, drooping, pink and blue star-shaped flowers are supported on fuzzy stems. Leaves and flowers taste like cucumber. Flowers attract bees.
Leaves:	Hairy, bluish green.
Habit:	24″–36″ (61–91cm) tall. Spreading.
Culture:	Prefers full sun in light, dry, poor soil. Propagate by seeds; will reseed.
Season of Bloom:	Spring to midsummer.
Hardiness:	Tender annual killed by frost.
Uses:	Attractive in an herb garden. The pretty flowers can be used to decorate cakes. Scrape hair off leaves before adding them to salads and drinks.

Popular for planting at the edge of beds and borders to create an informal effect, since plants have a tendency to droop, spilling over into lawn areas and onto pathways in an appealing, carefree manner.

Brachycome
iberidifolia

**Common
Name:**   Swan River daisy

Flowers: Native to Australia. Abundant clusters of
fragrant 1″ (2.5cm) daisylike blooms in white,
blue, rose, or violet.

Leaves: Narrow, toothed, medium green.

Habit: 12″ (31cm) tall. Bushy, mounded.

Culture: Prefers full sun in moist, rich, fertile, sandy or
loam soil. Propagate by seeds started indoors
eight weeks before outdoor planting.

**Season
of Bloom:**   June to frost.

Hardiness: Hardy annual that tolerates mild frost.

Uses: Good edging in mixed beds and borders and
in terrace planters. Beautiful accent in rock
gardens.

Most Swan River daisies are sold as mixtures. A very
fine exception is the variety 'Purple Splendor',
producing masses of deep purple-blue flowers with
contrasting golden yellow centers.

Browallia
speciosa

**Common
Name:**   Bush violet

Flowers: Native to South America. Clusters of tubular
blue, violet, or white flowers blanket this
compact plant.

Leaves: Narrow, oval, pointed, light green.

Habit: 12″–15″ (31–38cm) tall. Bushy, mounded.

Culture: Flourishes in partial shade in moist,
moderately rich soil. Propagate by seeds
started indoors ten weeks before outdoor planting. Cut back plants to desired size before
bringing them indoors.

**Season
of Bloom:**   Early to late summer. For winter blooms, grow
in pots on a sunny windowsill.

Hardiness: Tender annual killed by frost.

Uses: Popular in window boxes and hanging baskets
as well as massed plantings in shady beds.

'Blue Bells Improved'—a beautiful bright blue cultivar—
is especially good to grow cascading from shady window
boxes and hanging baskets.

Calceolaria integrifolia

Common Name: Pocketbook flower

Flowers: Native to South America. Canary yellow pouch-shaped flowers ½″ (13mm) across, borne in dense clusters.

Leaves: Heart-shaped, serrated, dark green.

Habit: To 12″ (31cm) tall. Bushy.

Culture: Prefers full sun in well-drained, sandy or loam soil. Best grown from seeds started indoors eight weeks before outdoor planting.

Season of Bloom: Summer; flowers best when summers are cool.

Hardiness: Moderately hardy annual killed by severe frost.

Uses: Massing in beds and borders. Good in containers, especially window boxes.

(Pictured above is a free-flowering hybrid, 'Sunshine', in a mixed bed of annuals.)

Calendula officinalis

Common Name: Pot marigold, calendula

Flowers: Native to northern Africa. Daisylike heads of single or double pale flowers. Flowering slows in midsummer heat, resumes in autumn. Colors include yellow, orange, and apricot.

Leaves: Lancelike, medium green; sticky and aromatic.

Habit: 12″–30″ (31–76cm) tall. Sprawling, branching.

Culture: Prefers full sun in well-drained, moist, fertile, sandy or loam soil during cool growing weather. Propagate by seeds, direct-sown.

Season of Bloom: Early summer to autumn.

Hardiness: Hardy annual that tolerates mild frost.

Uses: Popular in drifts in mixed beds and borders and in containers. Good cut flower.

The Dutch-bred variety, 'Fiesta Gitano' (meaning "gypsy festival"), is an especially fine mixture, having won a Fleuroselect award for its compact, 12″ (31cm) habit and large double flowers with dark centers.

Callistephus chinensis

Common Name: China aster

Flowers: Native to China. Daisy- or chrysanthemum-like double and semidouble flowers in white, yellow, pink, red, blue, and purple.

Leaves: Lancelike, toothed, green.

Habit: 12″–36″ (31–91cm) tall. Leggy, branching.

Culture: Grows in full sun or light shade in a wide range of well-drained soils. Propagate by seeds, direct-sown.

Season of Bloom: Bloom period is four weeks long. For summer-long blooms, purchase early, midseason, and late-summer flowering varieties or stagger sowings.

Hardiness: Tender annual killed by severe frost.

Uses: Cut flower or bedding plant.

The low-growing, cushionlike 'Dwarf Queen' asters can be used for edging and containers. Long-stemmed kinds are preferred for backgrounds and cutting. When tall asters are in peak bloom, the entire plant can be cut to create an instant bouquet.

Campanula medium

Common Name: Canterbury-bells

Flowers: Native to southern Europe. Plants grow erect stems clustered with gorgeous, nodding, bell-shaped flowers up to 2″ (5cm) across, mostly in white, blue, and pink.

Leaves: Spear-shaped, wavy, light green.

Habit: Up to 48″ (122cm) tall. Upright, spirelike.

Culture: Prefers full sun, cool nights, and moist but well-drained, fertile loam soil. Direct-sow in June for extra-early blooms the following spring. Some varieties may be grown as annuals started indoors twelve weeks before outdoor planting.

Season of Bloom: Early summer.

Hardiness: Hardy biennials and annuals, depending on variety. Overwinters in zones 5–8.

Uses: Good tall accent in mixed beds and borders. Excellent for cutting.

The above photograph shows plants combined with an edging of sweet Williams and foxgloves.

Catharanthus roseus

Common Name: Madagascar periwinkle

Flowers: Native to Madagascar. Starlike flowers with dark red centers. Colors include white, pink, rose, and salmon.

Leaves: Oval, pointed, glossy, dark green.

Habit: 6″–18″ (15–46cm) tall. Mounded.

Culture: Prefers full sun or partial shade in any well-drained soil. Tolerates city pollution and stress from heat, humidity, and drought. Dislikes overwatering and cool soil. Propagate by seeds started indoors six weeks before outdoor planting, or take cuttings.

Season of Bloom: All summer until autumn frost.

Hardiness: Tender annual killed by frost.

Uses: Popular massed as a ground cover in beds and borders. Also used as a trailing plant in containers and hanging baskets.

Periwinkles offer a nonstop flowering display. Dwarf kinds are excellent for edging. Plants thrive in difficult-to-plant places such as the edge of parking lots.

Celosia cristata

Common Name: Cockscomb

Flowers: Native to Africa. The crested types have flower heads that resemble a rooster's comb. The plume varieties resemble a bunch of feathers. Colors include yellow, orange, gold, pink, and red.

Leaves: Pointed, lancelike, in shades of yellow-green, deep green, or bronze, depending on variety.

Habit: 6″–48″ (15–122cm) tall. Upright spikes, bushy.

Culture: Prefers full sun in well-drained, fertile, loam soil. Propagate by seeds, direct-sown, since plants resent transplanting.

Season of Bloom: All summer. If old flowers are removed, smaller ones appear until frost.

Hardiness: Tender annual killed by frost.

Uses: Good for massing in beds and borders. Excellent in freshly cut or dried flower arrangements.

The cultivar 'Toreador' is extremely large-flowered with individual combs up to 10″ (25cm) across. All celosias are extremely sensitive to root disturbance and resent transplanting or any check in growth. Either sow seed directly where plants are to bloom after all danger of frost has passed, or start in peat pots that can be transplanted with just the bottom removed to minimize root disturbance and transplant shock.

Centaurea
cyanus

Common Name:	Bachelor's-button, cornflower
Flowers:	Native to Europe. Delicate heads of almost translucent doubled flowers on slender stems. Colors include sky blue, purple, pink, rose, and red.
Leaves:	Narrow, toothed, woolly, silver-gray.
Habit:	12"–36" (31–91cm) tall. Upright, wiry.
Culture:	Prefers full sun in well-drained, fertile, sandy or loam soil. Tolerates light shade, drought, and impoverished soil. Propagate by seeds, direct-sown; will reseed.
Season of Bloom:	Peaks in late spring and early summer, then blooms intermittently throughout the summer. May rebloom in autumn.
Hardiness:	Hardy annual that tolerates mild frost.
Uses:	Its beautiful blue color makes an excellent contrast against muted and red flower colors when massed in mixed beds and borders. Although the weak stems can cause droopiness in floral displays, it is used as a cut flower.

An excellent companion plant to Shirley poppies. The two are often combined in wildflower meadow mixes and look sensational blooming at the same time, especially when the wildflower mixture uses mostly blue varieties of *Centaurea* and red varieties of Shirley poppies.

Chrysanthemum
carinatum

Common Name:	Tricolor chrysanthemum
Flowers:	Native to northern Africa. Single or double daisylike flowers with contrasting rings next to a dark center tinted bronze or silver. Colors include white, pink, yellow, and red.
Leaves:	Feathery, deeply toothed, dark green.
Habit:	24"–36" (61–91cm) tall. Upright.
Culture:	Prefers full sun in well-drained, reasonably fertile soil. Propagate by seeds, direct-sown.
Season of Bloom:	Late spring to early summer. Prefers cool nights to bloom spectacularly. Cut plants back after flowering for late-season bloom.
Hardiness:	Reasonably hardy annual that tolerates mild frost.
Uses:	Popular in mixed beds and borders. Good cut flower. First chrysanthemum species to bloom.

A good flowering plant for cool coastal areas. 'Court Jesters' is an especially colorful mixture.

Clarkia
amoena

Common Name: Godetia, satin flower

Flowers: Native to California. Crinkled, shimmering, bell-like flowers. Colors include white, pink, red, lavender, and bicolors.

Leaves: Narrow, pointed, medium green.

Habit: 10"–30" (51–76cm) tall. Bushy.

Culture: Prefers full sun in well-drained, sandy or loam soil. Propagate by seeds, direct-sown. In mild-winter areas, seed may be sown outdoors in early autumn for extra-early spring blooms.

Season of Bloom: Midsummer to autumn. Flowers best during cool weather.

Hardiness: Hardy annual that tolerates mild frost.

Uses: Excellent in coastal gardens. Good for massing in mixed beds and borders. Tall kinds suitable for cutting.

'Monarch Mixed' is an outstanding dwarf, compact mixture of uniform height (10" [25cm]). 'Firelight' (a bright crimson) and 'Sybil Sherwood' (a lovely lavender pink) are superb color selections.

Cleome
hasslerana

Common Name: Spider flower

Flowers: Native to South America. Large open clusters of globular pink, rose, violet, and white flowers with elongated seed pods that create a spidery effect.

Leaves: Fan-shaped, deeply indented, sticky, dark green.

Habit: 3'–5' (.9–1.5m) tall. Upright, branching.

Culture: Prefers full sun in well-drained, sandy or loam soil. Propagate by seeds, direct-sown or started indoors six weeks before outdoor planting.

Season of Bloom: Midsummer to frost.

Hardiness: Tender annual killed by frost.

Uses: An excellent backdrop for other plants (including perennials) in beds and borders. Good in flower arrangements.

A nonstop flowering display midsummer to frost. Though pink tends to be the most widely planted color, the white looks sensational against a background of evergreens. The white variety is also a popular component of all-white gardens.

Consolida ambigua

Common Name:	Rocket larkspur
Flowers:	Native to southern Europe. Upright spikes of showy, delicate, many-petaled flowers in shades of blue and pink, plus white.
Leaves:	Feathery, medium green.
Habit:	36″ (91cm) tall. Upright spikes.
Culture:	Prefers full sun in cool locations, light shade in hot areas. Thrives in well-drained, humus-rich, sandy or loam soil. Propagate by seeds, direct-sown.
Season of Bloom:	Early to midsummer.
Hardiness:	Hardy annual that tolerates severe frost.
Uses:	A popular background plant massed in mixed beds and borders or along walls and fences. Good for floral arrangements.

Though the flowering display is generally brief, lasting perhaps two weeks in early summer, a massed bed of mixed larkspur can look sensational. They are particularly good to use in cutting gardens. Generally, best results are obtained from seeding in late summer and early autumn so plants bloom in late spring.

Coreopsis tinctoria

Common Name:	Calliopsis
Flowers:	Native to North America. Mostly single daisy-like flowers are supported on long, slender stems. Color ranges from gold and orange to red, plus bicolors, surrounding a dark center.
Leaves:	Delicate, narrow, bright green.
Habit:	12″–36″ (31–91cm) tall. Mounded, branching.
Culture:	Prefers full sun in well-drained, sandy or loam soil. One of the easiest plants to propagate by seeds, direct-sown.
Season of Bloom:	All summer.
Hardiness:	Hardy annual that tolerates severe frost.
Uses:	Brings brilliant color to mixed beds and borders. Good cut flower.

Both dwarf and tall types are available. The dwarf varieties make a good edging plant, while the tall kinds are a popular component in meadow wildflower mixtures. The tall varieties are old-fashioned flowers that mix well with cosmos, Shirley poppies, and four-o'clocks for an informal cottage garden appearance. Plants resent any root disturbance and are best seeded directly into the garden at two-week intervals so there is a succession of bloom.

Cosmos
bipinnatus

Common Name: Cosmos

Flowers: Native from southwestern United States to tropical America. Dainty single or double daisylike flowers up to 3″ (7.5cm) across nod with the slightest breeze on tall, upright, wiry stems. Colors include white, pink, rose, and crimson.

Leaves: Delicate, lacy, bright green.

Habit: 3′–5′ (.9–1.5m) tall. Upright, bushy, with an open, branching appearance.

Culture: Easy to grow. Prefers full sun in well-drained, sandy or loam soil. Propagate by seeds, direct-sown. Reseeds readily.

Season of Bloom: All summer.

Hardiness: Hardy annual that tolerates mild frost.

Uses: Delightful planted in the back of beds and mixed borders or along a fence in the vegetable or cutting garden.

Cosmos prefer to be direct-seeded where plants are to bloom. Save some of the seed packet to make a late sowing in mid-June so that plants reach peak bloom during autumn months. They are especially good in combination with perennial *Helianthus* and small-flowered annual sunflowers.

Cosmos
sulphureus

Common Name: Yellow cosmos

Flowers: Native to Mexico. Double and semidouble, serrated ray flowers in yellow, orange, or orange-red surrounding a yellow disc on many branched, open stems. Cut off faded flowers to encourage continuous flowering.

Leaves: Feathery, lancelike, dark green.

Habit: 18″–36″ (46–91cm) tall. Upright, bushy.

Culture: Easy to grow. Prefers full sun in well-drained, sandy or loam soil. Fertile soil produces more foliage than flowers. Propagate by seeds, direct-sown. May self-sow.

Season of Bloom: All summer.

Hardiness: Moderately hardy annual killed by severe frost.

Uses: Popular accent in mixed beds and borders and for containers. Good cut flower. Popular component of wildflower meadow mixtures.

'Lemon Twist', 'Sunny Gold', and 'Sunny Red' can be purchased as separate colors, though 'Lemon Twist' is the taller of the three (up to 30″ [76cm]). 'Ladybird Mixture' combines yellow, tangerine, and red of similar heights. All have good drought-resistance.

Dahlia ×
hybrida

**Common
Name:**   Bedding dahlia

Flowers: Native to Mexico. Bright, large, daisylike
heads with single or double petals grow
upright on strong, thin stalks. May require
staking. Flowers come in all colors except blue.
Prolific bloomer.

Leaves: Shiny, toothed, light green or bronze.

Habit: 12″–24″ (31–61cm) tall. Upright, bushy.

Culture: Prefers full sun and well-drained, fertile,
humus-rich soil. Propagate by seeds started
indoors six weeks before outdoor planting.

**Season
of Bloom:**   Late summer to frost.

Hardiness: Tender annual killed by frost.

Uses: Makes an excellent long-lasting cut flower.
Lovely massed in flower gardens or in mixed
beds. Dahlias will add a burst of color wherever
they are placed.

Many gardeners in areas with warm summers prefer
to start bedding dahlias late for transplanting in midsummer so that peak flowering occurs in autumn when
cool nights and reliable rainfall stimulate extra-heavy
flowering.

Delphinium
elatum

**Common
Name:**   English delphinium

Flowers: Native to Europe. Massive showy spikes are
surrounded with starlike, spurred flowers with
contrasting centers called a "bee." The bees
can be white or black. Most popular colors are
dark to light blue and white, but shades of
pink, purple, and yellow are also available.
May need staking.

Leaves: Broad, toothed, medium green.

Habit: 4′–6′ (1.2–1.8m) tall. Upright.

Culture: Prefers full sun in well-drained, moist, fertile
soil. Heavy feeder. Prefers a slightly alkaline
soil. Protect from strong winds. Propagate by
seeds, cuttings, or division. Start seeds
indoors eight weeks before outdoor planting.

**Season
of Bloom:**   Late spring to midsummer.

Hardiness: Hardy annual that tolerates mild frost.

Uses: A favorite old-fashioned flower massed in the
backgrounds of mixed beds or along fences.
Prized as a cut flower.

Delphiniums do not like hot summers and will burn up
in the heat. In order to obtain a worthwhile flowering
display by early summer, start delphiniums in late
summer and hold them in cold frames over winter for
transplanting to their permanent locations after the
soil warms in spring. The most spectacular delphinium
displays are in cool coastal regions.

Dianthus barbatus

Common Name: Sweet William

Flowers: Native to Europe. Fragrant single or double, flat-topped clusters of five-petaled flowers on upright stems. Colors include white, pink, rose, purple, violet, red, and bicolors. Cut back after flowering to encourage second crop of blooms in late summer.

Leaves: Lancelike, dark green.

Habit: 8″–20″ (20–51cm) tall. Mounded, spreading.

Culture: Easy to grow. Prefers full sun or light shade in well-drained, moist, fertile soil. Prefers light shade in hot areas. Propagate by seeds or cuttings. May self-sow if plants are not cut back.

Season of Bloom: May, June, and late summer.

Hardiness: Hardy biennial, some varieties best treated as hardy annuals (see note below).

Uses: Old-fashioned favorite. Popular in mixed beds, borders, edgings, rock gardens, and in containers. Attractive cut flower.

Though most sweet Williams are biennials, requiring two seasons to bloom, the varieties 'Wee Willie' and 'Red Monarch' will bloom within eight weeks from seed. 'Wee Willie' is a compact, low-growing mixture good for edging. 'Red Monarch' at 10″ (25cm) is taller and suitable for cutting.

Dianthus caryophyllus

Common Name: Carnation

Flowers: Native to the Mediterranean region. Fragrant double and semidouble fringed flowers on brittle, slender stems. Colors include white, red, pink, yellow, and bicolors.

Leaves: Narrow, pointed, silvery green.

Habit: 12″–18″ (31–46cm). Bushy, sprawling.

Culture: Prefers full sun in any well-drained garden soil, especially if it is slightly alkaline. Propagate by seeds, cuttings, or division. Start seeds indoors eight weeks before outdoor planting.

Season of Bloom: Late spring to early summer.

Hardiness: Hardy annual that tolerates mild frost.

Uses: A good accent for rock gardens, mixed beds and borders. Does well in coastal areas. Popular cut flower.

The variety 'Scarlet Luminette' won an All-America award for its extra-earliness and heat tolerance. Lightly scented, scarlet-red, 2½″ (6.5cm), fully double flowers form a compact mounded plant just 18″ (46cm) high. 'Perpetual-flowering' carnations are evergreen perennials that flower year-round when grown under glass.

Dianthus chinensis

Common Name: Rainbow pink

Flowers: Native to China. Fragrant, single or double, frilled, 1″ (2.5cm) flowers arranged in clusters on erect stems with branching occurring at the top. Colors include white, pink, red, lavender, purple, and bicolors. To extend bloom, deadhead spent blossoms.

Leaves: Narrow, pointed, silvery green.

Habit: 6″–12″ (15–31cm) tall. Low, mounded.

Culture: Prefers full sun in any well-drained garden soil, especially one that is slightly alkaline. Propagate by seeds, cuttings, or division. Start seeds indoors eight weeks before outdoor planting.

Season of Bloom: Late spring to early summer when nights are cool.

Hardiness: Hardy annual that tolerates mild frost. Perennial in mild winter areas.

Uses: A favorite flower massed in low edges, beds, and borders. Popular in rock gardens.

Many beautiful hybrids have been produced that flower spectacularly in early summer or autumn when nights are cool, or all summer in cool coastal locations. Especially noteworthy are 'Telstar' hybrids, an assortment of mostly red shades edged in white, and 'Snowfire' hybrids, bearing large, white, fringed flowers with a red "eye."

Digitalis purpurea

Common Name: Common foxglove

Flowers: Native to Europe. Drooping, spotted, tubular flowers on tall spikes. Colors include pink, purple, white, and yellow. To extend bloom, cut back main spike after blooms have faded so side shoots will develop.

Leaves: Oval, pointed, downy, gray-green; form a rosette around the base of each plant.

Habit: 2′–5′ (.6–1.5m) tall. Spirelike.

Culture: Prefers sun or partial shade in well-drained, humus-rich, fertile soil. Prefers an acid soil. Propagate by seeds started indoors eight weeks before outdoor planting.

Season of Bloom: Late spring to early summer when nights are cool.

Hardiness: Hardy biennial that grows almost anywhere if planted to flower during cool weather.

Uses: Excellent as a showy background plant in mixed beds and borders in shady or woodland gardens. Good cut flower.

Most foxgloves are really biennials, growing a crown of leaves the first season and flowering in spring the second season. However, the variety 'Foxy' will flower the first year as an annual if seed is started early indoors and transplanted after danger of frost has passed. Combines especially well with hostas, ferns, and Siberian iris.

Dimorphotheca
sinuata

Common Name: Cape marigold

Flowers: Native to South Africa. Shimmering daisylike flowers with dark centers. A wintertime favorite in dry warm-winter areas. Profuse bloomer. Colors include white, yellow, orange, and salmon.

Leaves: Coarsely toothed, dark green.

Habit: 12″–15″ (31–38cm) tall. Compact, mounded.

Culture: Prefers sun in well-drained, sandy or loam soil. Propagate by seeds, direct-sown.

Season of Bloom: Late spring to autumn when nights are cool.

Hardiness: Tender annual killed by frost.

Uses: Popular massed as a ground cover or in mixed beds and borders. Excellent in rock gardens and in coastal gardens. Pretty in flower arrangements.

These African daisies demand cool nights to flower well. They are sensational in cool coastal gardens, planted in drifts and seeded among cracks in dry walls. *D. Pluvialis* is a spectacular, free-flowering, shimmering white species with a purple circle surrounding a black "eye."

Dolichos
lablab

Common Name: Hyacinth bean

Flowers: Origin unknown, probably Asia. Pealike purple flowers on rapid-growing vines. The decorative flowers are followed by glossy magenta pods that prolong the ornamental display.

Leaves: Lustrous, triangular, green, borne in threes.

Habit: Up to 10′ (3m) tall. Dense, bushy, vining.

Culture: Direct-sow seeds into a sunny position in well-drained soil in spring, after the danger of frost has passed. Tolerates poor soil, heat, and drought. Needs support such as a trellis to climb.

Season of Bloom: Summer to autumn frost.

Hardiness: Tender annual killed by frost.

Uses: Beautifies fences, walls. Reddish beans are edible.

Equally at home in the vegetable garden as in the flower garden. Plants prefer warm, sunny summers to grow well. Also known as *Lablab dolichos*.

Dorotheanthus bellidiformis

Common Name: Livingstone daisy

Flowers: Native to South Africa. Glistening daisylike petals are highlighted by a white ring encircling the deep orange flower eye. Colors include pink, purple, orange, yellow, white, and bicolors.

Leaves: Small, fat, nubby, coated with silvery particles that appear to be crystals of ice.

Habit: 6″ (15cm) tall. Low, spreading.

Culture: Prefers full sun in well-drained, sandy or loam soil. Propagate by seeds, direct-sown.

Season of Bloom: Spring, but succession sowings can ensure flowers into autumn.

Hardiness: Tender annual that tolerates mild frost.

Uses: Edging to low mixed beds and borders.

Most seed catalogs list this flower under its old botanical name, *Mesembryanthemum.* 'Magic Carpet' is a particularly fine mixture. Also try 'Yellow Ice', a low-growing bright yellow flower that looks especially beautiful planted in a rock garden or as an edging to flower beds. All Livingstone daisies flower best during cool nights and prefer cool coastal locations.

Dyssodia tenuiloba

Common Name: Dahlberg daisy

Flowers: Native to south central Texas and Mexico. Pretty, delicate yellow daisies held erect by thin, wiry stalks.

Leaves: Narrow, bright green; overall billowing, airy appearance.

Habit: 6″–8″ (15–20cm) tall. Low, mounded.

Culture: Easy to grow, especially in hot climates. Prefers full sun in well-drained, sandy or loam soil. Propagate by seeds, direct-sown.

Season of Bloom: All summer.

Hardiness: Tender annual killed by frost.

Uses: Delightful one-season ground cover and massed edging for beds and borders. Makes an attractive hanging plant.

Spectacular summer-long flowering display. Though individual flowers are only ½″ (13mm), they are clustered in such a tight mass that the effect can be dazzling.

Erysimum hieraciifolium

Common Name: Siberian wallflower

Flowers: Native to Siberia. Sweetly scented, thick clusters of four-petaled, velvety flowers on erect, leafy stems. Colors include yellow and orange.

Leaves: Long, lancelike, bright green.

Habit: 12″–30″ (31–76cm) tall. Upright, branching.

Culture: Easy to grow. Prefers full sun or partial shade in well-drained, sandy or loam soil. Prefers cool weather. Propagate by seeds started indoors ten weeks before outdoor planting.

Season of Bloom: Spring to early summer.

Hardiness: Hardy biennial best treated as an annual. Tolerates mild frost.

Uses: Old-fashioned favorite. Good coastal plant. Popular planted in bulb beds or mixed beds and borders. Suitable for cutting.

The Siberian wallflower differs from the more colorful *Cheiranthus cheiri* (English wallflower) in several ways. Though its color range is restricted to yellow and orange, it will produce a magnificent early-spring display in warm summer climates where the English wallflower produces a weak display. The above photograph shows Siberian and English wallflowers combined in Monet's garden, Giverny, France.

Eschscholzia californica

Common Name: California poppy

Flowers: Native to California and Oregon. Shimmering 3″ (7.5cm) poppy flowers mostly range from deep orange to pale yellow, but white, rose, scarlet, and bronze are also available.

Leaves: Lacy, silvery green.

Habit: 12″–15″ (31–38cm) tall. Open, mounded, spreading.

Culture: Easy to grow. Performs best in full sun in well-drained, sandy soil. Tolerates desert conditions and poor soil. Propagate by seeds, direct-sown in early spring or—for earliest flowering—in early autumn.

Season of Bloom: Early summer, but successive sowings can ensure continuous flowering into autumn.

Hardiness: Hardy annual that grows almost anywhere if planted to flower during cool weather.

Uses: Popular in wildflower meadows. Attractive in mixed beds and borders.

The state flower of California. Though the wild species are mostly orange-flowered, plant breeders have not only extended the color range considerably, they have created flowers with "fluted" petals, such as 'Ballerina'.

Eustoma grandiflorum

Common Name: Prairie gentian

Flowers: Native to Texas. Single or double bell-shaped flowers, up to 4″ (10cm) across, with five overlapping petals on brittle stems. Colors include purple, white, pink, and blue.

Leaves: Heart-shaped, silvery green.

Habit: 12″–24″ (31–61cm) tall. Upright.

Culture: Prefers full sun in well-drained, fertile, sandy or loam soil. Propagate by seeds started indoors ten weeks before outdoor planting. Cut back for bushier plant.

Season of Bloom: All summer.

Hardiness: Tender annual killed by frost.

Uses: Good accent in mixed beds and borders. Sensational cut flower.

Also known as *Lisianthus russellianus*. The seed is tiny and germination slow. Challenging to grow from seed. 'Yodel Mixed Colors' is a balanced blend of the best colors. 'Blue Lisa' is an award-winning dwarf variety.

Gaillardia pulchella

Common Name: Blanket flower

Flowers: Native to North America. Single flowers up to 3″ (7.5cm) across resemble daisies; fully double forms have globular flowers. Colors include yellow, orange, red, and bicolors.

Leaves: Pointed, lancelike, downy, green.

Habit: 18″–24″ (46–61cm) tall. Upright, bushy.

Culture: Easy to grow. Prefers full sun in well-drained, sandy or loam soil. Tolerates dry impoverished soil. Propagate by seeds, direct-sown.

Season of Bloom: All summer.

Hardiness: Hardy annual that tolerates mild frost.

Uses: Popular component of meadow gardens, mixed beds and borders. Long-lasting cut flower.

'Gaiety Mixed' is a variety of *Gaillardia* that blooms quickly from seed sown directly into the garden, since they resent transplanting. 'Red-bloom' is an All-America award winner, with cinnamon-red fully double blooms that flower nonstop all summer until autumn frost. They are quite distinct from perennial gaillardias, which are daisy-flowered.

Gazania
rigens

**Common
Name:** Treasure flower

Flowers: Native to South Africa. Single daisylike flowers close at night and on cloudy days. Colors include shades of yellow, orange, bronze, salmon, and red.

Leaves: Rounded, narrow, dark green with white undersides; form a rosette.

Habit: 10″–12″ (25–31cm) tall. Upright, clump-forming.

Culture: Prefers full sun in light, well-drained, sandy soil. Tolerates poor soil, wind, drought, and heat, but not wet summers. Propagate by seeds, direct-sown.

**Season
of Bloom:** Early summer to frost.

Hardiness: Tender perennial best treated as a moderately hardy annual. Tolerates mild frost.

Uses: Excellent in rock gardens, between niches in dry walls, containers, and mixed beds and borders.

The variety 'Pinnata' has an especially wide color range and an unusual number of flowers with stripes along the petals, so that the effect on a sunny day is distinctive. Will overwinter in mild climates.

Gomphrena
globosa

**Common
Name:** Globe amaranth

Flowers: Native to India. Round, ³⁄₄″ (19mm) papery, cloverlike heads in white, yellow, pink, and purple.

Leaves: Oval, medium green.

Habit: 6″–18″ (15–46cm) tall. Upright, bushy.

Culture: Prefers full sun in well-drained, sandy or loam soil. Tolerates heat. Propagate by seeds, direct-sown after there is no longer a danger of frost, or start indoors six weeks before outdoor planting.

**Season
of Bloom:** Early summer to frost.

Hardiness: Tender annual killed by frost.

Uses: A good accent massed in beds and borders. Excellent cut or dried flower.

One of the finest "everlasting" flowers. An orange-red variety, 'Strawberry Fayre', is perhaps the most eye-catching separate color available. 'Buddy'—a magenta—is extra-dwarf and suitable for edging.

Gypsophila elegans

Common Name:	Baby's-breath
Flowers:	Native to Europe. Tiny, starlike flowers are massed on rigid, delicate, branched stems. Tall varieties may require staking. Colors include white and rose.
Leaves:	Small, slender, feathery green.
Habit:	12″–24″ (31–61cm) tall. Open, bushy.
Culture:	Prefers full sun in well-drained, sandy or loam soil. Propagate by seeds, direct-sown.
Season of Bloom:	Early summer for approximately six weeks.
Hardiness:	Hardy annual that tolerates mild frost.
Uses:	Popular in bridal bouquets and in dried arrangements. Attractive in rock gardens and edging beds and borders.

The floral display from annual baby's-breath is short-lived, and sowings should be made every few weeks to ensure a succession of bloom. Sow seeds directly into the garden as plants resent transplanting. Beautiful, billowing, cloudlike appearance.

Helianthus annuus

Common Name:	Common sunflower
Flowers:	Native to North America. Huge solitary heads are filled in the center with large black-and-white striped seeds surrounded by sunny, yellow petals supported by a towering stalk. On a hot summer day, you can see sunflowers all facing the same direction since they turn their heads to face the sun.
Leaves:	Gigantic, wide, pointed, hairy, green.
Habit:	3′–8′ (.9–2.4m) tall. Upright.
Culture:	Easy to grow. Prefers full sun in well-drained, sandy or loam soil. Propagate by seeds, direct-sown.
Season of Bloom:	Midsummer to autumn.
Hardiness:	Tender annual killed by frost.
Uses:	Grown for its edible sunflower seeds. Makes a good temporary screen or hedge and a nice accent in borders. Attractive in country flower arrangements.

The giant-headed sunflowers make wonderful highlights in old-fashioned cottage gardens, but actually the smaller-flowered mixtures such as 'Color Fashion'—with many bicolored flowers—can create a much more colorful tall background for annual flower borders. 'Teddy Bear' is a low-growing bushy variety with large double flowers similar to the sunflowers that the Impressionist painter van Gogh admired.

Helichrysum bracteatum

Common Name: Strawflower

Flowers: Native to Australia. Papery heads up to 3″ (7.5cm) across. Glossy yellow, orange, red, salmon, rose, purple, and white daisylike flowers.

Leaves: Narrow, pointed, green.

Habit: 18″–48″ (46–122cm) tall. Tall varieties are upright, dwarf forms are bushy.

Culture: Easy to grow. Prefers full sun in well-drained, sandy or loam soil. Propagate by seeds, direct-sown.

Season of Bloom: Mid- to late summer.

Hardiness: Tender annual killed by severe frost.

Uses: Popular in dried arrangements. Mostly grown in cutting gardens; dwarf kinds suitable for bedding.

Several dwarf varieties of strawflower are now available, including the 'Bikini' mixture, growing just 18″ (46cm) tall. Though one of the best flowers to grow as an everlasting, the stems tend to collapse soon after picking, and the brightly colored flowers are best stuck onto wires when making arrangements.

Heliotropium arborescens

Common Name: Heliotrope

Flowers: Native to Peru. Sweetly scented, branching, upright flower clusters grow as big as 12″ (31cm) wide. Colors include deep blue, purple, and white.

Leaves: Spear-shaped, pointed, dark green.

Habit: 12″–24″ (31–61cm) tall. Upright, bushy.

Culture: Prefers full sun or partial shade in well-drained, fertile, sandy or loam soil. Prefers partial shade in hot areas. Propagate by seeds.

Season of Bloom: All summer.

Hardiness: Tender perennial best treated as a tender annual. Killed by severe frost.

Uses: Popular for its fragrance. Good in borders, window boxes, and containers.

The compact variety, 'Marine', is popular as a greenhouse pot plant. Seeds sown in autumn will flower during winter and early spring, filling sunrooms with a vanillalike fragrance.

Helipterum roseum, Acroclinium roseum

Common Name: Rhodanthe

Flowers: Native to the Mediterranean region. Papery, double, daisylike flowers in red, pink, and white.

Leaves: Slender, indented, dark green.

Habit: 36″ (91cm) tall. Upright.

Culture: Prefers full sun, cool nights, and well-drained, sandy or loam soil. Propagate by seeds, direct-sown.

Season of Bloom: Early summer.

Hardiness: Killed by severe frost. Grows almost anywhere as a tender annual if planted to flower when nights are cool.

Uses: Beds and borders. Popular for drying.

The above photograph shows a representative range of colors. Combines well with dwarf forms of *Helichrysum bracteatum* (strawflowers).

Hibiscus moscheutos

Common Name: Southern hibiscus, common rose mallow

Flowers: Native to the eastern United States. Large, showy, shimmering, open, disc-shaped flowers with a contrasting yellow pistil in each center. Colors include white, pink, red, and bicolors. Profuse bloomer with individual flowers lasting for only one day.

Leaves: Wide, maple-shaped, dark green.

Habit: 3′–8′ (.9–2.4m) tall. Upright, shrubby.

Culture: Prefers full sun or partial shade in moist, fertile, loam soil. Propagate by seeds or plant division. Start seeds indoors six to eight weeks before outdoor planting.

Season of Bloom: Midsummer to frost.

Hardiness: Hardy perennial mostly grown as a tender annual. Though seedlings are killed by frost, established plants will survive several winters through dormant roots.

Uses: A single specimen accent, especially along stream banks and pond margins.

The hybrid 'Southern Belle' won an All-America award for its spectacular size and ability to flower from seed the first year. 'Disco Belle' is a bushier, more compact version of 'Southern Belle'. To improve germination, soak the pea-size seeds overnight in lukewarm water and start indoors in peat pots at 75°F (23.9°C) soil temperature. Plants flower continuously from midsummer until autumn frost.

Hunnemannia fumariifolia

Common Name: Mexican tulip poppy, golden-cup

Flowers: Native to Mexico. Related to California poppy. Shimmering, open, cup-shaped, yellow flowers, 4″ (10cm) across, on tall, wiry stems.

Leaves: Deeply indented, dark green.

Habit: 24″ (61cm) tall. Open, branching.

Culture: Easy to grow. Prefers full sun in dry, sandy or loam soil. Propagate by seeds, direct-sown.

Season of Bloom: Summer to autumn.

Hardiness: Tender annual that tolerates mild frost.

Uses: Effective massed in mixed borders. A long-lasting cut flower if stem ends are singed or dipped in hot water to prevent wilting.

Like most members of the poppy family, the Mexican tulip poppy dislikes transplanting, and its seeds should be sown directly into the garden where plants are to bloom. The bright yellow petals have an incredible satinlike sheen that is almost dazzling when plants are grown in clumps.

Iberis umbellata

Common Name: Globe candytuft

Flowers: Native to Europe. Easy to grow. Clusters of flat, circular flowers. Colors include white, lavender, pink, rose, purple, and carmine.

Leaves: Short, narrow, pointed, dark green.

Habit: 6″–12″ (15–31cm) tall. Low, spreading.

Culture: Prefers full sun in well-drained, sandy or loam soil. Propagate by seeds, direct-sown.

Season of Bloom: Spring.

Hardiness: Hardy annual that tolerates mild frost.

Uses: Popular in rock gardens and as an edging to beds and borders.

The variety 'Flash' is a distinct improvement over older varieties, containing a beautiful selection of bright colors best planted as a bold mass in front of mixed beds and borders. Prefers to be direct-sown. Flowers best during early summer when nights are still cool. Especially good to grow in coastal gardens; mixes well with perennials.

Impatiens balsamina

Common Name: Garden balsam

Flowers: Native to India and China. Single, semidouble, or double 2″ (5cm) roselike flowers. Colors include white, salmon, pink, red, purple, and bicolors.

Leaves: Lancelike, finely toothed, bright green.

Habit: 8″–36″ (20–91cm) tall. Upright.

Culture: Prefers full sun or partial shade in light, moist, humus-rich soil. Intolerant of wet or cold weather. Propagate by seeds, direct-sown or started indoors six weeks before outdoor planting.

Season of Bloom: Early summer to autumn.

Hardiness: Tender annual killed by frost.

Uses: Mostly massed in beds and borders.

A good flower to use in gardens that evoke an old-fashioned aura. 'Camellia-flowered' varieties are especially attractive—mostly red and purple flowers splashed with white arranged along stout stems like a miniature hollyhock.

Impatiens wallerana

Common Name: Busy Lizzie, patience plant

Flowers: Native to South America. Single and double flowers up to 2″ (5cm) across come in white, orange, red, rose, salmon, violet, and bicolors.

Leaves: Broad, pointed, glossy, light green or bronze.

Habit: 6″–18″ (15–46cm) tall. Compact, mounded.

Culture: Some varieties do well in full sun. However, most varieties prefer partial to full shade in well-drained, moist soil with plenty of organic matter. Propagate by seeds started eight weeks before outdoor planting, or from cuttings.

Season of Bloom: Early summer to frost.

Hardiness: Tender annual killed by frost.

Uses: Popular massed in shady beds and borders. Attractive in hanging baskets and as a container plant.

'Super Elfin' and 'Futura' are popular mixtures good for low bedding and mass displays. For something more distinctive, however, try the taller-growing orange 'Tango' and the award-winning 'Blitz', which has the largest flowers. In recent years an exotic race of impatiens called 'New Guinea' hybrids have become popular for their multicolored leaves and extra-large flowers, though they are more temperamental and demand constant irrigation.

Ipomoea tricolor

Common Name:	Morning-glory
Flowers:	Native to South America. Blue, purple, pink, red, white, striped, or bicolor trumpet-shaped flowers on twining stems. Flowers open only in the morning unless the day is cloudy.
Leaves:	Heart-shaped, medium green.
Habit:	10'–15' (3–4.6m) tall. Vining.
Culture:	Easy to grow. Prefers full sun in well-drained, humus-rich soil. Propagate by seeds soaked overnight in lukewarm water to aid germination.
Season of Bloom:	All summer.
Hardiness:	Tender annual killed by frost.
Uses:	Attractive as a ground cover and growing on fences, trellises, and posts.

The variety 'Heavenly Blue' is by far the most popular morning-glory. A beautiful effect can be achieved by planting 'Heavenly Blue' in combination with the night-flowering *Ipomoea alba* (moonflower) so that the colors intermingle. Also, consider planting a red, white, and blue to climb up the same trellis for a spectacular tricolor display.

Lantana camara

Common Name:	Lantana, yellow sage
Flowers:	Native to South America. Clusters of small flowers with contrasting eyes on upright, stiff-branching, thorny stems. Colors include yellow, orange, pink, red, white, and bicolors.
Leaves:	Spear-shaped, serrated, pungent, dark green.
Habit:	Dwarf spreading varieties, 12"–18" (31–46cm) tall. Shrub varieties, up to 36" (91cm) tall. Open, shrubby.
Culture:	Easy to grow. Prefers full sun in sandy or loam soil. Cut back in spring to prevent woodiness. Propagate mainly by cuttings.
Season of Bloom:	All summer.
Hardiness:	Tender perennial in zone 9. Best treated as a tender annual in colder areas.
Uses:	Dwarf varieties are effective in beds and borders. Larger varieties used as low hedges, specimen shrubs, and bank covers. Popular in containers.

Though strictly a perennial shrub, plants will flower the first year from seed if started early indoors. Soak seeds overnight in lukewarm water to encourage germination. A mixture called 'Hybrids & Species Mixed' can create a spectacular ground cover in a bright color range, the flowers continuing nonstop all summer until autumn frost.

Lathyrus
odoratus

Common Name:	Sweet pea
Flowers:	Native to Italy. Clusters of fragrant pea flowers consist of one upright, roundish petal (called a banner) and two narrow side petals (called wings). The wings form a keel which resembles a boat. Sweet peas come in every color except yellow.
Leaves:	Oval, deeply veined, gray-green leaflets arranged in sets of three with clasping, branched tendrils.
Habit:	4′–8′ (1.2–2.4m) tall. Vining.
Culture:	Prefers full sun in well-drained, sandy or loam soil. Propagate by seeds, direct-sown. Early-autumn sowings are best in areas with mild winters.
Season of Bloom:	All summer.
Hardiness:	Hardy annual that tolerates mild frost.
Uses:	An old-fashioned favorite. Attractive climber on fences and trellises. There's nothing more simple or elegant than the display of a vase full of freshly picked sweet peas.

'Antique Fantasy Mixed' is a special blend of highly fragrant sweet peas, though the plants tend to be weak and intolerant of high temperatures. More durable modern varieties include the 'Royal' mixture and 'Galaxy' series with extra-large flowers on long wiry stems.

Lavatera
trimestris

Common Name:	Rose mallow, satin flower
Flowers:	Native to the Mediterranean region. Masses of shimmering, 3″ (7.5cm), hibiscuslike flowers in white and shades of pink with dark "eyes."
Leaves:	Maplelike, serrated, dark green.
Habit:	Up to 42″ (107cm) tall. Bushy, branching.
Culture:	Prefers full sun, good drainage, and sandy or loam soil. Propagate by seeds, direct-sown or started indoors four weeks before outdoor planting.
Season of Bloom:	Summer.
Hardiness:	Hardy annual that tolerates mild frost.
Uses:	Good accent in mixed beds and borders. Spectacular as a temporary flowering hedge.

The flowers are borne in such profusion, they can almost completely hide the foliage. Particularly free-flowering in coastal gardens.

Limnanthes douglasii

Common Name: Meadow foam

Flowers: Native to California. Waxy, prominently veined, deeply lobed, five-petaled, saucer-shaped flowers with bicolor markings of white at the tips and yellow in the center.

Leaves: Trailing, deeply indented, medium green.

Habit: 4″ (10cm) tall. Low, spreading.

Culture: Easy to grow. Prefers full sun in moist, well-drained, garden soil. Propagate by seeds, direct-sown.

Season of Bloom: Spring to early summer when nights are cool.

Hardiness: Hardy annual that tolerates mild frost.

Uses: Suitable as a one-season ground cover and for edging beds and borders.

Self-seeds freely. Early-autumn sowings are best in areas with mild winters. Effective as a mass planting, especially as drifts at the forefront of perennial beds and around boulders in rock gardens.

Limonium sinuatum

Common Name: Statice

Flowers: Native to the Mediterranean region. Papery clusters of bright flowers on short, strong, winged stems. Colors include white, yellow, blue, pink, and lavender.

Leaves: Straplike, sharply notched, medium green; form a rosette.

Habit: 18″–24″ (46–61cm) tall. Upright.

Culture: Easy to grow. Prefers full sun in well-drained, sandy soil. Tolerates heat, drought, and salt spray. Propagate by seeds, direct-sown.

Season of Bloom: Summer and early autumn.

Hardiness: Tender annual killed by frost.

Uses: Suitable for cutting and coastal gardens. Popular in fresh and dried flower arrangements.

A popular everlasting flower excellent for cutting gardens. Other species of statice suitable for long-lasting dried arrangements include *Statice dumosa,* also called *Limonium dumosum* (German statice), with masses of tiny white flowers resembling baby's-breath, and *Statice suworowii,* producing elegant tapering pink flower spikes.

Linaria
maroccana

Common Name: Toadflax

Flowers: Native to Morocco. Tiny snapdragon flowers on vertical spikes. Most commonly seen as red, but also in blue, white, yellow, pink, and purple.

Leaves: Narrow, grasslike, bright green.

Habit: 12″ (31cm) tall. Upright.

Culture: Prefers full sun in well-drained, sandy or loam soil. Propagate by seeds, direct-sown.

Season of Bloom: Usually early summer when nights are cool.

Hardiness: Hardy annual that tolerates mild frost.

Uses: Perfect for massing in rock gardens and edging borders.

Best sown directly into the garden where plants are to bloom. Tolerates crowding, and looks especially beautiful as a mixture planted informally in clumps or drifts. 'Fairy Bouquet' is an All-America award winner.

Lobelia
erinus

Common Name: Edging lobelia

Flowers: Native to South Africa. Upright or trailing small, tubular flowers. Colors include white, blue, and pink.

Leaves: Slender, feathery, light green.

Habit: 6″ (15cm) tall. Low, mounded or trailing, lacy.

Culture: Prefers full sun in well-drained, sandy or loam soil. Propagate by seeds started indoors ten weeks before outdoor planting.

Season of Bloom: Summer to early autumn.

Hardiness: Tender annual killed by frost.

Uses: Suitable for edges and borders. Widely used in mixed hanging baskets, flower boxes, and containers.

'Blue Cascade' is a superb variety for hanging baskets. 'String of Pearls' is a colorful mixture for bedding. Flowers best when nights are cool, and in coastal areas. Combines well with white alyssum in balcony planters. Seed is tiny and initial growth is extremely slow.

Lobularia maritima

Common Name:	Sweet alyssum
Flowers:	Native to the Mediterranean region. Numerous tiny, four-petaled flowers arranged in dense clusters. Colors include white, pink, and purple. Fragrance is sweet, honeylike.
Leaves:	Slender, dark green; usually hidden by profuse blooms.
Habit:	3″–10″ (7.5–25cm) tall. Mounded, spreading.
Culture:	Prefers full sun in well-drained, sandy or loam soil. Tolerates light shade. Propagate by seeds, direct-sown.
Season of Bloom:	All summer. In midsummer, cut back plants to encourage more bloom.
Hardiness:	Hardy annual that tolerates mild frost.
Uses:	Excellent in rock gardens, between paving stones, as an edging in beds and borders. Also popular cascading over a wall, in containers and hanging baskets. Can be used as a one-season ground cover. Effective for hiding maturing leaves in bulb beds.

Plants in the 'Wonderland' series—a rosy red, snow white, and purple—have been specially bred to complement each other, each creating a compact mound of color. Can be direct-seeded in cracks to bloom among broken flagstone.

Matthiola incana

Common Name:	Stock
Flowers:	Native to southern Europe. Fragrant, single or double 1″ (2.5cm) flowers clustered on strong spikes. Colors include white, blue, yellow, pink, rosy red, and purple.
Leaves:	Broad, hairy, gray-green.
Habit:	12″–30″ (31–76cm) tall. Upright, spirelike.
Culture:	Prefers full sun or light shade in moist but well-drained, humus-rich, loam soil. Prefers cool weather. Propagate by seeds started indoors eight weeks before outdoor planting.
Season of Bloom:	Early to midsummer.
Hardiness:	Hardy annual that tolerates mild frost.
Uses:	Widely used cut flower in the floral industry. Good massed in mixed beds.

Flowers best when nights are cool. Easily stressed by heat. Other kinds of stock are also popular, including *Matthiola bicornis* (night-scented stock), which is extremely fragrant, and *Malcomia maritima* (Virginia stock), which is also fragrant and flowers within four weeks of sowing seed directly into the garden.

Mimulus × hybridus

Common Name: Monkey flower

Flowers: Derived from species native to North and South America. Small, spotted, velvety, trumpetlike flowers resemble the faces of smiling monkeys. Colors range mainly from bright shades of red to yellow.

Leaves: Broad, coarsely toothed, light green.

Habit: 12″–16″ (31–41cm) tall. Low, mounded.

Culture: Prefers full sun or light shade in wet or moist, humus-rich, loam soil. Prefers cool weather. Propagate by seeds.

Season of Bloom: Summer to autumn. Intolerant of summer heat.

Hardiness: Hardy annual that tolerates mild frost.

Uses: Excellent around moist banks and edges of ponds and streams, and in mixed beds and borders. Good container plant.

Where summers are hot, mimulus are rather short-lived, but interesting for their exotically spotted throats. 'Calypso' is an award-winning mixture.

Mirabilis jalapa

Common Name: Four-o'clock, marvel-of-Peru

Flowers: Native to Peru. Long, fragrant, trumpet-shaped flowers in shades of red, pink, yellow, and bicolors. Flowers open in late afternoon and on cloudy days. They attract moths for pollination.

Leaves: Broad, pointed, dark green.

Habit: Up to 30″ (76cm) tall. Bushy, shrublike.

Culture: Fast-growing. Prefers full sun or partial shade in well-drained, sandy or loam soil. Tolerates urban pollution and heat stress. Propagate by seeds, direct-sown or started indoors six weeks before outdoor planting. Mature plants have tubers that can be stored in a frost-free location over winter and replanted.

Season of Bloom: Summer to frost.

Hardiness: Tender annual killed by frost.

Uses: Good accent in mixed borders or as a temporary shrub.

An old-fashioned flower popular in cottage gardens. Though some plants are all one color, others may have several colors on the same plant, many mottled or striped with a contrasting color. Look, but don't touch, as all parts of this plant are poisonous.

Moluccella laevis

Common Name:	Bells-of-Ireland
Flowers:	Native to Asia. Tiny, fragrant, white flowers lie inside the showy, light green, bell-shaped calyx streaked with white veins.
Leaves:	Rounded, spade-shaped, coarsely serrated, light green.
Habit:	24″–36″ (61–91cm) tall. Bushy, spreading, spirelike.
Culture:	Prefers full sun in well-drained, moist, sandy or loam soil. Propagate by seeds, direct-sown or started early indoors six weeks before outdoor planting.
Season of Bloom:	All summer.
Hardiness:	Tender annual killed by frost.
Uses:	Suitable for cutting gardens and for massing in mixed beds and borders.

The flower stems can be dried to a papery texture for use in long-lasting dried arrangments. The seed is hard-coated and sensitive to cool temperatures. Germination is hastened by soaking overnight in lukewarm water. Plants tolerate crowding and look especially attractive massed together in a large clump.

Myosotis sylvatica

Common Name:	Garden forget-me-not
Flowers:	Native to Europe. Sprays of tiny, tightly clustered blue, white, and pink flowers with yellow eyes. If cut back, may rebloom.
Leaves:	Lancelike, hairy, silvery green.
Habit:	6″–18″ (15–46cm) tall. Open, mounded, branching.
Culture:	Adaptable to most conditions. Thrives in light shade in moist garden soil. Propagate by seeds started indoors ten weeks before outdoor planting or direct-sown in late summer for bloom the following year.
Season of Bloom:	Spring, with periodic flowering occurring to midsummer.
Hardiness:	Hardy annual that tolerates frost.
Uses:	Perfect along streams and in bog gardens, moist meadows, and woodlands. Makes an interesting underplanting for spring bulbs and a one-season ground cover. Effective edging in mixed beds and borders.

'Victoria' mixture has a balanced blend of blue, pink, and white, though it's best treated as a biennial, with plants started from seed in late summer to flower the following spring. 'Blue Ball' can be forced to bloom as an annual by starting seed early indoors and transplanting. Plants reseed themselves readily. Pink tulips growing through blue forget-me-nots is a spectacular combination.

Nemesia
strumosa

Common Name:	Nemesia
Flowers:	Native to South Africa. Clusters of orchidlike 1″ (2.5cm) flowers display a protruding lower lip on narrow, erect stems. Colors include white, yellow, bronze, pink, orange, and lavender.
Leaves:	Pointed, lancelike, serrated, medium green.
Habit:	12″ (31cm) tall. Bushy.
Culture:	Prefers full sun in well drained, moist, fertile, humus-rich soil. Prefers cool coastal and high-altitude regions. Propagate by seeds started indoors eight weeks before outdoor planting.
Season of Bloom:	All summer.
Hardiness:	Tender annual killed by severe frost.
Uses:	Excellent in coastal gardens massed in mixed borders and beds. Also effective in container plantings, especially in window boxes.

A good bedding plant for cool coastal locations, and a flowering pot plant grown under glass during winter. Tends to "burn" in very hot summer conditions.

Nicotiana
alata

Common Name:	Flowering tobacco
Flowers:	Native to South America. An unusual night-blooming flower with a protracted throat perfectly designed to attract moths. Flowers of modern hybrids do open during the day—their intense fragrance occurs only at night. Colors include white, pink, yellow, red, and green.
Leaves:	Sticky, hairy, fragrant, green, on branching stalks.
Habit:	12″–36″ (31–91cm) tall. Open, clump-forming.
Culture:	Prefers full sun or partial shade in well-drained, moist, sandy or loam soil. Propagate by seeds started indoors six to eight weeks before outdoor planting.
Season of Bloom:	Late spring to autumn.
Hardiness:	Tender annual killed by frost.
Uses:	Charming when massed or clustered in beds, borders, and containers. For evening enjoyment, plant near the house under windows, near paths, or on decks and terraces. Good cut flower.

Old-fashioned nicotianas used to close up in the afternoon, but newer hybrids stay open all day, especially the 'Nicki' hybrids, which are more compact and more free-flowering in the bargain. Plants that are finished flowering can be pruned back to force new growth.

Nicotiana sylvestris

Common Name:	Fragrant tobacco
Flowers:	Native to South America. Clusters of highly fragrant, pendant, tubular white flowers.
Leaves:	Large, broad, heart-shaped, green.
Habit:	Up to 6′ (1.8m) tall. Upright, spirelike. Tall, tobaccolike plants.
Culture:	Prefers full sun, fertile soil, and good drainage. Propagate by seeds started indoors six weeks before outdoor planting.
Season of Bloom:	Summer.
Hardiness:	Killed by frost. Grows almost anywhere as a tender annual.
Uses:	Tall highlight for mixed beds and borders.

A valuable component of all-white gardens and moon gardens since the flowers seem to glow in moonlight.

Nierembergia hippomanica

Common Name:	Cupflower
Flowers:	Native from Mexico to Chile and Argentina. Cup-shaped flowers with contrasting yellow throats and two-tone violet petals covered with a star pattern. There is also a white variety.
Leaves:	Narrow, pointed, green.
Habit:	6″–9″ (15–23cm) tall. Low, rounded.
Culture:	Prefers full sun or light shade in well-drained, average soil. Propagate by seeds.
Season of Bloom:	All summer, peaking in late summer.
Hardiness:	Tender annual killed by frost.
Uses:	Good in rock gardens, window boxes, and low bedding.

A member of the fascinating Solanaceae family of plants, *Nierembergia* is good for edging beds and borders. The variety 'Purple Robe' contrasts well with 'White Cascade' petunias in container plantings.

Oenothera speciosa

Common Name: Pink evening primrose

Flowers: Native to Texas. Pink, 3″ (7.5cm), cup-shaped flowers, usually with pale pink or white centers. There is also a white form.

Leaves: Slender, smooth, gray-green.

Habit: Up to 12″ (31cm) tall. Spreading, delicate, wispy stems.

Culture: Prefers full sun, good drainage. Tolerates crowding and impoverished soil. Propagate by seeds, direct-sown.

Season of Bloom: Spring to early summer.

Hardiness: Hardy perennial in zones 5–9, but usually grown as a hardy annual since plants will flower the first year from seed.

Uses: Massing in beds and borders. Effective in wildflower meadow mixtures.

A good companion to white daisies—especially the hardy *Chrysanthemum leucanthemum* (oxeye daisy) and tender *C. frutescens* (marguerite), shown here.

Papaver nudicaule

Common Name: Iceland poppy

Flowers: Native to the Canadian Rockies. Crinkled, papery, cup-shaped flowers and nodding buds on tall, wiry, erect stems. Bright colors include red, orange, yellow, pink, and white.

Leaves: Hairy, toothed, gray-green; form a rosette.

Habit: 24″–36″ (61–91cm) tall. Upright.

Culture: Easy to grow. Prefers full sun in well-drained, sandy or loam soil. Propagate by seeds, direct-sown after danger of frost in spring or in early autumn in areas with mild winters.

Season of Bloom: Spring to summer.

Hardiness: Tender perennial best treated as a hardy annual. Plants tolerate mild frost, but not heavy freezing.

Uses: Effective massed in beds and borders or as an accent plant. Suitable for cutting if stems are scorched to prevent wilting.

Plants resent root disturbance, so seeds are best broadcast into bare soil where they are to bloom. 'Oregon Rainbows' is a superior mixture with individual blooms up to 8″ (20cm) across. Flowers best during cool nights. Another good annual poppy is *Papaver rhoeas* (Shirley poppy) with colors that predominate in red, white, and pink. Both kinds are a popular component of wildflower meadow mixtures.

Papaver rhoeas

Common Name: Corn poppy, Shirley poppy

Flowers: Native to Europe, especially the Mediterranean region. Slender, wiry stems are topped by saucerlike, 3″ (7.5cm) flowers that shimmer in the sunlight. Colors include crimson, white, and shades of pink, with handsome black markings.

Leaves: Hairy, indented, light green.

Habit: Up to 48″ (122cm) tall. Clump-forming.

Culture: Prefers full sun, good drainage, sandy or loam soil. Propagate by seeds, direct-sown, as plants will usually wilt and die if transplanted.

Season of Bloom: Late spring to early summer.

Hardiness: Hardy annual that grows almost anywhere if planted to flower during cool nights.

Uses: Sensational accent in mixed beds and borders. Spectacular planted as a component of wildflower meadow mixtures, especially combined with cornflowers *(Centaurea cyanus)*.

One of the most beautiful sights of early summer is the sight of Shirley poppies flowering in fruit tree orchards. Sensational scattered among perennials.

Pelargonium × hortorum

Common Name: Zonal geranium, bedding geranium

Flowers: Native to South Africa. Single, double, or semidouble dense clusters of five-petaled flowers. Colors include white, red, pink, salmon, and some bicolored.

Leaves: Kidney-shaped, scalloped, velvety, green with variegated markings; exudes a distinct odor when bruised.

Habit: 12″–24″ tall (31–61cm) tall. Branching.

Culture: Easy to grow. Prefers full sun in well-drained, moist, fertile soil. Propagate by seeds or stem cuttings. Seeds should be started indoors eight to ten weeks before outdoor planting.

Season of Bloom: All summer.

Hardiness: Tender annual killed by frost.

Uses: Popular in containers, hanging baskets, and mixed beds and borders.

Deadheading considerably enhances the flowering of these dependable bedding plants. Modern hybridizing has produced numerous varieties that flower within nine weeks from seed. 'Multibloom' hybrids produce more flowering stems per plant over a longer period than other mixtures.

Penstemon ✕ gloxinioides

Common Name: Beard-tongue

Flowers: Derived from species native to Mexico. Nodding, tubular flowers with flared bicolored lip on erect spikes. Colors include white, red, pink, lavender, and scarlet.

Leaves: Spear-shaped, dark green.

Habit: 24″–36″ (61–91cm) tall. Upright, spirelike.

Culture: Easy to grow. Prefers full sun or light shade in well-drained, sandy or loam soil. Propagate by seeds started indoors six to eight weeks before outdoor planting.

Season of Bloom: All summer.

Hardiness: Moderately hardy annual that survives mild frost.

Uses: Attractive massed in beds and borders, especially when used in mixed colors. Long-lasting cut flower.

Blooms best when nights are cool. 'Hyacinth-flowered Mixed' is an award-winning mixture. Popular in coastal gardens.

Petunia ✕ hybrida

Common Name: Common garden petunia

Flowers: Derived from species native to South America. Many different varieties. Single or double funnel-shaped flowers may have plain, ruffled, or fringed petals that can be deeply veined or striped. Some are scented. Colors are solid or bicolor and include white, cream, yellow, salmon, pink, rose, red, lavender, and violet.

Leaves: Oval, pointed, sticky, light green.

Habit: 8″–15″ (20–38cm) tall. Trailing or mounded.

Culture: Easy to grow. Prefers full sun or partial shade in well-drained, sandy or loam soil. Propagate by seeds started indoors six weeks before outdoor planting.

Season of Bloom: Spring to early autumn.

Hardiness: Tender annual killed by frost.

Uses: Popular massed in beds, borders, flower boxes, containers, and hanging baskets.

Petunias are mostly classified as Grandiflora (giant-flowered) and Multiflora (many-flowered), with the Multifloras making a quicker recovery after inclement weather and creating a longer-lasting display. The 'Ultra' series of Grandifloras has an extremely free-flowering, basal-branching habit, while the 'Joy' series is a superb Multiflora hybridizing achievement. Largest-flowered of all petunias are the old-fashioned *Petunia fimbriata* types, notably 'Can Can', a mixture with highly ruffled petals.

Phlox
drummondii

Common Name: Annual phlox

Flowers: Native to Texas. Prolific tight clusters of showy 1″ (2.5cm), star-shaped flowers on strong stems. Colors include pink, red, yellow, lavender, white, and bicolors.

Leaves: Lancelike, sticky, light green.

Habit: 6″–18″ (15–46cm) tall. Mounded.

Culture: Easy to grow. Prefers full sun or light shade in well-drained, sandy or loam soil. Propagate by seeds started indoors six weeks before outdoor planting. In areas with mild winters, direct-sow seeds in late summer or early autumn.

Season of Bloom: Peaks in early summer and repeats in late autumn.

Hardiness: Hardy annual that tolerates mild frost.

Uses: Attractive in rock gardens and massed in beds and borders. A good choice for window boxes.

'Dwarf Beauty' is a handsome, compact, free-flowering mixture that contains mostly solid colors with contrasting eyes. 'Twinkle Dwarf Star' is an unusual form with pointed petals and many bicolors.

Portulaca
grandiflora

Common Name: Rose moss

Flowers: Native to South America. Prolific, dainty, bright single or double 2″ (5cm) flowers resemble tiny roses. Life of the individual flower lasts one full day; deadhead for abundant blooms. Colors include pink, red, yellow, orange, and white.

Leaves: Succulent, needlelike, trailing, medium green.

Habit: 6″–8″ (15–20cm) tall. Low, spreading.

Culture: Easy to grow. Thrives in full sun in well-drained, sandy soil. Propagate by seeds, direct-sown.

Season of Bloom: For several weeks in summer. Flowers close in the late afternoon.

Hardiness: Tender annual killed by frost.

Uses: Popular in rock gardens, edgings, and container plantings. Makes an excellent one-season ground cover.

Succession sowings every two weeks are necessary to maintain continuous bloom. The variety 'Calypso' is an especially good mixture with a high percentage of semidouble blooms. The hybrid 'Sundial' blooms up to two weeks earlier and creates a more densely packed floral display, but the seed is expensive and should be started indoors in pots for transplanting to the garden after there is no longer a danger of frost.

Rudbeckia
hirta

Common Name:	Gloriosa daisy, black-eyed Susan
Flowers:	Native to North America. Bright, single or double yellow, orange, mahogany, or bicolored daisy flowers with contrasting brown or green centers on erect, stiff stems. Cut frequently to encourage new blooms.
Leaves:	Spear-shaped, coarse, hairy, dark green.
Habit:	36″ (91cm) tall. Upright, branching.
Culture:	Easy to grow. Prefers full sun in well-drained, sandy or loam soil. Propagate by seeds, direct-sown or started indoors six weeks before outdoor planting.
Season of Bloom:	All summer.
Hardiness:	Fairly hardy annual that tolerates mild frost.
Uses:	Excellent way to brighten up drab spots in beds and borders. Long-lasting cut flowers.

Many good varieties have been developed from *Rudbeckia* (black-eyed Susans) that grow wild along the waysides of North America, including 'Irish Eyes', with bright green "eyes," 'Double Gold', with large double flowers, and 'Marmalade', a compact dwarf variety with clear orange petals.

Salpiglossis
sinuata

Common Name:	Painted-tongue
Flowers:	Native to South America. Loose clusters of velvety, open-throated, trumpet-shaped flowers that are usually deeply veined and speckled. Colors include yellow, gold, pink, red, and blue.
Leaves:	Lancelike, sticky, light green.
Habit:	18″–24″ (46–61cm) tall. Upright, branching.
Culture:	Prefers full sun in well-drained, sandy or loam soil. Stops flower production in hot weather. Propagate by seeds started indoors six weeks before outdoor planting.
Season of Bloom:	All summer in cool climates, in early summer in hot climates.
Hardiness:	Tender annual killed by frost.
Uses:	Suitable for mixed beds and borders. May need staking.

Autumn-sown under glass, *Salpiglossis* can make spectacular flowering pot plants for winter and early-spring bloom. Except in areas with cool summers, plants tend to be short-lived since they demand cool nighttime temperatures to flower well. 'Casino' and 'Splash' are hybrids with a spectacular color range.

Salvia
farinacea

**Common
Name:**   Mealy-cup sage

Flowers: Native to Texas. Small pale blue, violet-blue, or white, lavenderlike flowers are densely clustered on upright spikes.

Leaves: Lancelike, coarsely toothed, gray-green; on square stems.

Habit: 24″–36″ (61–91cm) tall. Upright.

Culture: Prefers full sun in well-drained, moist garden soil. Propagate by seeds started indoors six weeks before outdoor planting.

**Season
of Bloom:**   Midsummer to frost.

Hardiness: Tender annual killed by frost.

Uses: Popular massed in background plantings or in mixed beds and borders. Grows well in containers. Also makes an excellent freshly cut or dried flower. To dry, cut stalks before the flowers fully open and hang upside down in a dark, cool, airy place.

The award-winning variety, 'Victoria', has bold flower spikes of a rich violet-blue; 'White Porcelain' is a spectacular white that is most often used in gardens with an all-white theme. The blues combine especially well with orange-flowered cosmos.

Salvia
splendens

**Common
Name:**   Scarlet sage

Flowers: Native to South America. Showy clusters of tubular flowers on erect spikes. Most popular color is red; other colors include purple, pink, orange, lavender, and white.

Leaves: Spear-shaped, green; on square stems.

Habit: 8″–30″ (20–76cm) tall. Upright, spirelike.

Culture: Prefers full sun in well-drained, moist, loam soil. In desert areas, plant in partial shade. Propagate by seeds started indoors six to eight weeks before outdoor planting.

**Season
of Bloom:**   Summer to frost.

Hardiness: Tender annual killed by frost.

Uses: Effective in beds, borders, and containers. Dwarf types are suitable for edging. Good cut flower.

Though the scarlet-red varieties, such as 'Carabiniere', are the most popular, many beautiful mixtures have started to appear, including 'Panorama' and 'Phoenix'. Blue *S. farinacea* and scarlet *S. splendens* make a colorful combination.

Sanvitalia procumbens

Common Name:	Creeping zinnia
Flowers:	Native to Mexico. Small, single, 1″ (2.5cm) yellow to orange daisy flowers with contrasting dark purple centers on trailing purple stems.
Leaves:	Creeping, oval, hairy, dark green.
Habit:	6″ (15cm) tall. Low, spreading.
Culture:	Prefers full sun in well-drained sandy or loam soil. Tolerates light shade, heat, drought, humidity, and poor soil. Propagate by seeds, direct-sown.
Season of Bloom:	Early summer to frost.
Hardiness:	Tender annual killed by frost.
Uses:	Lovely massed as a ground cover. Attractive as an edging in mixed beds and borders. Also suitable for containers, hanging baskets, rock gardens, and in rock walls and paths.

Like most zinnias, this variety resists root disturbance and prefers to be sown directly into the garden where plants are to bloom. Flowering will begin within five weeks of sowing if plants are encouraged to grow fast by watering, though once established they are drought-tolerant.

Scabiosa atropurpurea

Common Name:	Pincushion, sweet scabious
Flowers:	Native to Europe. Delicate, round flower heads with stamens appearing like pins in a cushion. Colors include white, lavender, purple, pink, red, yellow, and black.
Leaves:	Oblong, deeply divided, medium green.
Habit:	12″–36″ (31–91cm) tall. Upright.
Culture:	Easy to grow. Prefers full sun in well-drained, humus-rich, loam soil. Propagate by seeds, direct-sown.
Season of Bloom:	Early summer to frost.
Hardiness:	Moderately hardy annual that tolerates mild frost.
Uses:	Attractive accent in cutting gardens and mixed beds and borders. Makes a lacy addition to summer bouquets.

Plants tolerate crowding and look best in a mass. A related annual species, *S. stellata*, produces a dome of dried flower parts and is popular among flower arrangers as an everlasting.

Schizanthus × wisetonensis

Common Name: Butterfly flower, poor-man's orchid

Flowers: Native to Chile. Clusters of colorful, orchidlike flowers with speckled throats on upright spikes. Colors include pink, rose, lavender, purple, yellow, or white. May need staking.

Leaves: Delicate, fernlike, green.

Habit: Up to 24″ (61cm) tall. Upright, bushy.

Culture: Prefers full sun or filtered shade in well-drained, humus-rich garden soil. Popular in cool coastal regions. Propagate by seeds, direct-sown or started indoors eight weeks before outdoor planting.

Season of Bloom: Summer.

Hardiness: Tender annual killed by frost.

Uses: Excellent in window boxes. Attractive massed in beds and borders. Frequently found potted in greenhouses and conservatories.

Except in cool high-elevation and cool coastal areas, where it will bloom outdoors in early summer, *Schizanthus* is mostly grown under glass, seeded in autumn to flower during winter months and early spring.

Tagetes erecta

Common Name: American marigold, African marigold

Flowers: Native to Mexico. Pungent, dense heads of white, yellow, and orange flowers up to 5″ (13cm) across. Deadhead to prolong bloom.

Leaves: Feathery, aromatic, deeply indented, dark green.

Habit: Three varieties: Dwarf, 10″–14″ (25–36cm) tall; medium, 15″–20″ (38–51cm) tall; and tall, 24″–36″ (61–91cm) tall. Upright, branching.

Culture: Easy to grow. Prefers full sun in well-drained, sandy or loam soil. Tolerates some dryness. Propagate by seeds, direct-sown or started indoors six weeks before outdoor planting. May self-sow.

Season of Bloom: All summer.

Hardiness: Tender annual killed by severe frost.

Uses: All-purpose flower. Good massed in beds and borders. Suitable for cutting. An important component to all-yellow gardens.

The 'Lady' series is an especially good display flower because the hybrid plants produce an extraordinary number of blooms—sometimes fifty open blooms on one plant at the same time. Compact, bushy plants don't need staking. Since seed is expensive, plants are best started indoors for transplanting into the garden after there is no longer a danger of frost.

Tagetes
patula

Common Name: French marigold

Flowers: Native to Mexico. Aromatic, tidy, single or double flower heads in yellow, gold, orange, red, and bicolors. Deadhead to prolong bloom.

Leaves: Feathery, aromatic, sharply indented, dark green.

Habit: 10″–16″ (25–41cm) tall. Dense, bushy, mounded.

Culture: Easy to grow. Prefers full sun in well-drained, sandy or loam soil. Tolerates some dryness. Propagate by seeds, direct-sown or started indoors four to six weeks before outdoor planting.

Season of Bloom: Early summer to frost.

Hardiness: Tender annual killed by severe frost.

Uses: All-purpose flower. Attractive massed in beds and borders and for edgings. Suitable for cutting.

The dozens of varieties from which to choose include award-winning 'Queen Sophia', a yellow and red bicolor, and 'Golden Gate', a golden yellow with a hint of bronze. Plant breeders have crossed French marigolds with African marigolds to produce a series known as triploid hybrids (or Mules). 'Red Seven Star' is a beautiful scarlet, while 'Fireworks Mixed' is a dazzling mixture. These triploid hybrids are sterile and cannot set viable seed, so all their energy is directed into producing a nonstop flowering display that can last for ten weeks.

Tagetes
tenuifolia

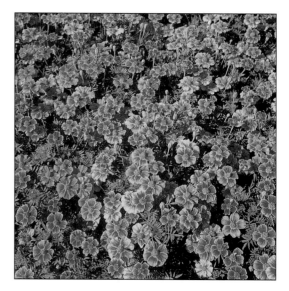

Common Name: Signet marigold

Flowers: Native to Mexico. Aromatic, single, open-faced, ½″ to 1″ (1 to 2.5cm) flowers. Colors include yellow, orange, and burnt red. For prolonged and abundant blooms, deadhead regularly.

Leaves: Feathery, aromatic, heavily indented, dark green.

Habit: 12″ (31cm) tall. Dense, bushy, mounded.

Culture: Easy to grow. Prefers full sun in well-drained, sandy or loam soil. Tolerates some dryness. Propagate by seeds, direct-sown or started indoors four to six weeks before outdoor planting.

Season of Bloom: Midsummer to frost.

Hardiness: Tender annual killed by severe frost.

Uses: Popular as an edging in mixed beds and borders. Good container plant. Can be used along dry walls and in rock gardens.

The botanical name for these cheerful, low-growing marigolds used to be *T. signata*. 'Paprika' is a glorious rusty red variety; 'Golden Gem' and 'Lemon Gem' are other good colors.

Thunbergia alata

Common Name:	Black-eyed Susan vine
Flowers:	Native to South Africa. Funnel-shaped, five-petaled, white, yellow, or orange flowers with black eyes; flowers borne in the axils of twining vines.
Leaves:	Heart-shaped, light green.
Habit:	3'–6' (.9–1.8m) tall. Climbing.
Culture:	Easy to grow. Prefers full sun in moist, humus-rich, loam soil. Propagate by seeds started indoors six weeks before outdoor planting.
Season of Bloom:	Summer to autumn. Blooms best when nights are cool.
Hardiness:	Tender annual killed by frost.
Uses:	Excellent as a quick cover for a screen or to beautify trellises and fences. Valuable as a trailing plant for containers, window boxes, and hanging baskets.

'Susie Mixed Colors' includes a balanced blend of orange, yellow, and white varieties. A popular plant to grow under glass for winter flowering.

Tithonia rotundifolia

Common Name:	Mexican sunflower
Flowers:	Native to Mexico. Sunny daisy flowers borne on upright stems. Flowers are generally orange-red, but can be bright yellow. Taller varieties may need staking. Pinch back young plants to encourage branching.
Leaves:	Heart-shaped, velvety, serrated, gray-green.
Habit:	2½'–6' (.8–1.8m) tall. Upright, shrubby.
Culture:	Easy to grow. Prefers full sun in well-drained, sandy or loam soil. Tolerates heat and drought. Propagate by seeds, direct-sown.
Season of Bloom:	Summer.
Hardiness:	Tender annual killed by frost.
Uses:	Attractive accent for backgrounds and to add color to dreary spots along a border. Makes a good screen. Suitable as a cut flower although must be treated by searing the end of the hollow stem to prevent wilting.

The variety 'Torch' is tall-growing, while 'Sundance' produces more robust, compact plants that generally do not need staking.

Torenia
fournieri

Common Name: Bluewings, wishbone flower

Flowers: Native to Africa. Two-lipped tubular flowers are white, violet, or pink with gold nectar markings at the base of the throat where pairs of yellow stamens are bent in the shape of a wishbone. Pinch back plants to encourage branching.

Leaves: Oval, serrated, green; on a square stem.

Habit: 12″ (31cm) tall. Mounded.

Culture: Easy to grow. Prefers light to full shade in well-drained, moist, humus-rich soil. Thrives in cool weather. Propagate by seeds started indoors eight weeks before outdoor planting.

Season of Bloom: Early summer to frost.

Hardiness: Tender annual killed by frost.

Uses: Popular massed in shaded beds, especially as borders and edgings. Attractive in pots, window boxes, and hanging baskets.

'Clown Mixed' is an award-winning variety with rose-pink, violet, white, and blue in a balanced blend.

Tropaeolum
majus

Common Name: Garden nasturtium

Flowers: Native to South America. Cheerful, trailing, single and double, upward-facing flowers with nectar-bearing spur. Colors include shades of yellow, orange, pink, red, and white.

Leaves: Circular, long-stemmed, bright green.

Habit: 12″ (31cm) mounds or 2½′–6′ (.8–1.8m) trailing habit, depending on variety.

Culture: Easy to grow. Prefers full sun in well-drained, sandy or loam soil. Tolerates impoverished soil and drought conditions. Rich soils produce lush leaf growth with few flowers. Propagate by seeds, direct-sown.

Season of Bloom: Spring and autumn; throughout the summer in cooler areas.

Hardiness: Tender annual killed by frost.

Uses: Popular as bedding plants or short trailers in beds, borders, containers, and hanging baskets. Attractive when allowed to cascade down walls. Useful as a screen if tied to a support.

'Whirlibird' is a "spurless" strain that causes the flowers to face up at the sky, creating a more colorful display when planted in beds and borders. 'Fordhook Favorites' are climbers that will grow to 6′ (1.8m) and can be trained up a trellis or left to creep across the ground.

Venidium fastuosom

Common Name: Cape daisy

Flowers: Native to South Africa. Bright daisylike flowers with a glistening black center surrounded by a purplish brown zone. Colors include orange, yellow, and white. Blossoms close during the night and in cloudy weather.

Leaves: Feathery, hairy, silver-white, with an interesting shimmering effect.

Habit: 24″ (61cm) tall. Bushy.

Culture: Easy to grow. Prefers full sun and light, well-drained, sandy or loam soil. Propagate by seeds, direct-sown.

Season of Bloom: All summer.

Hardiness: Tender annual killed by frost.

Uses: Attractive accent in mixed beds and borders. Good cut flower.

'Zulu Prince' is an unusual white variety with black markings around a dark eye. Make successive sowings to ensure summer-long displays.

Verbena × hybrida

Common Name: Garden verbena

Flowers: Native to South America. Abundant, scented, upright or creeping, flat clusters on short stalks. Colors include white, pink, red, blue, and purple. Frequently, flowers have contrasting white centers.

Leaves: Narrow, toothed, gray-green.

Habit: 12″ (31cm) tall. Low; erect or spreading, depending on variety.

Culture: Easy to grow. Prefers full sun in humus-rich, sandy or loam soil. Propagate by seeds started indoors six to eight weeks before outdoor planting.

Season of Bloom: Summer.

Hardiness: Tender annual killed by frost.

Uses: Old-fashioned garden favorite for edging and bedding. Also good for rock gardens and window boxes. Makes a colorful one-season ground cover.

Dozens of good varieties are offered by seed growers. 'Blaze' is a dazzling bright red that won an All-America award; 'Showtime' is a superb mixture with a good balance of red, white, blue, and pink varieties, many with contrasting eyes.

Zinnia angustifolia

Common Name: Classic zinnia

Flowers: Native to Mexico. Single, daisylike flowers have bright orange petals encircling deeper orange centers.

Leaves: Narrow, pointed, lancelike, green.

Habit: 12″ (31cm) tall. Spreading.

Culture: Easy to grow. Prefers full sun in well-drained, fertile, sandy or loam soil. Propagate by seeds, direct-sown.

Season of Bloom: July to frost.

Hardiness: Tender annual killed by frost.

Uses: Excellent massed as a ground cover or massed in beds, especially as an edging. Attractive as an accent plant in rock gardens. Also can be used in pots, window boxes, and hanging baskets.

'Rose Pinwheel' is an incredibly beautiful zinnia that resulted from crossing *Z. angustifolia* with *Z. elegans*. It has good mildew resistance. Flowering all summer, the blooms open pink and turn a lovely shade of deep rose. Growing just 10″–12″ (25–31cm) tall, the flowers are exquisite in dainty floral arrangements.

Zinnia elegans

Common Name: Common zinnia

Flowers: Native to Mexico. Single, double, or semi-double, daisylike flowers may have flat, twisted, or tubular petals. The petals encircle a center of yellow to purple disc flowers. The flowers come in every color except blue; some varieties are bicolored. Attracts butterflies.

Leaves: Long, spear-shaped, rough, green.

Habit: 6″–36″ (15–91cm) tall. Mounded or upright and bushy.

Culture: Easy to grow. Prefers full sun in well-drained, fertile, sandy or loam soil. Propagate by seeds, direct-sown.

Season of Bloom: Summer to frost.

Hardiness: Tender annual killed by frost.

Uses: Eye-catching when massed in beds and borders. Small varieties are effective as edgings or planted in containers. Good cut flower.

There are dozens of varieties to choose from. 'Burpee's Zenith' hybrids are among the largest-flowered, up to 5½″ (14cm) across. The Ruffles series are smaller-flowered, but they race into bloom within five weeks of sowing seed into the garden and don't stop until autumn frost. Cutting stimulates more buds to bloom. The Ruffles are highly mildew-resistant and cold-tolerant.

Perennials

Acanthus spinosus, A. spinossimus

Common Name:	Bear's-breech
Flowers:	Native to Greece. Stately clusters of tubular flowers with a protruding lower lip borne on erect spikes. Bicolors include white and purple, or white and rose.
Leaves:	Giant, shiny, deeply lobed, dark green, with prominent white veins. Often planted for the beauty and size of its decorative leaves.
Habit:	24″–48″ (61–122cm) tall. Upright, bushy.
Culture:	Prefers partial shade in hot, dry areas in well-drained, fertile soil. Can be planted in full sun in cooler areas. Tolerates drought conditions. Propagate by seeds, division, or cuttings.
Season of Bloom:	Mid- to late summer.
Hardiness:	Zones 5–9.
Uses:	Ideal for coastal gardens. Makes an excellent foliage plant and a good ground cover. Suitable for fresh and dried arrangements.

The variety *Acanthus mollis* 'Latifolius' has a more attractive leaf than *A. spinosus*. Though it is more free-flowering, it is not hardy north of zone 8.

Achillea filipendulina

Common Name:	Fern-leaf yarrow
Flowers:	Native to Europe. Bright, compact, flattened clusters of small yellow flowers. Remove flower stalks as they finish blooming to prolong flowering over several months.
Leaves:	Fernlike, aromatic, indented, bright green.
Habit:	36″–48″ (91–122cm) tall. Upright, clump-forming.
Culture:	Easy to grow. Prefers full sun in well-drained, loam soil. Propagate by seeds, division, or cuttings.
Season of Bloom:	Late spring to midsummer.
Hardiness:	Zones 3–9.
Uses:	Popular in mixed borders. Excellent fresh or dried flower.

So easy to grow, even in poor soils and subjected to total neglect, plants will crowd out weeds and spread vigorously. May need dividing every other year. A number of other *Achillea* species and hybrids are popular in home gardens, including *A. ptarmica* (a double white valued by flower arrangers), and *A. millefolium* (especially the variety 'Fire King' with its deep rosy red flowers). *A.* 'Debutante' is a sensational hybrid mixture, resulting from crosses with *A. taygetea*, which is native to Greece. Colors include yellow, white, pink, orange, lemon, and scarlet red.

Achillea millefolium

Common Name: Common yarrow

Flowers: The variety 'Fire King' is a selection of the species native to Europe. Similar to fern-leaf yarrow except for the color of the flat flower clusters, which is mostly rose-pink or orange-red.

Leaves: Feathery, fragrant, dark green.

Habit: Up to 36″ (91cm) tall. Clump-forming, aggressive.

Culture: Prefers full sun and well-drained soil; tolerates poor soil. Propagate by division in spring and autumn. Invasive if not divided after two years of growth.

Season of Bloom: Late spring to early summer.

Hardiness: Zones 3–9.

Uses: Good accent in beds and borders. Makes a long-lasting cut or dried flower.

The hybrid mixture 'Summer Shades' is a beautiful blend of pastel colors, including white, pink, lavender, yellow, and red.

Aconitum carmichaelii

Common Name: Monkshood

Flowers: Native to Japan. Clusters of hooded blue flowers on erect stems.

Leaves: Finely divided, rich green.

Habit: Up to 5′ (1.5m) tall. Upright, clump-forming.

Culture: Grows in full sun or light shade; prefers well-drained, sandy or loam soil. Generally needs staking. Propagate by seeds or division.

Season of Bloom: Late summer to autumn.

Hardiness: Zones 4–8.

Uses: Tall accent in mixed beds and borders.

A related species, *A. napellus*, native to Europe and Asia, is similar in appearance, but more prone to wind damage. The roots of all monkshoods are deadly poisonous.

Ajuga
reptans

Common Name:	Carpet bugleweed
Flowers:	Native to Europe. Showy tubular flowers of blue, purple, pink, or white surround a square stem.
Leaves:	Deciduous to evergreen. Oval; dark green, bronze, purple, or variegated; form a rosette.
Habit:	6″–9″ (15–23cm) tall. Low, spreading.
Culture:	Easy to grow. Prefers full sun or shade and moist but well-drained soil; tolerates poor soil. Propagate by seeds or division.
Season of Bloom:	Early to late spring.
Hardiness:	Zones 3–9.
Uses:	Popular as a ground cover, especially in lightly shaded areas. Attractive as an edging and massed in rock gardens.

So easy to grow, it's almost indestructible, crowding out weeds and even reseeding. The variegated forms are good for foliage effect but weak-flowering. 'Burgundy Glow' is a tricolor variety, with green, cream, and pink all in the same leaf. It makes an especially good edging. (The above photograph shows the blue and white varieties in combination.)

Alchemilla
mollis

Common Name:	Lady's-mantle
Flowers:	Native to Europe. Lacy, small, yellowish green flowers borne upright on branching spikes.
Leaves:	Ornamental, scalloped, velvety, silver-green; centers tend to collect rounded drops of morning dew or raindrops.
Habit:	10″–18″ (25–46cm) tall. Spreading.
Culture:	Easy to grow. Grows in full sun or partial shade in well-drained, rich soil. Prefers cool temperatures. Propagate by seeds or division.
Season of Bloom:	Late spring to early summer.
Hardiness:	Zones 4–7.
Uses:	Attractive as a ground cover, or as drifts in mixed beds and borders. Good as a fresh or dried cut flower.

Hardly anyone notices this plant until it's missing from the garden. It's virtually foolproof—just tuck it between tall perennials at the edge of the border and see how it lights up the entire garden. Also known as *A. vulgaris*, this is a good plant to use at the edge of perennial borders to spill into pathways and also at the edge of pools and ponds so that the leaves and flowers spill into the water.

Amsonia
tabernaemontana

Common Name:	Bluestar
Flowers:	Native to North America. Clusters of light blue, starlike flowers protrude from upright spikes.
Leaves:	Long, slender, pointed, medium green, with a prominent middle vein.
Habit:	24″ (61cm) tall. Upright, clump-forming.
Culture:	Prefers full sun in well-drained, moist, light soil. Propagate by division.
Season of Bloom:	Early to late spring.
Hardiness:	Zones 4–10.
Uses:	Adds interest to spring gardens when planted in clumps in mixed beds and borders. Good cut flower. An important component of all-blue gardens.

Tolerates crowding, and best grown in rock gardens as a drift of blue (as shown above). Combines well with *Baptisia,* which is a deeper blue-flowered perennial, blooming about the same time.

Anchusa
azurea

Common Name:	Italian bugloss, alkanet
Flowers:	Native to the Mediterranean region. Masses of dainty, five-petaled, blue flowers with white contrasting centers borne on branched stems.
Leaves:	Spear-shaped, hairy, medium green.
Habit:	2′–5′ (.6–1.5m) tall. Upright, branching.
Culture:	Prefers full sun in well-drained, moist, fertile soil. Tolerates partial shade. May require staking. Propagate by seeds, division, or cuttings.
Season of Bloom:	Late spring to midsummer.
Hardiness:	Zones 3–9.
Uses:	Handsome in informal gardens. A tall accent in mixed beds and borders.

The dwarf kinds are good summer-flowering substitutes for forget-me-nots, but you must find room for the tall kinds as a sensational early summer accent. 'Loddon Royalist' has especially large flowers, up to 3″ (7.5cm) across, borne in handsome clusters, and the floral spike reaching to 5′ (1.5m) tall. A more compact variety, 'Little John', grows just 18″ (46cm) tall, and is suitable for edging.

Anemone × hybrida

Anigozanthos flavidus

Common Name: Japanese anemone

Flowers: Native to Japan. Showy, solitary, single or double pure white or pink, roselike flowers with nodding, fuzzy silver buds.

Leaves: Large-toothed, partially lobed, dark green.

Habit: 24″–36″ (61–91cm) tall. Upright, branching.

Culture: Prefers full sun or partial shade in well-drained, fertile, humus-rich soil. Propagate by seeds or division of tubers.

Season of Bloom: Late summer to early autumn.

Hardiness: Zones 4–8.

Uses: Attractive planted among ferns, hostas, and asters. Good accent in borders and in rock gardens. Pretty cut flower.

Absolutely indispensable for the late-summer garden—clump them generously at the back of every border and admire their profusion of pastel colors. Also known as *A. japonica*. Many good varieties are available, including 'Whirlwind', a semidouble white (pictured above), and 'September Sprite' (a single-flowered pink).

Common Name: Kangaroo-paw

Flowers: Native to western Australia. Clusters of yellow, tubular flowers with tip curled under resemble a paw.

Leaves: Slender, sword-shaped, green.

Habit: Up to 48″ (122cm) tall. Upright, clump-forming.

Culture: Prefers full sun, warm, dry summers, and mild winters; demands excellent drainage and a sandy or gritty soil. Propagate primarily by division.

Season of Bloom: Summer.

Hardiness: Zones 8–10.

Uses: Good tall accent in mixed borders. Suitable for cutting.

There is a rusty red form generally listed as *A. coccineus.*

Anthemis tinctoria

Common Name: Golden marguerite

Flowers: Native to Europe. Prolific, golden yellow daisy flowers on tall, narrow stems. Rarely bothered by insects.

Leaves: Fernlike, dark green; pungent when crushed.

Habit: 24″–36″ (61–91cm) tall. Upright, bushy.

Culture: Prefers full sun in any well-drained, fertile soil. Propagate by division or cuttings.

Season of Bloom: Summer.

Hardiness: Zones 4–10.

Uses: Excellent planted in clumps for mixed beds and borders. Good cut flower.

It's impossible to have enough yellow in the garden for cheerful, sunny floral displays to brighten up the dark greens of summer, and the golden marguerite is so appealing, it's worth growing in containers. The variety 'Kelwayi' is especially popular in home gardens, having deep golden yellow flowers on compact, bushy plants, usually 18″–24″ (46–61cm) tall.

Aquilegia hybrids

Common Name: Columbine

Flowers: Most species native to the American Rockies and Japan. Attractive, unusual flowers with five petals that curve backward to form spurs with knob endings. The knobs contain nectar that is principally enjoyed by hummingbirds. Colors include white, yellow, blue, purple, red, pink, and bicolors.

Leaves: Four-lobed, toothed, gray-green.

Habit: 12″–18″ (31–46cm) tall. Upright, open, branching.

Culture: Prefers full sun or partial shade in well-drained, moist, loam soil. Propagate by seeds or division.

Season of Bloom: Late spring.

Hardiness: Zones 3–9.

Uses: Good for informal cottage-style gardens. Attractive in mixed beds and borders. Pretty cut flower.

The variety 'McKana Giants' is an especially beautiful mixture that will often bloom the first year from seed sown early indoors. In recent years, the blue columbines have become extremely popular, including *A. caerulea,* the Rocky Mountain columbine suitable for naturalizing. *A. canadensis,* a wild red columbine native to the eastern United States, is sensational combined with primroses and haphazardly planted along fern-fringed woodland paths.

Arabis
caucasica

Common Name:	Wall rock cress
Flowers:	Native to Europe. Fragrant clusters of cross-shaped, four-petaled, white or pink flowers on upright stems.
Leaves:	Small, spear-shaped, ruffled, dark green.
Habit:	12″ (31cm) tall. Mounded, spreading.
Culture:	Prefers full sun or partial shade in well-drained, loam soil. Propagate by seeds, division, or cuttings.
Season of Bloom:	Spring.
Hardiness:	Zones 4–10.
Uses:	Popular in rock gardens, near stone walls, and as an edging along the front of borders.

One of those diminutive plants that is so valuable for early spring color. Though hardly anyone notices it against the more brilliant tulip displays, it bridges the gap between lawn-level and knee-high color. Combines well with *Iberis sempervirens* (edging candytuft), and *Aurinia saxatilis* (perennial yellow alyssum), especially cascading over dry walls.

Armeria
maritima

Common Name:	Sea pink, thrift
Flowers:	Native to Europe. Globelike clusters of small flowers borne on stiff, erect stems partially covered by a papery filament. Colors include pink, red, lavender, and white.
Leaves:	Evergreen tufts are pointed, grasslike, gray-green.
Habit:	6″–10″ (15–25cm) tall. Mounded, clump-forming.
Culture:	Prefers full sun in well-drained, dry, sandy soil. Propagate by seeds or division. Clumps have a tendency to die out in the middle and should be divided every three years.
Season of Bloom:	Late spring to midsummer.
Hardiness:	Zones 4–8.
Uses:	Well adapted to coastal gardens. Popular in rock gardens, along pathways, or edging mixed beds and borders. Excellent cut flower.

Especially beautiful planted in drifts on slopes. Highly wind- and salt-tolerant. Sensational planted in cracks between flagstones.

Aruncus dioicus

Common Name: Goatsbeard

Flowers: Native to the Pacific Northwest. Graceful, feathery flower spikes are ivory white, almost dazzling in sunlight. Plants resemble astilbe, but are more dominant in the landscape.

Leaves: Pointed, serrated, bright green leaflets. Beautiful for foliage effect alone.

Habit: 4'–5' (1.2–1.5m) tall. Bushy.

Culture: Prefers light shade, but tolerates full sun; demands fertile, humus-rich soil, or boggy ground. Propagate by seeds or division.

Season of Bloom: Late spring to early summer.

Hardiness: Zones 4–9.

Uses: Attractive background accent for perennial borders. Best seen close to a water feature such as a pond or stream.

Sometimes listed as *Dioicus sylvester.* The variety 'Kneiffii' is a dwarf form, especially beautiful when contrasted with blue Siberian iris.

Asclepias tuberosa

Common Name: Butterfly weed

Flowers: Native to North America. Vibrant clusters of orange, red, or yellow star-shaped flowers borne on branching, erect stalks.

Leaves: Pointed, lancelike, medium green; spiral upward toward the flower cluster.

Habit: 24"–36" (61–91cm) tall. Upright, open, mounded.

Culture: Prefers full sun in dry, sandy soil or well-drained soil. Propagate by seeds or division.

Season of Bloom: Late spring to midsummer.

Hardiness: Zones 3–9.

Uses: Excellent in meadow gardens and in mixed beds and borders. Good cut flower.

The combination of orange butterfly weed and red or pink Shirley poppies is enchanting. 'Gay Butterflies' is an attractive mixture, containing not only the common orange, but also yellow, lemon, and bright red. If seeds are started early indoors, plants may bloom the first year. Grows best where summers are warm and sunny.

Asphodeline
lutea

Common
Name: Asphodel, king's-spear

Flowers: Native to Sicily. Erect flower spikes are studded with 1″ (2.5cm) yellow, star-shaped florets that are lightly fragrant.

Leaves: Grasslike, blue-green.

Habit: Up to 42″ (107cm) tall. Clump-forming, with poker-straight flower stems.

Culture: Prefers full sun, good drainage, and fertile, loam soil. Propagate by seeds or division.

Season
of Bloom: Early summer.

Hardiness: Zones 5–9.

Uses: Best as a stately accent in mixed beds and borders.

After flowering, the spent flower spikes can be harvested and hung to dry for use in decorative arrangements.

Aster
novae-angliae

Common
Name: New England aster, Michaelmas daisy

Flowers: Native to New England. Masses of small, yellow-eyed, daisylike flowers bunched together in one large mound. Colors range from pink to deep violet-purple and sometimes white. If plant grows leggy, trim to bushy form. Pruning stimulates flowering.

Leaves: Small, narrow, serrated, green.

Habit: 3′–5′ (.9–1.5m) tall. Upright, mounded.

Culture: Prefers full sun in well-drained, sandy or loam soil. Propagate by division in spring.

Season
of Bloom: Late summer to early autumn.

Hardiness: Zones 3–8.

Uses: Excellent plant for autumn bloom. Good in mixed beds and borders. Left unpruned, it is good for background planting. Long-lasting cut flower.

The variety 'Harrington's Pink' (pictured above) produces masses of large pink flowers. Also consider varieties of *A. novi-belgii* (New York aster), which bloom about the same time. Combines well with dahlias, cosmos, and multiflora sunflowers.

Astilbe × arendsii

Common Name: Astilbe

Flowers: Native to Asia. Graceful, showy, feathery white or pink flower plumes grow erect on slender spikes.

Leaves: Serrated, deeply indented, medium green.

Habit: 2′–4′ (.6–1.2m) tall. Upright, bushy.

Culture: Prefers partial shade in well-drained, moist, humus-rich, garden soil. Propagate by seeds or division in spring.

Season of Bloom: Early to midsummer.

Hardiness: Zones 4–9.

Uses: Excellent for wet and shady areas, along stream banks and pond margins. Popular in mixed beds and borders. Flower plumes add interest in dried arrangements.

It's hardly possible to have too many astilbe in the garden, they are so appealing. 'Fanal' is a brilliant fiery red variety, 'Peach Blossom' a beautiful light pink, and 'Snowdrift' a striking pure white. All are similar in height. *A. chinensis* 'Pumila' is a dwarf astilbe suitable for edging.

Aubrieta deltoidea

Common Name: False rock cress

Flowers: Native to Europe. Clusters of four-petaled pink, rose, lavender, or purple flowers on erect, short stalks.

Leaves: Oval, gray-green; form rosettes.

Habit: 6″ (15cm) tall. Low, compact, mounded.

Culture: Prefers full sun in well-drained, sandy or loam soil. Propagate by seeds, division, or cuttings.

Season of Bloom: Early to mid-spring.

Hardiness: Zones 4–8.

Uses: Makes a good rock garden plant. Perfect lodged in stone walls or along the edges of perennial gardens.

Aubrietas do not come true to color from seed, but 'Royal Cascade' is a trailing kind that predominates in rosy red and pink tones. *Aubrieta novalis* 'Blue' displays sensational medium-blue flowers twice the size of other aubrietas. This, too, is a trailing plant excellent for growing along dry walls.

Aurinia
saxatilis

**Common
Name:**   Basket-of-gold

Flowers: Native to Europe. Compact masses of four-petaled, yellow flowers arranged in showy clusters.

Leaves: Oval, hairy, gray-green.

Habit: 9"–12" (23–31cm) tall. Low, mounded, spreading.

Culture: Prefers full sun in well-drained, moist, sandy or loam soil. If soil is too rich, plant will appear coarse and leggy. Propagate by seeds or division.

**Season
of Bloom:**   Early to mid-spring.

Hardiness: Zones 3–7.

Uses: Good for trailing over rock walls and edging raised beds.

This used to be listed in catalogs as *Alyssum saxatile*. 'Citrina' is a good lemon-yellow variety; 'Compacta' a golden yellow that is more spreading in habit. 'Flore Plenum' is a double-flowered version of 'Compacta'. Combines well with tulips and blue flowers such as forget-me-nots and Jacob's-ladder.

Baptisia
australis

**Common
Name:**   Wild blue indigo

Flowers: Native to North America. Erect lupinelike spikes of indigo-blue flowers borne on tall stems. Taller plants may need staking. Deadhead spent flowers to prolong blooming period.

Leaves: Oval, cloverlike, bright green.

Habit: 36"–48" (91–122cm) tall. Upright, bushy, spirelike.

Culture: Prefers full sun or partial shade in well-drained, sandy or loam soil. Propagate by seeds or division. If grown by seeds, plants will flower in two or three years. Deadhead faded flowers to prolong flowering.

**Season
of Bloom:**   Mid- to late spring.

Hardiness: Zones 3–8.

Uses: Superb background plant for mixed beds and borders. Attractive in herb gardens. Seed pods are good in dried flower arrangements.

Almost impossible to kill. An important component of all-blue gardens. *B. pendula* is white-flowered.

Bergenia
cordifolia

Common Name:	Heartleaf bergenia
Flowers:	Native to Siberia. Clusters of small, pink, bell-shaped flowers are borne at the top of short, fleshy stalks.
Leaves:	Evergreen, attractive, succulent, heart-shaped, shiny, displaying a blush of purple or pink during the winter.
Habit:	12″ (31cm) tall. Clump-forming.
Culture:	Prefers full sun or partial shade in well-drained, fertile, humus-rich soil. Propagate by division in spring.
Season of Bloom:	Early to late spring.
Hardiness:	Zones 3–8.
Uses:	Attractive as a spring-flowering ground cover. Popular in rock gardens and along stream banks and pond margins.

Many new varieties and hybrids have been produced by German plant breeders. 'Silver Light' is a beautiful white that turns pink with age; 'Evening Glow' has crimson-purple flowers and striking maroon-colored leaves in winter. The plants look especially attractive planted next to old brick.

Boltonia
asteroides

Common Name:	Boltonia
Flowers:	Native to North America. Spectacular billowing mound of daisylike flowers, each up to 1″ (2.5cm) across. So free-flowering, foliage is almost completely hidden. Usually white, but can be pink.
Leaves:	Slender, gray-green; on wiry stems.
Habit:	Up to 6′ (1.8m) tall. Cloudlike, generally needs staking to stay upright.
Culture:	Prefers full sun and good drainage. Propagate by division in autumn, by tip cuttings in spring.
Season of Bloom:	Late summer to early autumn.
Hardiness:	Zones 3–8.
Uses:	Excellent background plant for mixed beds and borders. Popular as an accent plant, prized for its height and brilliance.

The variety 'Snowbank' is a more compact plant than the species, growing 4′ (122cm) tall. Combines well with autumn-flowering *Sedum* 'Autumn Joy', *Anemone* × *hybrida*, and *Aster novae-angliae*, and also with ornamental grasses such as *Miscanthus* (pictured above).

Caltha
palustris

Common Name:	Marsh marigold
Flowers:	Native to northern Europe. Waxy, bright yellow buttercup flowers held upright on long, fleshy stems.
Leaves:	Heart-shaped, rounded, dark green.
Habit:	6″–12″ (15–31cm) tall. Clump-forming.
Culture:	Prefers full sun or partial shade and constant moisture or boggy soil. Propagate by division.
Season of Bloom:	Early spring.
Hardiness:	Zones 4–9.
Uses:	Excellent for wet soil areas around streams, ponds, or water gardens.

Blooms even before the last snowfall of winter. 'Alba' is a white variety with a conspicuous dome of yellow stamens; 'Flore Pleno' is double-flowered and more free-flowering than the single-flowered species.

Campanula
glomerata

Common Name:	Clustered bellflower
Flowers:	Native to Europe. Dense clusters of delicate, bell-shaped flowers face upward toward the sun. Colors include blue, violet-blue, and white.
Leaves:	Long, pointed, lancelike, bright green.
Habit:	12″–36″ (31–91cm) tall. Upright, clump-forming.
Culture:	Easy to grow. Prefers full sun or partial shade in moist soil. Can be invasive. Propagate by seeds or division in spring or autumn.
Season of Bloom:	Late spring to early summer.
Hardiness:	Zones 3–9.
Uses:	Popular as an accent in mixed borders and in rock gardens.

By far the showiest of bellflowers—and the easiest to grow. 'Crown of Snow' is a beautiful white-flowered form; 'Superba' has large violet-blue flowers and is taller than most other varieties. A valuable component of all-blue gardens, it is pictured here with *Salvia sclarea* and yellow columbine.

Campanula persicifolia

Common Name: Peach-bells, willow bellflower

Flowers: Native to Europe. Long, upright spikes of powdery blue or white bell-shaped flowers. For prolific flowering, pick off spent flowers and cut back stems to encourage second bloom cycle.

Leaves: Drooping, willowlike, medium green.

Habit: 24″–36″ (62–91cm) tall. Upright, clump-forming.

Culture: Easy to grow. Prefers full sun or partial shade in well-drained, sandy or loam soil. Propagate by seeds, division, or cuttings.

Season of Bloom: Late spring to early summer.

Hardiness: Zones 3–8.

Uses: Suitable in front of mixed borders or planted as drifts in rock gardens. Excellent cut flower.

'Alba' has beautiful white flowers. Other popular bellflowers for the perennial border include *C. medium* (Canterbury-bells), actually a biennial (see **Annuals**); *C. carpatica* (tussock bellflower), creating a mound of bell-shaped blue flowers; and *C. portenschlagiana* (Dalmatian bellflower), low-growing and excellent for edging beds.

Catananche caerulea

Common Name: Cupid's-dart

Flowers: Native to the Mediterranean region. Papery blue flowers with jagged petals resemble cornflowers. Borne erect on tall, wiry stems.

Leaves: Slender, grasslike, gray-green.

Habit: 18″–24″ (46–61cm) tall. Upright.

Culture: Prefers full sun in well-drained, sandy or loam soil. Intolerant of wet soil. Propagate by seeds or division.

Season of Bloom: Midsummer.

Hardiness: Zones 3–9.

Uses: Good massed in borders. Fine for fresh and dried flower arrangements.

'Alba' has white flowers; 'Blue Giant' pale blue flowers. An old-fashioned favorite for cottage gardens. Thrives in coastal gardens. Combines well with ornamental grasses.

Centranthus ruber

Common Name: Red valerian

Flowers: Native to the Mediterranean region. Large, fragrant clusters of pink, red, or white flowers on erect spikes. Prune after flowering to encourage late-season blossoms.

Leaves: Oval, pointed, smooth, gray-green.

Habit: 24"–36" (61–91cm) tall. Upright, clump-forming.

Culture: Prefers full sun in well-drained, slightly alkaline soil. Propagate by seeds or division.

Season of Bloom: Usually late spring or early summer. In cool climates, flowering continues throughout the summer.

Hardiness: Zones 4–7.

Uses: Old-fashioned favorite. Makes an excellent accent in mixed beds or borders. Good in rock gardens and next to stone walls. Suitable for cutting.

'Albus' has white flowers; 'Roseus' has rosy pink flowers. Plants grown from seeds offer considerable variation in color, so be on the alert for anything distinctive to propagate by division. Thrives in coastal gardens. Sensational planted near old-fashioned roses.

Cerastium tomentosum

Common Name: Snow-in-summer

Flowers: Native to Europe. Cheerful masses of starlike white flowers with notched petals.

Leaves: Small, lancelike, smooth, covered with a silvery down.

Habit: 3"–6" (7.5–15cm) tall. Spreading.

Culture: Prefers full sun in well-drained soil. Propagate by seeds, division, or cuttings.

Season of Bloom: Mid- to late spring.

Hardiness: Zones 4–8.

Uses: Excellent in rock gardens, massed as a ground cover, and in nooks and crannies of stone walls.

A seemingly insignificant plant, like perennial candytuft, that is easily overshadowed by more spectacular perennials but helps weave colors together. A popular component of all-white gardens. The silvery foliage helps make this plant especially good for coastal gardens where sea mists diffuse light and make silver-foliaged plants look mysterious.

Chrysanthemum coccineum, Tanacetum coccineum

Common Name: Painted daisy

Flowers: Native to Africa. Cheerful white, pink, or red daisylike flowers with golden button centers stand erect on strong, wiry stems.

Leaves: Feathery, light green.

Habit: 24″ (61cm) tall. Upright, clump-forming.

Culture: Prefers full sun in moist, humus-rich, sandy or loam soil. Propagate by seeds or division. If spent flower stems are cut to the ground, the plant may rebloom.

Season of Bloom: Late spring to early summer.

Hardiness: Zones 4–9.

Uses: Popular massed in mixed beds and borders. Fine cut flower.

Create as big a planting as possible, for you will not resist cutting the flowers to create cheerful indoor floral arrangements. The petals are a source of pyrethrum insecticide. 'Hybrid Double Mixed' is a good variety to grow from seed, flowering the second year. Plants are sometimes listed as *Pyrethrum roseum.*

Chrysanthemum × morifolium

Common Name: Garden mum, florists' chrysanthemum

Flowers: Hybrid of species native to China. Ranges in size and shape from globular heads to daisylike flowers. Colors include white, yellow, bronze, orange, red, lavender, and purple. Pinch back plant in spring and summer for compact, rounded look.

Leaves: Notched, dark green.

Habit: 12″–24″ (31–61cm) tall. Mounded.

Culture: Easy to grow. Prefers full sun in well-drained, fertile, sandy or loam soil. Propagate by division or cuttings.

Season of Bloom: Midsummer to frost.

Hardiness: Zones 5–8.

Uses: Delightful planted in drifts among mixed beds and borders, in edgings, and in containers. Cascading kinds are popular for balcony planters. Popular cut flower.

The so-called "cushion" mums are the most popular, though there is considerable variation in hardiness among them. 'Autumn Glory' is a beautiful mixture that can be grown from seed to flower the first year. However, ready-to-bloom potted mums are so inexpensive in autumn, it's hardly worth maintaining plants in your beds and borders the whole year.

Chrysanthemum ×
parthenium

**Common
Name:** Feverfew

Flowers: Native to Europe. Dainty, daisylike, small white flowers on long, upright, branching stalks. Can be invasive.

Leaves: Narrow, pointed, medium green.

Habit: 24″–36″ (61–91cm) tall. Upright, clump-forming.

Culture: Easy to grow. Prefers full sun in well-drained, sandy or loam soil. Propagate by seeds or division.

**Season
of Bloom:** Summer.

Hardiness: Zones 6–8.

Uses: Attractive in back of borders or in mixed beds. Good in naturalized settings. Long-lasting cut flower.

Well-grown plants present a billowing mass of white blossoms. Indispensable in mixed perennial borders, especially with yarrow and garden lilies. Sometimes listed as *Matricaria*. 'Butterball' has double yellow blooms that will flower the first year from seed sown early indoors and is sufficiently compact to consider for edging and containers, especially window boxes.

Chrysanthemum ×
superbum

**Common
Name:** Shasta daisy

Flowers: Developed from species native to Europe. Up to 4″ (10cm) single or double white daisylike flowers with yellow discs borne on sturdy, erect stems. Pinch back young shoots to encourage bushy growth.

Leaves: Narrow, pointed, toothed, dark green.

Habit: 12″–36″ (31–91cm) tall. Upright, clump-forming.

Culture: Easy to grow. Prefers full sun in well-drained, fertile, sandy or loam soil. Propagate by seeds or division.

**Season
of Bloom:** Summer.

Hardiness: Zones 4–9.

Uses: Suitable for mixed beds and borders and cutting gardens. Dwarf types are good for edgings. Attractive in containers. Long-lasting cut flower.

Often confused with *C. leucanthemum* (oxeye daisies), which are earlier flowering and not so large-flowered. Best to have them both in your garden. 'Marconi' is a large-flowered double white shasta daisy with individual flowers up to 6″ (15cm) across. 'Snow Lady' is a dwarf variety that will flower the first year from seed sown early indoors.

Cimicifuga racemosa

Common Name:	Black cohosh, black snakeroot
Flowers:	Native to North America. Lacy, creamy white, bottlebrushlike flowers borne erect on tall, branching, swaying spikes. May need staking.
Leaves:	Serrated, feathery, dark green.
Habit:	4'–6' (1.2–1.8m) tall. Upright, clump-forming.
Culture:	Easy to grow. Prefers partial sun in moist, humus-rich soil. Propagate mainly by seeds.
Season of Bloom:	Late summer to early autumn.
Hardiness:	Zones 3–8.
Uses:	Excellent in woodland settings or the rear of a shaded border. Attractive cut flower.

A related species, *C. simplex,* flowers for several weeks in late summer. The flower plumes are graceful and arching, not so tall as *C. racemosa,* and superb for all-white gardens. The variety 'White Pearl' is extremely free-flowering, growing 48″ (122cm) tall.

Coreopsis lanceolata

Common Name:	Tickseed, lance-leaf coreopsis
Flowers:	Native to North America. Bright, sunny bursts of yellow, double-petaled flowers on erect stems. Clip spent blossoms to prolong flowering.
Leaves:	Sparse, lancelike, light green.
Habit:	24″–36″ (61–91cm) tall. Spreading, clump-forming.
Culture:	Easy to grow. Performs best in full sun in well-drained, fertile, sandy or loam soil. Tolerates dry and moist soil. Propagate by dividing clumps every two or three years in spring.
Season of Bloom:	Early to late summer.
Hardiness:	Zones 4–10.
Uses:	Attractive accent in mixed beds and borders and in meadow gardens. Good cut flower.

The appeal of this easy-to-grow perennial was considerably enhanced by the introduction of the award-winning, everblooming 'Early Sunrise', which will flower the first year from seed and cover itself with large semidouble flowers up to 4″ (10cm) across. Other good related coreopsis species for perennial gardens include *C. verticillata,* creating a 24″ (61cm) mound of starry yellow flowers, and *C. rosea,* of similar habit but pink-flowered.

Dianthus plumarius

Common Name:	Cottage pink
Flowers:	Native to Europe. Fragrant, single or double, fringed, carnationlike flowers. Colors include white, pink, rose, purple, and bicolors.
Leaves:	Narrow, grasslike, blue-gray; form dense evergreen tufts.
Habit:	12″ (31cm) tall. Dense, mounded.
Culture:	Prefers full sun in well-drained, alkaline soil. Enjoys cool coastal conditions, but can flourish in hot climates if well watered. Propagate by seeds, division, cuttings, or layering.
Season of Bloom:	Late spring to early summer.
Hardiness:	Zones 3–9.
Uses:	Sensational in coastal gardens. Attractive in rock gardens and for edging mixed borders. Excellent cut flower.

A hybrid of *D. plumarius* and *D. caryophyllus* (perennial carnations) was produced in England, called Allwood hybrids, or *D. × Allwoodii*. It has inherited the hardiness of *D. plumarius* and the color range of carnations.

Dicentra spectabilis

Common Name:	Bleeding-heart
Flowers:	Native to Japan. An old-fashioned favorite. Nodding sprays of pink and white, or just white, heart-shaped flowers borne on fleshy stems.
Leaves:	Attractive, dainty, deeply cut, gray-green. The leaves die back after blooming and reappear the following spring.
Habit:	24″–36″ (61–91cm) tall. Bushy, rounded, with arching stems.
Culture:	Prefers partial shade in fertile, humus-rich, moist but well-drained soil that is well mulched. Propagate by seeds, root cuttings, or division in spring or autumn.
Season of Bloom:	Late spring to early summer.
Hardiness:	Zones 2–9.
Uses:	Attractive accent alone or in groups in mixed, shady borders or planted at the edge of woods. Suitable for cutting.

'Alba' is a beautiful white-flowered variety. *D. eximia*—a ground cover bleeding-heart, native to the mountains of the northeastern United States—is another excellent perennial for shade. The variety 'Luxurient' is especially free-flowering.

Digitalis grandiflora, D. ambigua

Common Name: Yellow foxglove

Flowers: Native to Greece. Enchanting clumps of erect, creamy yellow flower spikes with nodding tubular florets resembling the common foxglove.

Leaves: Evergreen, broad, pointed.

Habit: Up to 30″ (76cm) tall. Clump-forming. Shorter than the tall common foxglove.

Culture: Prefers full sun in a moist but well-drained, humus-rich, acid soil. Propagate by seeds or division.

Season of Bloom: Early summer.

Hardiness: Zones 4–8.

Uses: Good accent in mixed beds and borders, especially in combination with blue perennial salvias.

The above photograph shows *D. grandiflora* with clumps of blue *Salvia × superba* 'Blue Queen' in the background.

Doronicum caucasicum

Common Name: Leopard's-bane, dogbane

Flowers: Native to Europe. Bright, daisylike, yellow flowers borne upright on slender stems.

Leaves: Stem-clasping, heart-shaped, coarsely toothed, green. May die back after flowering to reappear in the spring.

Habit: 24″ (61cm) tall. Upright, clump-forming.

Culture: Prefers partial shade in hot climates, full sun in cooler climates, and well-drained, moist soil. Plants should be heavily mulched to preserve moisture around the shallow roots. Propagate by seeds or division in late summer.

Season of Bloom: Early to mid-spring.

Hardiness: Zones 4–7.

Uses: Excellent spring flower for mixed borders. Attractive in rock gardens. Good cut flower.

Combines well with tulips and primroses. Looks good in a small clump or massed as a sweep of color. 'Miss Mason' (pictured above) is a superior hybrid form. A related species, *D. grandiflorum*, is low-growing, compact, and suitable for rock gardens.

Echinacea
purpurea

Common Name: Purple coneflower

Flowers: Native to North America. Solitary heads of colorful, swept-back 4″ (10cm) purple flowers with domed orange-brown centers.

Leaves: Spear-shaped, coarsely toothed, dark green.

Habit: 24″–48″ (61–122cm) tall. Upright, clump-forming.

Culture: Easy to grow. Prefers full sun in well-drained, sandy or loam soil. In extreme hot weather, mottled shade will produce brighter flowers. Tolerates drought. Propagate mainly by cuttings or division every three or four years in the spring.

Season of Bloom: Summer.

Hardiness: Zones 3–8.

Uses: Popular accent in mixed borders or in naturalized meadow gardens. Good, long-lasting cut flower.

'Bright Star' (pictured above with double pink hollyhocks) is a popular bright rosy red selection of the species. 'White Swan' is an attractive white. Combines well with *Rudbeckia hirta* (black-eyed Susan), especially planted in large groups, and as meadow plantings.

Echinops
ritro

Common Name: Small globe thistle

Flowers: Native to Greece. Stately, globular heads of sharp, spiny bracts and deep, metallic blue tubular flowers borne on long, tough stems.

Leaves: Thistlelike, sharply toothed, medium green, with downy undersides.

Habit: 36″–48″ (91–122cm) tall. Upright, branching.

Culture: Prefers full sun, good drainage, and fertile sandy soil. Tolerates partial shade, heat, and drought. Propagate by cuttings or division in the spring.

Season of Bloom: Midsummer to early autumn.

Hardiness: Zones 3–8.

Uses: Excellent accent in mixed borders. Combines well with summer phlox. Good for fresh and dried flower arrangements.

The variety 'Taplow Blue' (pictured above) creates an especially good highlight. Low-growing annuals and daylilies are best clustered around the base of these plants, as lower stems tend to be bare.

Erigeron glaucus and hybrids

Common Name: Fleabane, beach aster

Flowers: Native to coastal California and Oregon. Clusters of daisylike purple or pink flowers with yellow centers.

Leaves: Stem-clasping, lancelike, medium green.

Habit: 18″–24″ (46–61cm) tall. Bushy, rounded.

Culture: Prefers full sun in well-drained, sandy or loam soil. Tolerates salt spray and high winds. Propagate by cuttings in spring or by division every two or three years.

Season of Bloom: Midsummer, with sporadic blooming through autumn.

Hardiness: Zones 4–8.

Uses: Popular in rock gardens and mixed borders, especially in coastal gardens. Attractive cut flower.

'Adria' is an especially good free-flowering variety bearing masses of deep rosy pink flowers with bright yellow centers. 'Azure Beauty' has beautiful blue flowers. Combines well with ornamental grasses.

Eryngium giganteum

Common Name: Eryngo, giant sea holly

Flowers: Native mostly to the Mediterranean region. Unusual silver flowers up to 4″ (10cm) across, surrounded by a circle of bracts that resemble spiny holly leaves.

Leaves: Three-lobed, white-veined, gray-green.

Habit: Up to 36″ (91cm). Upright, branching.

Culture: Prefers full sun, good drainage, and sandy soil. Propagate by cuttings or division.

Season of Bloom: Summer.

Hardiness: Zones 6–9.

Uses: Grown primarily for its unusual, white-veined foliage. Makes an excellent accent in mixed borders, or a specimen plant. Interesting fresh or dried; if flowers are picked just as they open, they will retain color when dried.

Other good species to consider that are not so large-flowered include *E. amethystinum* (bears many small, amethyst-blue flower heads) and *E. bourgatii* (low-growing mounded plants just 24″ [61cm] tall). A larger-flowered species, *E. alpinum*, exhibits frilly blue bracts.

Eupatorium coelestinum

Common Name:	Hardy ageratum
Flowers:	Native to the eastern United States. Flat-topped, tight clusters of fuzzy blue, purple, or white flowers borne erect on branching stems.
Leaves:	Lancelike, serrated, hairy, green.
Habit:	12″–24″ (31–61cm) tall. Upright, bushy, branching.
Culture:	Easy to grow. Prefers full sun in well-drained, sandy or loam soil. Tolerates partial shade. Propagate by seeds or division in spring.
Season of Bloom:	Midsummer to frost.
Hardiness:	Zones 5–10.
Uses:	Attractive in mixed beds and borders. Frequently planted for late-season flowering. Also grown as a cutting flower.

Other good eupatorium species for the perennial garden include *E. fistulosum* and *E. purpureum* (Joe-Pye weed). These produce mounded, dusky rose-pink blooms on 5′ (1.5m) stems. Flowering in late summer and early autumn, they are highly attractive to butterflies.

Euphorbia epithymoides

Common Name:	Spurge, cushion spurge
Flowers:	Native to eastern Europe. Unusual 3″ (7.5cm) flower clusters are bright chartreuse-yellow and appear in the middle of bright yellow bracts.
Leaves:	Needlelike, grayish green, turning a rust color in autumn. Exudes a milky sap when broken.
Habit:	12″–18″ (31–46cm) tall. Compact, mounded.
Culture:	Easy to grow. Prefers full sun in well-drained, sandy or loam soil. Propagate by seeds or division in spring.
Season of Bloom:	Early to midsummer.
Hardiness:	Zones 5–9.
Uses:	Suitable for dry walls, edging borders, and ground cover.

Also listed as *E. polychroma*. Other good perennial euphorbias include *E. griffithii* 'Fireglow', producing 36″ (91cm) clumps with bright red floral bracts, and *E. myrsinites*, a low, spreading ground cover with early-flowering yellow bracts.

Filipendula rubra

Common Name:	Queen-of-the-prairie, pink meadowsweet
Flowers:	Native to the eastern United States. Fluffy pink flower clusters, up to 12″ (31cm) across, on strong, wiry stems.
Leaves:	Sharply indented, medium green.
Habit:	Up to 6′ (1.8m) tall. Clump-forming, aggressive.
Culture:	Prefers full sun or light shade and moist, fertile, loam soil. Tolerates boggy soil. Propagate primarily by division.
Season of Bloom:	Early summer.
Hardiness:	Zones 4–8.
Uses:	Good tall background accent to mixed perennial borders.

Several species of *Filipendula* (mostly white-flowered) are grown in perennial gardens, but *F. rubra* is generally considered the best. A good companion to lilies.

Gaillardia × grandiflora

Common Name:	Blanket flower
Flowers:	Native to North America. Colorful heads of yellow, burgundy, red, and bicolored flowers with yellow or purple centers. Prolific bloomer.
Leaves:	Deeply lobed, grayish green.
Habit:	24″–36″ (61–91cm) tall. Bushy, sprawling.
Culture:	Prefers full sun in light, well-drained, reasonably fertile soil. Propagate by seeds, cuttings, or division in spring.
Season of Bloom:	Summer.
Hardiness:	Zones 4–10.
Uses:	Popular in mixed beds and borders. Excellent cut flower.

Sensational combined with nasturtiums and coreopsis. 'Baby Cole' and 'Goblin' are two mounded, dwarf varieties suitable for edging and rock gardens. 'Monarch Mixed' is a good tall variety to grow from seed. Others, such as 'Burgundy', displaying large wine-red flowers, should be bought as plants or propagated by division.

Geranium himalayense

Common Name: Blue cranesbill

Flowers: Native to the Himalayas. Attractive, five-petaled, 2″ (5cm), lilac-colored flowers with purple veins. Although this variety is not a true blue color, it is considered a blue perennial.

Leaves: Hairy, deeply indented, dull green.

Habit: 12″–18″ (31–46cm) tall. Mounded, spreading.

Culture: Prefers partial shade in moist, humus-rich, loam soil. Tolerates full sun in cool climates. Propagate by seeds, cuttings, or division in spring or autumn.

Season of Bloom: Late spring to summer during cool weather. In hot areas, flowering is restricted to late spring. A hybrid, 'Johnson's Blue' (pictured above), may bloom from mid-spring to early autumn.

Hardiness: Zones 4–10.

Uses: Attractive in mixed beds and borders when planted in drifts. Good ground cover.

Other good perennial species for the perennial border include *G. sanguineum* (cerise-colored flowers) and *G. macrorrhizuum* (cheerful pink flowers.)

Geum chiloense, G. quellyon

Common Name: Avens, geum

Flowers: Native to Chile. Double and semidouble roselike flowers in shades of yellow, orange, and red. To increase flowering period, remove spent blooms.

Leaves: Hairy, deeply lobed, medium green.

Habit: 12″–18″ (31–46cm) tall. Upright, branching.

Culture: Prefers full sun or partial shade in well-drained, sandy or loam soil. Propagate by seeds or division.

Season of Bloom: Spring to summer during cool weather.

Hardiness: Zones 5–9.

Uses: Grown primarily in cutting gardens and as an accent in mixed beds and borders. Sensational in coastal gardens combined with foxgloves.

'Lady Stratheden' is a semidouble golden yellow that grows true to color from seed; 'Mrs. Bradshaw' is a rich orange-red semidouble that also grows true from seed. There is no color quite like 'Mrs. Bradshaw' in all the world of perennials. It is outstanding in any garden where there is a preponderance of orange and yellow flowers.

Gypsophila paniculata

Common Name:	Baby's-breath
Flowers:	Native to Europe. From a distance, plants appear to be a delicate mist of dainty white or pink flowers with an open, airy, branching pattern.
Leaves:	Small, lancelike, green.
Habit:	12″–24″ tall (31–61cm). Mounded, billowing.
Culture:	Prefers full sun in well-drained, nutrient-poor soil. Propagate primarily by seeds or by division in spring or autumn.
Season of Bloom:	Early summer. Flowering can be extended by successive plantings timed two to three weeks apart.
Hardiness:	Zones 3–9.
Uses:	Attractive in cutting gardens or rock gardens. Dried flowers are prized in wedding bouquets and flower arrangements. Often planted below tall-growing perennials such as lilies and phlox to hide bare or mildewed lower stems.

'Pink Fairy' has double pink flowers. 'Bristol Fairy' is probably the best double white-flowered variety, creating a cloudlike mass. *G. elegans* is a low-growing, spreading, annual baby's breath good for the front of borders.

Helenium autumnale

Common Name:	Sneezeweed
Flowers:	Native to North America. Sunny, daisylike flowers up to 1½″ (4cm) across are held upright on branching stems. Colors range from yellow to orange or reddish brown. Usually needs staking.
Leaves:	Pointed, lancelike, serrated, medium green.
Habit:	2½′–6′ (8–1.8m) tall. Upright, bushy.
Culture:	Prefers full sun in moist, sandy or loam soil. Tolerates wet, soggy soils. Propagate by division every three years.
Season of Bloom:	Late summer to frost.
Hardiness:	Zones 3–8.
Uses:	Popular in cutting gardens and as a tall accent in mixed borders.

The variety 'Brilliant' is a beautiful rusty red; 'Butterpat' is a bright yellow. The two in combination (pictured here) create a stunning mass of color, especially in combination with pink asters and ornamental grasses.

Helianthemum nummularium

Common Name: Rock rose

Flowers: Native to Europe. Dainty, crinkled, five-petaled 1″ (2.5cm) flowers surrounding a center of numerous yellow stamens. Colors include yellow, orange, pink, red, and bicolors. Petals resemble crepe paper.

Leaves: Small, oblong, grayish green.

Habit: 6″–12″ (15–31cm) tall. Low, mounded, spreading.

Culture: Prefers full sun in well-drained, sandy or loam soil that is on the dry side and preferably alkaline. Mulch for winter protection. Propagate by division in spring or by cuttings in summer.

Season of Bloom: Late spring to early summer.

Hardiness: Zones 5–7.

Uses: A good rock garden or border plant. Grown as a ground cover and in dry walls.

Sensational planted in cracks between paving. 'Buttercup', a clear yellow (pictured above), and 'Fire Dragon', a rusty red, are two outstanding colors. For best results, shear plants to within several inches (cm) of the ground after flowering, and again in spring, before flowering, to maintain a compact, mounded habit.

Helianthus × multiflorus

Common Name: Perennial sunflower

Flowers: A hybrid of species native to North America. Solitary brilliant yellow heads of single or double petals on erect, stiff stems.

Leaves: Wide, oval, serrated, pointed at the tip, green; with hairy undersides.

Habit: 3′–5′ (.9–1.5m) tall. Large, upright, bushy.

Culture: Prefers full sun in well-drained, reasonably fertile soil. Propagate by division every three to four years.

Season of Bloom: Midsummer to autumn.

Hardiness: Zones 3–8.

Uses: Good accent in mixed perennial borders. Suitable for mass planting in an island bed. Good cut flower.

The variety 'Flora Pleno' bears masses of bright yellow double flowers that resemble miniature dahlias. Closely related to the swamp sunflower *(H. angustifolius)*, which tolerates boggy ground. Similar in appearance to *Heliopsis helianthoides* but flowers about four weeks later. Combines well with *Rudbeckia fulgida* (pictured here).

Heliopsis
helianthoides

Common Name: Oxeye, false sunflower

Flowers: Native to North America. Bright gold single or double daisylike flowers up to 4″ (10cm) across have brownish yellow centers. Double varieties are reminiscent of zinnias.

Leaves: Heart-shaped, pointed, sharply serrated, dark green.

Habit: 36″–48″ (91–122cm) tall. Upright, branching.

Culture: Prefers full sun or partial shade in moist, fertile, loam soil. Plants may need staking. Propagate by seeds or division in the spring or autumn.

Season of Bloom: Midsummer.

Hardiness: Zones 3–9.

Uses: Excellent for mixed perennial borders. Good cut flower.

Forget all the regular varieties and grow only 'Karat', a special large-flowered selection from Europe that has flowers at least 1″ (2.5cm) larger than other varieties. Cut and displayed in water, the flowers resemble sunflowers and last up to ten days.

Helleborus
niger

Common Name: Christmas rose

Flowers: Native to Europe. Resembling single-flowered wild roses, the pure white flowers have five petals that surround a center of numerous yellow stamens. As the flower ages, the petals turn from white to green. Flowers are 2½″ (6.5cm) across, borne one to three per stem.

Leaves: Evergreen, tough, leathery, deeply divided, dark green; resemble pachysandra.

Habit: 12″–15″ (31–38cm) tall. Mounded.

Culture: Prefers full sun or partial shade in well-drained, moist, rich soils. Leaves can become scorched if left unprotected from severe freezing or the sun. Propagate by seeds, since plant division is unreliable.

Season of Bloom: Winter to early spring.

Hardiness: Zones 4–8.

Uses: Excellent woodland accent or border plant. Mass near walkways where flowers can be easily seen.

'Potter's Wheel' is a special large-flowered selection grown from seed and originating from a British nursery. Closely related is the Lenten rose, *H. orientalis*, offering white, pink, and maroon in its color range, and generally more widely adapted than the Christmas rose, especially in southern gardens.

Helleborus orientalis

Common Name:	Lenten rose
Flowers:	Native to Japan. Up to 3″ (7.5cm) across, five-petaled, nodding. Colors include white, pink, maroon, and green, usually with spots leading to a crown of yellow stamens.
Leaves:	Evergreen, lustrous, serrated, dark green; resemble pachysandra.
Habit:	12″–24″ (31–61cm) tall. Bushy, clump-forming.
Culture:	Prefers partial shade in moist, humus-rich soil. Propagate by division in spring or by seeds (which must be fresh). Plants will not bloom the first year after division, and flowering from seed generally takes two years. Self-seeds and naturalizes easily.
Season of Bloom:	Winter to early spring, depending on location (blooms earliest in the south).
Hardiness:	Zones 4–9.
Uses:	Good as ground cover under deciduous trees or combined with early tulips and daffodils in mixed beds and borders. Ideal for winter gardens.

The pink and white varieties (shown above) are flowering with white *Pieris floribunda* and pink *Gaylussacia brachycera*. Much less demanding than its cousin, the Christmas rose *(Helleborus niger)*. Seedlings spring up around the mother plants, and are easily transplanted when young to help establish large colonies.

Hemerocallis hybrids

Common Name:	Daylily
Flowers:	Native to China. Fragrant, trumpet-shaped flowers up to 6″ (15cm) across are borne on long, leafless stems. Colors include yellow, orange, red, mahogany, pink, lavender, and bicolors.
Leaves:	Long, slender, pointed, arching, green.
Habit:	36″–48″ (91–122cm) tall. Upright, clump-forming.
Culture:	Prefers full sun or partial shade in well-drained, loam soil that is high in organic matter. Rich soils produce more foliage than flowers. Propagate by division in spring or autumn every four to six years.
Season of Bloom:	Each variety blooms for about a month in summer. Bloom time can be extended from early summer to frost by planting several different kinds of cultivars.
Hardiness:	Zones 3–10, depending on variety.
Uses:	Spectacular massed in borders, also in mixed beds. Dwarf types can be used for rock gardens or as a ground cover. Attractive cut flower, although the blossoms last only one day.

'Stella d'Oro' is a dwarf variety with orange flowers that will bloom continuously all summer and into autumn, provided faded blooms are removed to prevent seed formation. 'Hyperion' is a large-flowered, clear yellow, fragrant variety that is highly popular.

Heuchera
sanguinea

Common Name: Coralbells, alumroot

Flowers: Native to the Rocky Mountains. Branched spikes of delicate red, pink, or white bell-shaped flowers borne erect on wiry stems. Prolong flowering period by cutting back spent flower stalks.

Leaves: Heart-shaped, hairy, green; form rosettes. Remain evergreen in mild climates.

Habit: 12″–30″ (31–76cm) tall. Upright, mounded.

Culture: Prefers full sun or partial shade in well-drained, moist soil that is high in organic matter. Intolerant of direct hot sun in warm climates. Propagate by seeds, stem and leaf cuttings, or division in late autumn when center of plant becomes woody.

Season of Bloom: Late spring to early summer.

Hardiness: Zones 3–8.

Uses: Old-fashioned favorite that attracts hummingbirds. Good in mixed beds and borders, or as an accent in rock gardens.

Numerous varieties are available in mixtures and separate colors. 'Bressingham hybrids' is a mixture of white, pink, and coral-red that is easy to propagate from seed. 'Chatterbox' has rose-pink flowers with a June-to-September flowering period.

Hosta
seiboldiana

Common Name: Plaintain lily

Flowers: Native to Japan. Clusters of lilac or nearly white flowers are held aloft over the handsome foliage.

Leaves: Large, paddle-shaped, outstretched bluish green with prominent veins. This plant is grown primarily for the ornamental value of its leaves.

Habit: 24″–36″ (61–91cm) tall. Low, clump-forming.

Culture: Prefers partial shade in well-drained, moist, humus-rich, acid soil. Propagate by division throughout the growing season.

Season of Bloom: Midsummer, though leaves are ornamental all season.

Hardiness: Zones 3–9.

Uses: Excellent ground cover in shady beds or edgings. Spectacular planted along stream banks and pond margins.

The variety 'Frances Williams' has handsome blue-green leaves and a bold golden leaf margin, considered one of the best for ground-cover effect. Many other species and hybrids are popular for either their exotic leaf patterns or their conspicuous flowers. 'Royal Standard' is one of the best for flowering display, producing huge white flower spikes that are deliciously fragrant. 'Royal Standard' combines especially well with *Rudbeckia fulgida* (pictured above).

Iberis
sempervirens

Common Name: Edging candytuft

Flowers: Native to Europe and the Mediterranean region. Fragrant flat clusters of tiny, white flowers cover the entire plant, forming a flowering cushion.

Leaves: Evergreen, needlelike, glossy, dark green.

Habit: 6″–12″ (15–31cm) tall. Low, mounded, spreading.

Culture: Prefers full sun in well-drained, sandy or loam soil. Cut back stems by half after blooming to promote vigorous growth. Propagate by seeds, cuttings, or division in the spring.

Season of Bloom: Spring. Some varieties will repeat-bloom in September.

Hardiness: Zones 3–9.

Uses: Perfect for edgings and rock gardens. May also be planted in nooks and crannies of stone walls.

A good companion plant to yellow perennial alyssum, pink aubrieta, and blue forget-me-nots. The variety 'Snowflake' makes a 10″ (25cm) mound of evergreen leaves that are almost hidden when the extra-large dazzling white flowers are in bloom.

Iris ensata,
I. kaempferi

Common Name: Sword-leaved iris, Japanese iris

Flowers: Native to Japan. Flattened iris flowers are up to 6″ (15cm) across on erect stems. Mostly blue, white, and pale pink; also bicolors.

Leaves: Erect, sword-shaped, blue-green.

Habit: Up to 48″ (122cm) tall. Clump-forming.

Culture: Grows in sun or dappled shade, tolerates boggy soil, and will survive with roots permanently immersed in water. Propagate by division.

Season of Bloom: Early summer.

Hardiness: Zones 4–8.

Uses: Sensational accent along stream banks and pool margins.

Invaluable for adding an oriental aura to gardens, especially Japanese-style gardens (as pictured above).

Iris × germanica

Common Name: Bearded iris

Flowers: Developed from species native to Europe. Distinct flower form, rounded, up to 5″ (13cm) across. Each bloom is composed of three tongue-shaped petals that sweep up and three that sweep down, each lower petal accented with a cluster of powdery yellow stamens resembling a beard. Colors include white, yellow, orange, pink, red, blue, lavender, purple, brown, and almost black.

Leaves: Sword-shaped, blue-green.

Habit: 24″–48″ (61–122cm) tall. Upright, spreading, clump-forming.

Culture: Prefers full sun in well-drained, loam soil. Propagate by dividing the rhizomes after flowering.

Season of Bloom: Late spring to early summer.

Hardiness: Zones 3–9.

Uses: Popular in mixed beds and borders. Makes a stunning spring display when massed in island plantings.

Several hundred varieties are offered by specialist iris nurseries. Some of the best include 'Tollgate', a blue and white bicolor, 'Beverly Sills', a huge ruffled pink, and 'Raspberry Ripple', a glowing purple.

Iris sibirica

Common Name: Siberian iris

Flowers: Native to Europe. Up to 4″ (10cm) beardless flowers on erect, slender stems. Colors include white, blue, and purple. Attractive seed pods add interest after blooms have faded.

Leaves: Long, narrow, arching, green.

Habit: 24″–48″ (61–122cm) tall. Upright, clump-forming.

Culture: Prefers full sun or partial shade in moist or boggy, humus-rich, slightly acid soil. Tolerates poor and dry soil. Propagate by dividing the rhizomes after flowering.

Season of Bloom: Late spring to early summer.

Hardiness: Zones 3–8.

Uses: Attractive clumped around ponds, along stream banks, and as border plants, especially mixed with oxeye daisies (*Chrysanthemum leucanthemum*).

'Tealwood', a dark violet-blue, is a popular variety. Siberian iris are good planted in combination with *I. pseudacorus* (yellow flag), which blooms at the same time, and also *I. ensata* (Japanese or sword-leaved iris), which blooms a little later. All three will thrive in boggy soil.

Kniphofia
uvaria

Common Name:	Red-hot-poker
Flowers:	Native to South Africa. Thick clusters of tubular red and yellow flowers top a fleshy, tall stem.
Leaves:	Spiky, medium green.
Habit:	Up to 48″ (122cm) tall. Upright, clump-forming.
Culture:	Prefers full sun in well-drained, sandy or loam soil. Intolerant of wet feet. Propagate by seeds (will flower in two or three years) or by division in spring.
Season of Bloom:	Summer.
Hardiness:	Zones 6–8.
Uses:	Use sparingly as an accent in mixed beds and borders. Performs especially well in coastal gardens. Unusual cut flower.

A popular variety is 'Royal Standard', displaying red flowers at the top of the "poker" and yellow at the bottom (pictured above).

Lathyrus
latifolius

Common Name:	Perennial pea
Flowers:	Native to South Africa. Old-fashioned favorite. Clusters of white, pink, and rose flowers borne on a hardy vine. Prolific grower.
Leaves:	Oval with tendrils, light green.
Habit:	4′–8′ (1.2–2.4m) tall. Vining.
Culture:	Easy to grow. Prefers full sun in dry, loam soil. Propagate by seeds.
Season of Bloom:	Late spring to midsummer.
Hardiness:	Zones 4–10.
Uses:	Attractive on fences, trellises, and posts. Makes a lovely bouquet.

A good plant to consider for controlling soil erosion, especially on slopes. Effective in the perennial border when trained up the inside of a wire cylinder.

Lavandula angustifolia

Common Name: English lavender

Flowers: Native to the Mediterranean region. Old-fashioned favorite. Spicy whorls of violet-blue or white flowers borne on erect spikes. The scent receives widespread use in perfume, potpourri, and sachets.

Leaves: Needlelike, fragrant, grayish green.

Habit: 12″–36″ (31–91cm) tall. Compact, mounded.

Culture: Easy to grow. Prefers full sun in well-drained, sandy or loam soil. Propagate by seeds, cuttings, or division in autumn.

Season of Bloom: Summer.

Hardiness: Zones 5–9.

Uses: Popular in herb gardens or mixed beds and borders. A wonderful scented "hedge" along paths. Perfect for bouquets, fresh or dried.

'Hidcote' is the most desirable variety, but 'Munstead' is hardier. There is little difference between the two except that 'Hidcote' (pictured above) has deeper violet-blue flowers. 'Jean Davis' is a white variety.

Liatris spicata

Common Name: Blazing-star, gay-feather

Flowers: Native to North America. Feathery spikes of rose-pink, lavender, or white flowers.

Leaves: Small, almost needlelike, medium green.

Habit: 1½′–5′ (.5–1.5m) tall. Upright.

Culture: Easy to grow. Prefers full sun or light shade in well-drained, loam soil. Propagate by seeds or by rhizome division every four years in spring.

Season of Bloom: Midsummer to late autumn.

Hardiness: Zones 3–9.

Uses: Good accent in mixed beds and borders. Popular in fresh or dried bouquets. Combines well with ornamental grasses.

The variety 'Kobold' is a dwarf, compact plant that can be used at the front of perennial borders. A related species, *L. pycnostachya,* is twice as tall and is available in white as well as purple.

Ligularia dentata

Common Name: Ligularia

Flowers: Native to China. Yellow daisylike, clustered flowers on top of tall stems that rise 3' to 4' (.9–1.2m) above the main body of leaves.

Leaves: Large, rounded, dinner-plate size, dark green; highly ornamental with a metallic sheen.

Habit: Up to 6' (1.8m) tall when flowering. Bushy before flower spikes appear.

Culture: Prefers a semishaded location and moist but well-drained, humus-rich soil. Propagate by seeds or division.

Season of Bloom: Midsummer.

Hardiness: Zones 5–8.

Uses: Popular accent in mixed beds and borders, and along pond and stream margins. One plant makes a dominant accent.

The variety 'Othello' (pictured above) has a darker leaf coloration and a leaf underside that is a bronzy red. A bold, handsome foliage plant; its flowers are a bonus.

Ligularia × przewalskii

Common Name: Rocket ligularia

Flowers: Native to China. Bold spikes of starry, bright yellow flowers are thrust upright on dark, naked, slender stems.

Leaves: Arrow-shaped, serrated, light green; stay below the tall stalk.

Habit: 5'–6' (1.5–1.8m) tall. Upright, clump-forming.

Culture: Prefers partial shade in moist but well-drained soil that is high in organic matter. Propagate by division.

Season of Bloom: Early to midsummer.

Hardiness: Zones 4–8.

Uses: Effective background accent in mixed beds and borders. Attractive next to ponds or streams. Good cut flower.

Leaves will wilt during the heat of the day unless protected by some shade. Listed in some catalogs as *L. stenocephala*.

Lilium
lancifolium

Common Name: Tiger lily

Flowers: Native to Japan. Attractive nodding "Turk's cap" up to 4″ (10cm) across with brown speckles on orange petals.

Leaves: Pointed, lancelike, medium green.

Habit: 4′–6′ (1.2–1.8m) tall. Upright.

Culture: Prefers full sun or partial shade in moist, humus-rich, loam soil. May need staking. Propagate by division or black bulblets that form in the leaf axils.

Season of Bloom: Summer.

Hardiness: Zones 3–8.

Uses: Attractive background plant in mixed beds and borders. Excellent cut flower, although the pistils should be cropped to keep the brown, powdery pollen from staining clothes.

Perhaps the most widely grown and most reliable of all *Lilium* species. Other good lily species to consider are *L. speciosum* (pink-and-white spotted deep rose), *L. regale* (a white trumpet species), and *L. canadense* (an American native popular in woodland gardens).

Linum
perenne

Common Name: Perennial flax

Flowers: Native to Europe. Delicate sky-blue flowers held erect on stiff stems.

Leaves: Small, lancelike, light green.

Habit: 12″–24″ (31–61cm) tall. Upright, branching.

Culture: Prefers full sun or partial shade in well-drained, loam soil. Propagate by seeds or cuttings.

Season of Bloom: Late spring to summer.

Hardiness: Zones 5–8.

Uses: Excellent in wildflower meadow gardens. Good accent in herb, rock, or perennial gardens. Not suitable as a cut flower since the flowers are short-lived.

Several linums are popular in home gardens, including *L. flavum* (golden flax), displaying golden yellow flowers; and *L. grandiflorum* (flowering flax), a rosy red grown as a hardy annual.

Liriope
spicata

**Common
Name:**   Creeping lilyturf

Flowers: Native to China and Japan. Showy, short,
dense spikes of violet, lilac, lavender, purple, or
white flowers. Ornamental black fruits follow
and persist through winter.

Leaves: Grasslike, dark green; form dense evergreen
tufts.

Habit: 8″–12″ (20–31cm) tall. Mounded, fountainlike.

Culture: Prefers partial shade in well-drained, moist,
humus-rich, acid soil. Some cultivars will
tolerate full sun. Propagate by division in
spring.

**Season
of Bloom:** Summer.

Hardiness: Zones 6–10.

Uses: Popular ground cover since it is so dense that
it crowds out weeds. Edging in mixed beds and
borders.

The variety 'Variegata' has yellow striped leaves and
violet flowers, creating an especially beautiful ground
cover for shaded locations. A related species, *L. muscari*,
forms a larger clump but is not so hardy.

Lobelia
cardinalis

**Common
Name:**   Cardinal flower

Flowers: Native to the eastern United States and
Canada. Distinctive red flowers clustered
around a tall spike.

Leaves: Spear-shaped, toothed, dark green.

Habit: 36″–48″ (91–122cm) tall. Upright, clump-
forming.

Culture: Prefers light shade in moist soil. Enjoys being
mulched. Propagate by seeds or division.

**Season
of Bloom:** Early to late summer.

Hardiness: Zones 2–9.

Uses: Attractive in naturalized areas, near ponds
and streams, and in mixed beds and borders.
Highly attractive to hummingbirds.

Combines well with yellow *Coreopsis verticillata*
(pictured above). A related species, *Lobelia siphilitica*
(great lobelia) is similar to the scarlet lobelia but
displays sky-blue flowers and is not so tall.

Lupinus
'Russell' hybrids

Common Name:	'Russell' hybrid lupines
Flowers:	Developed from species native to North America. Showy spires of pealike blue, purple, white, red, pink, yellow or bicolored flowers. May need staking.
Leaves:	Oval, medium green; leaflets form a fan shape.
Habit:	36″–48″ (91–122cm) tall. Upright, clump-forming.
Culture:	Prefers full sun or partial shade in cool, moist, acid soil. Propagate by seeds or root cuttings.
Season of Bloom:	Early summer when nights are cool.
Hardiness:	Zones 4–8.
Uses:	Popular in wildflower meadow gardens. Attractive accent in mixed beds and borders.

Especially popular in coastal gardens if sheltered from high winds. Several dwarf varieties of lupines have been developed, such as 'Lulu Mixed Colors', growing just 24″ (61cm) tall and including the full color range of 'Russell' hybrids.

Lychnis
chalcedonica

Common Name:	Maltese-cross
Flowers:	Native to Russia. Bright, 4″ (10cm) clusters of red flowers individually looking like a Maltese cross.
Leaves:	Lancelike, dark green.
Habit:	36″–48″ (91–122cm) tall. Upright, clump-forming.
Culture:	Easy to grow. Prefers full sun or partial shade in well-drained, fertile, humus-rich soil. Propagate by seeds or division every three or four years in spring or autumn.
Season of Bloom:	Summer.
Hardiness:	Zones 4–9.
Uses:	Attractive massed in mixed beds or borders. Combines well with yellow perennials, such as heliopsis. Good cut flower.

Several other species of *Lychnis* are popular in perennial borders, especially *L. coronaria* 'Atrosanguinea', which bears masses of rosy red flowers on silvery foliage, the bushy plants growing just 30″ (76cm) tall.

Lynchnis coronaria

Common Name:	Mullein pink, rose campion
Flowers:	Native to southern Europe. Star-shaped, rose-red flowers.
Leaves:	Lancelike, woolly, silvery.
Habit:	Up to 36″ (91cm) tall. Upright, numerous branching stems.
Culture:	Prefers full sun, good drainage; tolerates poor soil. Propagate by seeds for plants that may flower the first year if started early indoors.
Season of Bloom:	Summer.
Hardiness:	Zones 4–8.
Uses:	Good accent in mixed beds and borders. Self-sows readily.

Shown above is *L. coronaria* in combination with *L. flosjovis* and yellow *Verbascum olympicum.*

Lysichiton americanus

Common Name:	Skunk cabbage, yellow skunk cabbage
Flowers:	Native to the Pacific Northwest. Bright yellow, hooded flowers with a fragrant, yellow, powdery spadix.
Leaves:	Paddle-shaped, upright, bright green.
Habit:	Up to 48″ (122cm) tall. Upright, clump-forming.
Culture:	Demands sun or light shade, boggy soil. Propagate mostly by division or seeds. Slow to become established.
Season of Bloom:	Early spring; one of the earliest spring-flowering perennials.
Hardiness:	Zones 7–9.
Uses:	Sensational along stream banks and pond margins.

Sometimes called yellow skunk cabbage, but this is an unfair description. Though the green leaves resemble *Symplocarpus* species (skunk cabbage), the leaves are not malodorous and, indeed, the flower has a pleasant sweet fragrance.

Lysimachia punctata

Common Name: Garden loosestrife

Flowers: Native to Europe and Asia. Golden yellow starlike flowers clustered in the leaf axils of erect spires.

Leaves: Whorled, hairy, green; run up and down the floral spike in groups of four.

Habit: 18″–30″ (46–76cm) tall. Upright, spreading.

Culture: Easy to grow. Prefers full sun or partial shade in moist but well-drained soil. Can be invasive. Propagate by seeds or division in spring.

Season of Bloom: Late spring to early summer.

Hardiness: Zones 5–10.

Uses: Plant as an accent in mixed beds and borders where it can form a generous clump. Good massed along stream banks and pond margins.

So easy to grow because it self-seeds readily. (The plant pictured above is in Monet's garden, Giverny, France.) A related species, *L. clethroides,* produces masses of attractive white flower spikes that end in a curious "twist" like a gooseneck; it grows bushy, to 36″ (91cm), and is prized for cutting.

Lythrum salicaria

Common Name: Purple loosestrife

Flowers: Native to North America. Attractive dense spikes of purple florets borne erect on woody stems.

Leaves: Narrow, pointed, medium green.

Habit: 3′–5′ (.9–1.5m) tall. Upright, clump-forming.

Culture: Easy to grow. Prefers full sun in any soil, wet or dry. Propagate by cuttings or by division in spring or autumn. The wild species can be invasive.

Season of Bloom: Mid- to late summer.

Hardiness: Zones 3–9.

Uses: Superb for low, wet areas along stream banks or pond margins. May also be planted in back of mixed beds and borders. Good cut flowers.

In the United States, some states have started to ban this species, as it becomes a pest in wetlands. However, the garden hybrids involving the European species, *L. virgatum,* rarely self-seed. 'Morden Pink' is undoubtedly the most appealing of the hybrids, producing masses of rose-pink flower spikes (pictured above).

Malva
alcea

Common Name: Mallow

Flowers: Native to Italy. Pink flowers resembling miniature hibiscus are borne in profusion.

Leaves: Heavily lobed, blue-green; similar to a maple.

Habit: 36"–48" (91–122cm) tall. Upright, bushy.

Culture: Prefers full sun or light shade in any well-drained soil. Propagate mostly by seeds sown in summer of the year before flowering. Also propagate by cuttings.

Season of Bloom: Throughout the summer until frost.

Hardiness: Zones 5–8.

Uses: Attractive among other perennials, especially white shasta daisies. May need staking late in the season. Especially good for coastal gardens.

A related species, *M. sylvestris mauritiana,* has gorgeous purple flowers that are heavily veined. Plants are sometimes sold as dwarf hollyhocks.

Meconopsis
grandis

Common Name: Tibetan poppy, blue poppy

Flowers: Native to the Himalayas. Nodding, saucer-shaped, four-petaled, poppylike, sky-blue flowers, up to 4" (10cm) across, with powdery, yellow centers.

Leaves: Spear-shaped, upright, hairy, serrated, green.

Habit: Up to 42" (107cm) tall. Upright, growing one main stem, branching on top.

Culture: Prefers light shade; demands cool, moist conditions to bloom well. Soil should be humus-rich, acid. Hot summers and winds will kill the plants. Propagate by seeds or division; usually does best from autumn planting.

Season of Bloom: Early summer.

Hardiness: Mostly restricted to Zone 8.

Uses: Perhaps the most prized of all hardy perennials. Sensational in colonies planted among rhododendrons and azaleas.

A hybrid between *M. grandis* × *M. betonicifolia,* known botanically as *M.* × *sheldonii,* grows the largest flowers. The variety 'Branklyn' has produced flowers up to 8" (20cm) across.

Mertensia
virginica

Common Name: Virginia bluebells

Flowers: Native to the northeastern United States. Nodding, blue, bell-shaped flowers held in clusters like English cowslips; there is a rare white form.

Leaves: Tongue-shaped, mottled gray and green.

Habit: Up to 24″ (61cm) tall. Upright, clump-forming.

Culture: Prefers light shade under deciduous trees in moist but well-drained, humus-rich, acid soil. Propagate by seeds or division in autumn.

Season of Bloom: Spring.

Hardiness: Zones 3–9.

Uses: Pretty in shady beds and borders, and naturalized in woodland, especially when combined with daffodils.

Since the foliage dies down by early summer, Virginia bluebells should be grown next to plants that will spread over them, such as hostas.

Monarda
didyma

Common Name: Bee balm, bergamot

Flowers: Native to North America. Aromatic tubular flowers create a dense floral cluster resembling a crown held erect on stiff, square stems. Colors include scarlet, mahogany, pink, and white.

Leaves: Spear-shaped, pointed, serrated, green; when crushed, put out a scent similar to that of mint, to which the plant is related.

Habit: 36″–48″ (91–122cm) tall. Upright, bushy, clump-forming.

Culture: Prefers full sun in moist, loam soil. Propagate by seeds, softwood cuttings, or division in spring. Can be invasive.

Season of Bloom: Summer.

Hardiness: Zones 4–8.

Uses: Popular in meadow or herb gardens. A bold accent in mixed beds and borders.

Flowers are attractive to butterflies and hummingbirds. 'Cambridge Scarlet' is probably the most popular variety on account of its intense red flowers; 'Mahogany' is more unusual, displaying wine red flowers; 'Croftway Pink' (pictured above) is an attractive rose-pink; 'Snow Queen' is probably the best of the whites. 'Panorama Mixed' is a good mixture to grow from seed.

Nepeta × faassenii

Common Name: Ornamental catmint

Flowers: Hybrid developed from species native to Europe. Splendid clusters of small, lavender, trumpet-shaped flowers stud the upright, square stems.

Leaves: Oval, downy, silvery, gray-green; redolent with a mint fragrance.

Habit: 18″–36″ (46–91cm) tall. Spreading.

Culture: Prefers full sun in moist but well-drained, sandy or loam soil. Propagate only by division.

Season of Bloom: Early summer to autumn.

Hardiness: Zones 1–9.

Uses: A good edging plant along paths. Good accent in herb gardens or mixed beds and borders.

A great way to please cats since they love catmint almost as much as they do catnip. Unscrupulous nursery growers sometimes substitute the inferior *N. mussinii* for *N. × faassenii* because the former is cheaper to grow from seed, while the latter commands a higher price.

Nymphaea × marliacea

Common Name: Marliac water lily

Flowers: Hardy hybrid water lilies developed mostly from *N. alba* (European white water lily), *N. mexicana* (the yellow Mexican water lily), and *N. odorata* (fragrant water lily) by a French nurseryman. Flowers are large—up to 6″ (15cm) across—star-shaped and brightly colored, mostly white, yellow, orange, and deep carmine pink.

Leaves: Rounded, green; float on the surface of water.

Habit: Roots are submerged in water and leaves float on top, the flowers usually projecting above the leaves by long, pliable stems.

Culture: Prefers full sun. Plants like their roots in clay or loam soil, covered with 12″–14″ (31–36cm) of still water. Propagate by root division.

Season of Bloom: Summer until autumn frost.

Hardiness: Zones 5–10.

Uses: Decorates the surface of ponds, forming islands of foliage and beautiful flowers.

Shown above is 'Escarboucle', one of the best 'Marliac' hybrids.

Oenothera tetragona

Common Name:	Sundrop
Flowers:	Native to North America. Sunny golden yellow, four-petaled flowers open to a cup-shaped appearance.
Leaves:	Willowlike, dark green; cover stiff, brown stems.
Habit:	18″–24″ (46–61cm) tall. Bushy, spreading.
Culture:	Prefers full sun in well-drained, sandy soil. Tolerates drought and poor soils. Propagate by cuttings or seeds in spring or autumn.
Season of Bloom:	Summer.
Hardiness:	Zones 3–9.
Uses:	Attractive in mixed beds and borders, especially when allowed to form a dense, low-growing, cushionlike mass of blooms.

Sometimes listed in catalogs as *O. fruticosa*. There are many beautiful *Oenothera* species worth growing in home gardens, including *O. speciosa* (winecups), which self-seeds freely, and *O. missourensis* (Missouri primrose), which grows spectacular large flowers.

Paeonia officinalis

Common Name:	Herbaceous peony
Flowers:	Native to China. The beautiful large, solitary, single or double flowers measure up to 6″ (15cm) across, and are sometimes so heavy the stems cannot hold them erect. Colors include white, pink, and deep red.
Leaves:	Deeply lobed, dark green.
Habit:	36″–48″ (91–122cm) tall. Bushy.
Culture:	Prefers full sun in well-drained, fertile, humus-rich soil. Tolerates some shade. Propagate by dividing clumps into sections containing three to five buds. Set buds 1″ (2.5cm) below the soil surface. Plants require three years maturation before flowering occurs.
Season of Bloom:	Early to late spring.
Hardiness:	Zones 3–8.
Uses:	Excellent accent in mixed beds and borders. Superb flowering "hedge" to line a driveway. Good cut flower.

Estate hybrid peonies, developed by a nursery grower near Chicago, grow some of the biggest blooms. Outstanding varieties include 'Barrington Belle' (a double-flowered red), 'Glory Hallelujah' (a vivid pink), and 'Raspberry Sunday' (a pure white with pink flecks). For tree peonies, see *Paeonia suffruticosa* under **Shrubs.**

Papaver orientale

Common Name: Oriental poppy

Flowers: Native to Asia. Cheery, single or double blooms have crinkled, rounded petals surrounding a circle of delicate black stamens. Colors range from white to orange, pink, red, and bicolors.

Leaves: Hairy, sharply indented, green, turning brown and dying back in midsummer, then reappearing in autumn and staying green through winter.

Habit: 36″–48″ (91–122cm) tall. Upright, clump-forming.

Culture: Prefers full sun or partial shade in well-drained, loam soil. Propagate by seeds, root cuttings, or division in late summer. Poppies resent any kind of root disturbance.

Season of Bloom: Late spring to early summer.

Hardiness: Zones 3–8.

Uses: Popular planted as drifts in meadow gardens. Attractive as clumps in mixed beds and borders. Poppies make excellent cut flowers if stems are seared. The seed pods may be used in dried arrangements.

'Beauty of Livermore' is a mammoth among Oriental poppies, with individual flowers, up to 8″ (20cm) across, crimson-red with handsome black markings. 'Allegro' is a new dwarf type from France, growing less than 24″ (61cm) tall and displaying orange-red flowers up to 6″ (15cm) across.

Pelargonium peltatum

Common Name: Ivy-leaf geranium

Flowers: Native to South Africa. Loose, open clusters of five to seven starlike flowers borne on erect stems. Color range includes white, red, pink, and lavender.

Leaves: Five-lobed, resembling ivy; dark green, sometimes marked with red.

Habit: 12″–18″ (31–46cm) tall. Mounded, spreading.

Culture: Easy to grow. Prefers full sun in well-drained, moist, fertile soil. Water frequently and deadhead to encourage continuous blooming. Propagate by seeds or cuttings.

Season of Bloom: All summer.

Hardiness: Zones 8–10. Tender to frost.

Uses: Attractive in containers, hanging baskets, and as house plants. Can be massed in beds, borders, and as a one-season ground cover in cold winter climates.

Though truly a perennial in frost-free areas of North America, ivy-leaf geraniums are mostly grown as a temporary ground cover for decorating slopes and as a flowering pot plant for sunrooms and greenhouses. The vast majority of ivy-leaf geraniums are grown from cuttings, but 'Summer Showers' is a mixture that can be propagated from seed for flowering within sixteen to seventeen weeks. The Balcan series, grown from cuttings, are extremely free-flowering.

Penstemon barbatus

Common Name: Beard-tongue, Colorado penstemon

Flowers: Native to Colorado. Tubular, foxglovelike flowers in rose-pink and scarlet form an attractive spike.

Leaves: Slender, lancelike, surrounding the flower stem, green.

Habit: Up to 30″ (76cm) tall. Clump-forming.

Culture: Prefers full sun in well-drained, fertile soil. Propagate by seeds, cuttings, or division.

Season of Bloom: Late spring.

Hardiness: Zones 4–8.

Uses: Good accent in mixed beds and borders. Superb rock garden plant.

The above photograph shows *P. barbatus* in a rock garden, with dark blue *Salvia × superba* in the background.

Perovskia atriplicifolia

Common Name: Russian sage

Flowers: Native to Afghanistan. Small, lavender-blue flowers whorl around tall, erect spires, presenting a "misty" appearance.

Leaves: Narrow, aromatic, silvery gray; with attractive silvery stems in autumn.

Habit: 36″–48″ (91–122cm) tall. Bushy, sprawling.

Culture: Prefers full sun in well-drained, sandy or loam soil. Plants may need staking. Propagate by seeds or cuttings.

Season of Bloom: Summer through autumn.

Hardiness: Zones 6–9.

Uses: Popular accent in mixed borders and in herb gardens. Foliage is attractive fresh or dried.

A finer blue-flowering perennial is hard to imagine! Combines especially well with ornamental grasses, such as varieties of *Miscanthus, Helenium,* and purple coneflower.

Phlox divaricata

Common Name:	Blue phlox
Flowers:	Native to the northeastern United States. Blue or mauve star-shaped flowers borne in loose clusters.
Leaves:	Lancelike, green.
Habit:	12″–18″ (31–46cm) tall. Creeping.
Culture:	Grows in sun or light shade; prefers a moist but well-drained, humus-rich soil. Propagate by seeds or division.
Season of Bloom:	Spring.
Hardiness:	Zones 4–8.
Uses:	Good for use in edging paths and in mixed beds and borders, as well as for massing in woodland gardens. Especially beautiful underplanted in a bed of tulips.

Similar in appearance to *P. stolonifera,* which has an excellent white form, 'Bruce's White'.

Phlox maculata

Common Name:	Dwarf summer phlox
Flowers:	Native to the east coast of North America. Resembles tall summer phlox *(P. paniculata),* but shorter in stature, earlier flowering. Flowers borne in columnlike clusters. Colors include white and rose-pink with contrasting "eyes."
Leaves:	Slender, lancelike, green; resistant to mildew.
Habit:	Up to 36″ (91cm) tall. Clump-forming.
Culture:	Prefers full sun in a well-drained, fertile, loam soil. Propagate primarily by division.
Season of Bloom:	Early summer.
Hardiness:	Zones 4–8.
Uses:	Strong accent in mixed beds and borders. Suitable for rock gardens. Good for cutting.

Deserves to be much more widely grown. The above photograph shows variety 'Alpha' planted with pale pink *Oenothera speciosa,* yellow 'Stella d'Oro' daylily, and blue common sage.

Phlox
paniculata

Common Name: Summer perennial phlox

Flowers: Native to the southeastern United States. Large, showy panicles of white, pink, purple, salmon, lilac, and scarlet flowers. Some have noticeable yellow "eyes." Taller varieties may need staking.

Leaves: Spear-shaped, medium green; susceptible to mildew.

Habit: 24″–48″ (61–122cm) tall. Upright, clump-forming.

Culture: Prefers full sun or partial shade in moist but well-drained, fertile soil. Powdery mildew can be controlled by spraying. Propagate by division every three to four years.

Season of Bloom: Mid- to late summer.

Hardiness: Zones 3–9.

Uses: Popular accent in mixed beds and borders. Suitable for cutting.

Many good varieties are available, but the best would include 'Pinafore Pink', which produces short stems that require no staking. Summer perennial phlox combines well with globe thistle and yellow-flowering perennials such as black-eyed Susan and perennial sunflower.

Phlox
subulata

Common Name: Moss pink, moss phlox

Flowers: Native to North America. Small clusters of five-petaled flowers form a dense carpet of blooms on short stems. Colors include white, salmon, pink, rose, and lavender.

Leaves: Almost evergreen. Feathery, gray-green.

Habit: 3″–6″ (7.5–15cm) tall. Low, ground-hugging.

Culture: Prefers full sun in well-drained, sandy or loam soil that is slightly akaline. Propagate by division after blooming or by autumn cuttings.

Season of Bloom: Mid- to late spring.

Hardiness: Zones 2–9.

Uses: Popular flowering ground cover and edging plant. Attractive in nooks and crannies of walls.

Combines well with spring-flowering bulbs such as tulips. 'Crimson Beauty', 'White Delight', and 'Oakington Blue' are all good selections, as are any varieties named 'Millstream', after a Connecticut nursery specializing in creeping phlox.

Physalis franchetii, P. alkekengi

Common Name: Chinese lantern

Flowers: Native to Japan. Inconspicuous, tiny, white flowers are followed by showy, bright orange, papery lanterns that are actually seed cases. Lanterns turn a reddish color in autumn.

Leaves: Oval, pointed, wavy, green like a pepper plant.

Habit: 18″–24″ (46–61cm) tall. Branching, spreading.

Culture: Prefers full sun in well-drained, sandy or loam soil. Propagate by seeds and division. Can be invasive.

Season of Bloom: The unusual lanterns appear in late summer.

Hardiness: Zones 4–10.

Uses: Though suitable for mixed beds and borders, plants are usually grown in a bed of their own and in cutting gardens. Popular in dried winter arrangements. To harvest, pick the lanterns before they begin to turn color and hang stems upside down in a dry, dark, well-ventilated room.

'Gigantea' (pictured above) is by far the best variety, displaying 2″ (5cm) orange-scarlet lanterns that command a premium price when offered for sale as a dried flower. A related species, *P. alkekengi,* native to China, is similar but bears small lanterns and is more aggressive.

Physostegia virginiana

Common Name: Obedience, false dragonhead

Flowers: Native to North America. Panicled spikes of attractive flower clusters resembling snapdragons are borne on square stems. Colors include snowy white, rosy pink, and vivid purple.

Leaves: Lancelike, evenly spaced, green.

Habit: 24″–48″ (61–122cm) tall. Upright, clump-forming.

Culture: Prefers full sun or partial shade; tolerates wet or dry soil. Can be invasive, but sandy soils will check spreading tendencies. Propagate by seeds or division every two years in spring.

Season of Bloom: Late summer to early autumn.

Hardiness: Zones 2–9.

Uses: Suitable for mixed beds and borders. Popular companion to autumn-flowering roses. Good cut flower.

'Vivid' is a dwarf variety that does not become overpowering like its taller cousins. 'Summer Snow' has beautiful white flowers. 'Variegata' has creamy margins to its leaves, making it a good foliage plant with pink flowers as a bonus.

Platycodon grandiflorus

Common Name: Balloon flower

Flowers: Native to Japan. The buds of these 2″ (5cm) wide, bell-shaped flowers pop like balloons when burst, hence the common name. Colors are blue, white, or pink.

Leaves: Broadly oval, serrated along the edge, grayish green.

Habit: 24″–36″ (61–91cm) tall. Upright, mounded.

Culture: Prefers full sun or partial shade in well-drained, slightly acid, sandy or loam soil. Hates wet feet. Propagate by seeds or cuttings. Does not like to be disturbed.

Season of Bloom: Early summer to early autumn.

Hardiness: Zones 3–9.

Uses: Attractive planted as drifts in rock gardens and as accents in perennial borders. Good cut flower, providing stem ends are seared.

'Albus' is a beautiful pure white, 'Mother of Pearl' a pale pink, and 'Baby Blue' a dwarf compact variety growing less than 10″ (25cm) tall. Plant breeders in Japan have produced a dwarf annual form named 'Sentimental Blue'. A moderate number of flowers are produced the first season, with more flowers on slightly larger plants the second and subsequent years.

Polemonium reptans

Common Name: Jacob's-ladder

Flowers: Native to the northeastern United States. Small, blue, slightly nodding, bell-shaped flowers in generous clusters. Resemble forget-me-nots.

Leaves: Oval, light green leaflets arranged evenly on arching stems.

Habit: 12″–15″ (31–38cm) tall. Clump-forming.

Culture: Prefers partial shade in well-drained, moist, humus-rich soil. Propagate by seeds or division in spring or autumn.

Season of Bloom: Mid-spring to early summer.

Hardiness: Zones 4–8.

Uses: Interesting in rock gardens as an edging and as a ground cover. Good massed in naturalized areas, particularly in woodlands.

An important component of all-blue gardens. Combines well with yellow perennial alyssum, wild red columbine, and primrose. Deserves to be much more widely used in spring gardens. Sensational as an underplanting to tulips.

Polygonum bistorta

Common Name: Snakeweed

Flowers: Native to Europe and Asia. Attractive clusters of pink pokerlike flowers are borne erect on long, slender stems.

Leaves: Rosette-forming, straplike, green with a prominent white midrib down the leaf's center.

Habit: 24″–36″ (61–91cm) tall. Spreading, clump-forming.

Culture: Prefers full sun or partial shade in moist or damp soil high in organic matter. Propagate by seeds or division in spring.

Season of Bloom: Late spring to midsummer.

Hardiness: Zones 4–8.

Uses: Superb for edging paths and planted as drifts in mixed beds and borders. Good massed along stream banks or pond margins.

Several types of *Polygonum* are popular for ground covers in perennial gardens, notably *P. affine,* which is more diminutive than *P. bistorta,* of which 'Superbum' is the best selection. Even more diminutive is *P. capitatum,* most often seen creating a dense carpet on dry slopes and in rock gardens, with pink, buttonlike flowers.

Primula japonica

Common Name: Japanese primrose; candelabra primrose

Flowers: Native to Japan and China. Distinct primroselike clusters arranged in tiers on top of a slender tall stem. Colors include white, pink, purple, and red.

Leaves: Oblong, wrinkled, apple green; form rosettes.

Habit: 12″–24″ (31–61cm) tall. Upright stems but ground-hugging leaves.

Culture: Prefers light shade in moist, acid soil high in organic material. Propagate by seeds in spring, or by division when dormant.

Season of Bloom: Late spring to early summer.

Hardiness: Zones 6–8.

Uses: Attractive in shady perennial borders or along stream banks and pond margins.

Mostly grown as a mixture of colors in boggy ground. However, the deep cerise-red variety, 'Valley-Red', will grow true to color from seed. While *P. japonica* displays colors in the red area of the spectrum, *P. beesiana* displays colors in the yellow range. Separate mass plantings of each kind in a swampy area are sensational.

Primula × polyantha

Common Name:	Polyanthus primrose
Flowers:	Hybrid of species native to Europe. Bright clusters of white, yellow, blue, or red primrose-like flowers stand upright on slender stems.
Leaves:	Oblong, wrinkled, light green; form rosettes.
Habit:	Up to 12″ (31cm) tall. Upright, compact, clump-forming.
Culture:	Prefers light shade in moist soil that is high in organic material such as peat. Propagate by seeds or division.
Season of Bloom:	Spring.
Hardiness:	Zones 3–8.
Uses:	Popular in shady mixed beds and borders or along streams. Combines well with ferns, bluebells, and forget-me-nots along woodland paths.

Hybrids of the English primrose *(P. vulgaris)* and the English cowslip *(P. veris)*. The most popular strain is 'Pacific Giants', developed in Japan (pictured here in Monet's garden, Giverny, France).

Rudbeckia fulgida

Common Name:	Coneflower, black-eyed Susan
Flowers:	Native to North America. Sunny, golden, daisy-like flowers with contrasting brownish purple centers are borne upright on hairy stems.
Leaves:	Lancelike, hairy, medium green.
Habit:	24″–36″ (61–91cm) tall. Upright, spreading.
Culture:	Easy to grow. Prefers full sun in moist, well-drained, loam soil but is adaptable to most soil conditions. Propagate by seeds or division in spring.
Season of Bloom:	Mid- to late summer.
Hardiness:	Zones 3–9.
Uses:	Popular for its intense yellow color. Grow in meadow gardens or in mixed beds and borders. One of the top perennials for sunny locations. Combines well with the purple coneflower.

Also known as *Rudbeckia hirta*, the most popular variety is 'Goldsturm', which is sterile, does not set viable seed, and is propagated by division. The sterility of 'Goldsturm' imbues the plant with extraordinary vigor, creating a bold mass of flowers unlike anything else in the perennial flower kingdom. (Shown here is 'Goldstrum' with variegated *Miscanthus* grass.)

Salvia × superba

Common Name: Perennial sage

Flowers: Hybrid of species native to Europe. Tall spikes of tightly clustered, violet-purple flowers on strong, upright stems.

Leaves: Spear-shaped with serrated edges, dark green.

Habit: 24″–36″ (61–91cm) tall. Upright, clump-forming.

Culture: Easy to grow. Prefers full sun in well-drained, loam soil. Tolerates drought. Mulch for winter protection. Propagate by cuttings or division in spring.

Season of Bloom: Early to late summer.

Hardiness: Zones 5–8.

Uses: Good for massing in a bed or as an accent in mixed beds and borders. Indispensable component of all-blue gardens.

'Blue Queen', with deep violet-blue flowers, and 'East Friesland' with violet flowers, are the most free-flowering varieties. 'Blue Queen' (pictured above) is generally capable of a more dramatic display because of its more compact habit—18″ (46cm) compared to 30″ (76cm).

Santolina chamaecyparissus

Common Name: Lavender cotton

Flowers: Native to the Mediterranean region. Grown primarily for its decorative leaves, although the blossoms are attractive—they are yellow, buttonlike, held erect on stiff stems.

Leaves: Small, narrow, pungent, silvery gray.

Habit: 12″–24″ (31–61cm) tall. Low, mounded, cushionlike.

Culture: Prefers full sun in well-drained, sandy or loam soil. Tolerates seashore conditions. Prune to retain compactness. Propagate by seeds or cuttings.

Season of Bloom: Midsummer.

Hardiness: Zones 6–9.

Uses: Excellent small formal hedge and edging in mixed beds and borders. Dried leaves are an insect repellant, especially disliked by moths. Popular for herbal knot gardens, though heavy pruning prevents flowering.

A related species, *S. virens*, is identical in habit, except its leaves are green instead of silvery gray. An appealing tapestry effect can be achieved by planting the two together in intermingling drifts or a checkerboard design. Both are popular components of drought-tolerant landscapes.

Saponaria
ocymoides

**Common
Name:** Rock soapwort

Flowers: Native to the Maritime Alps. Small, pink, starlike flowers create a ground-hugging carpet, clustered so tightly they hide the foliage.

Leaves: Short, lancelike, dark green, with reddish branching stems.

Habit: 4″–5″ (10–13cm) tall. Low, flat, spreading.

Culture: Easy to grow. Prefers full sun in well-drained, sandy or loam soil. Tolerates impoverished soil. Propagate by seeds or division in spring.

**Season
of Bloom:** Late spring, with sporadic flowering occurring throughout summer.

Hardiness: Zones 2–7.

Uses: Popular in rock gardens, on walls, and edging beds and borders. Superb for lining sandy paths, especially through a wildflower meadow or up a rocky slope.

An often-overlooked plant for ground-cover effect, especially on dry slopes. Provides a carpet of color when in bloom.

Scabiosa
caucasica

**Common
Name:** Pincushion flower

Flowers: Native to Europe. Ruffled petals of sky-blue flowers surround a round cushion of white stamens. Deadhead flowers to encourage new blooms.

Leaves: Spear-shaped, segmented, dark green.

Habit: 18″–24″ (46–61cm) tall. Upright, open, branching.

Culture: Prefers full sun in well-drained, rich, neutral soil. Enjoys cool, moist climates. Propagate by seeds or division in spring.

**Season
of Bloom:** All summer.

Hardiness: Zones 4–8.

Uses: Suitable for mixed beds and borders. Makes a good addition to a cutting garden; try to include both the white and blue types.

Though its presence in a perennial border is rather understated compared to garish phlox and screaming yellow black-eyed Susans, it is eye-catching. 'Clive Greave' (pictured above) is a popular large-flowered blue, but 'Fama' has deeper blue coloring. 'Alba' is a beautiful white.

Sedum spectabile

Common Name: Stonecrop

Flowers: Native to Japan. Spectacular late-season flower that has a long bloom cycle. The white, pink, or red flowers form wide, dense, colorful plates that are borne erect on tough, stiff stems. Highly attractive to butterflies.

Leaves: Succulent, oval, grayish green, slightly toothed at the edges.

Habit: 18"–24" (46–61cm) tall. Upright, mounded, clump-forming.

Culture: Prefers full sun in well-drained, sandy or loam soil. Propagate by stem cuttings or division in spring.

Season of Bloom: Late summer to frost.

Hardiness: Zones 3–10.

Uses: Attractive massed in perennial borders, as an accent plant in mixed beds, or planted as drifts in rock gardens.

The hybrid 'Autumn Joy' is one of the top ten hardy perennials. Its rose-pink flower clusters turn deep red and then bronze as the plant ages. Even in winter the dried flower clusters are ornamental.

Sedum spurium

Common Name: Dragon's blood

Flowers: Native to Asia. Masses of rosy red, starry flowers.

Leaves: Succulent, small, green, serrated, with orange margins.

Habit: 6" (15cm) tall. Spreading.

Culture: Prefers full sun, good drainage; tolerates high heat and poor, stony soil. Propagate by division.

Season of Bloom: Summer.

Hardiness: Zones 4–9.

Uses: Good ground cover for dry slopes, edging beds and borders, dry walls, and rock gardens.

The above photograph shows a clump of *S. spurium* spilling onto a mosslike, ground-hugging planting of *Arenaria* species, commonly called sandworts.

Stachys byzantina, S. olympia

Common Name: Lamb's-ears, woolly betony

Flowers: Native to Turkey. Masses of downy spikes of deep pink or purple flowers are held erect on stiff stems.

Leaves: Fuzzy, silvery gray; texture resembles silky lamb's ears.

Habit: 12″–18″ (31–46cm) tall. Low, spreading.

Culture: Prefers full sun in well-drained, fertile, loam soil. Divide plants every few years to prevent overcrowding. Propagate by division in autumn or spring. Takes two years for plants to flower from seeds.

Season of Bloom: Summer.

Hardiness: Zones 4–9.

Uses: The attractive silvery leaf color makes this a wonderful edging plant or ground cover with ornamental flowers as a bonus. Leaves are used in bouquets and wreaths.

Widely cultivated as an ornamental in perennial gardens and herb gardens. 'Silver Carpet' is a sterile form that produces no flower spikes and therefore makes the best ground-cover effect.

Stokesia laevis

Common Name: Stokes' aster

Flowers: Native to the southern United States. Feathery, asterlike, blue flowers with yellow centers, up to 3″ (7.5cm) across.

Leaves: Spear-shaped, medium green; clasp closely to the stems.

Habit: 12″–18″ (31–46cm) tall. Sprawling.

Culture: Prefers full sun in well-drained, sandy or loam soil. Propagate by seeds, root cuttings, or division in spring.

Season of Bloom: Summer.

Hardiness: Zones 5–8.

Uses: Low accent in mixed beds and borders. Good cut flower.

Stokes' aster, a supportive player in the perennial garden, is generally placed at the front below taller-growing subjects such as phlox and poppies. 'Blue Danube' has clear blue flowers, 'Blue Moon', lilac flowers, and 'Silver Moon', white flowers.

Thymus
praecox

**Common
Name:**   Thyme, mother-of-thyme

Flowers: Native to Europe. Clusters of delicate pink to pale lavender flowers blanket the stems.

Leaves: Small, oval, fragrant, evergreen.

Habit: Up to 4″ (10cm) tall. Low, spreading, carpetlike effect.

Culture: Prefers full sun in well-drained, loam soil. Propagate by seeds or division.

**Season
of Bloom:**   Spring.

Hardiness: Zones 4–9.

Uses: Pretty in crevices of walkways or as an edging to paths in herb gardens. Superb ground cover, especially for slopes. Popular culinary herb.

Dozens of varieties of thyme are available from specialist herb catalogs. Two especially good varieties for planting among flagstone are *T.* × *citriodorus* 'Aureus' (golden lemon thyme) and *T.* × *citriodorus* 'Argenteus' (silver lemon thyme). *T. vulgaris* (garden thyme) grows bushy and mounded, (up to 12″ [31cm] tall).

Trollius
europaeus

**Common
Name:**   Globeflower

Flowers: Native to swampy areas of the northern temperate zone. Creamy yellow globular flowers are directly related to buttercup. Flowers grow up to 2″ (5cm) across, held high above the foliage on branching stems.

Leaves: Lustrous, with serrated edges; dark green.

Habit: 18″–24″ (46–61cm) tall. Upright, clump-forming.

Culture: Prefers full sun or partial shade in moist, humus-rich, loam soil. Intolerant of drought. Propagate by seeds or by division every five years in late summer.

**Season
of Bloom:**   Late spring, with sporadic flowering to midsummer.

Hardiness: Zones 5–8.

Uses: Enjoys being planted along stream banks and pond margins. Long-lasting cut flower.

Yellow flowers are not as prolific in the spring as they are in summer. This is one of the best early-flowering yellow perennials, since it also provides valuable height to a display. 'Superbus' (pictured above with a variegated hosta) has bright lemon yellow flowers. The hybrid 'Orange Princess', with bright orange flowers, is especially appealing.

Verbascum olympicum

Common
Name: Mullein, giant mullein

Flowers: Native to Europe. Towering, multiflowered, branching spikes of bright yellow florets. If main flower spike is cut back, it will send out several smaller flower spikes.

Leaves: Long, broad, woolly, silver-gray; arranged in a basal rosette.

Habit: 5'–6' (1.5–1.8m) tall. Upright, spirelike.

Culture: Easy to grow. Prefers full sun in well-drained, sandy or loam soil. Propagate by seeds. Plants self-sow and die after flowering since they are biennials.

Season
of Bloom: Mid- to late summer.

Hardiness: Zones 6–9.

Uses: Plant in groups of at least three in the back of mixed beds and borders, or display as a single specimen plant.

The variety 'Silver Candelabra' is an extremely free-flowering tall plant. There are many other kinds of *Verbascum* suitable for mixed perennial borders. Though most of them are tall-growing and best used at the back of the border, *V. chaixii* is low-growing (36″ [91cm]), with beautiful columnar white flower spikes and purple "eyes."

Veronica spicata

Common
Name: Speedwell

Flowers: Native to Russia. Majestic spikes of royal blue, white, and pink flowers.

Leaves: Spearlike, pointed, dark green.

Habit: 36″ (91cm) tall. Upright, spreading.

Culture: Easy to grow. Prefers full sun in any well-drained soil. May need staking. Propagate by seeds or division.

Season
of Bloom: Early to midsummer.

Hardiness: Zones 3–8.

Uses: Colorful planted in drifts among mixed beds and borders.

'Blue Peter' is a stunning deep blue variety, producing masses of flowers; 'Red Fox' is a deep rose-pink; 'Icicle' is a magnificent white. The blues among *Veronica* are especially appealing. *V. latifolia* 'Crater Lake' is low-growing and can create a sea of blue when planted in drifts in rock gardens and along the edges of beds and borders.

Viola
tricolor

Common Name:	European wild pansy, Johnny-jump-up
Flowers:	Native to Europe. Smiling faces of whiskered flowers painted with several colors. Violet, yellow, and maroon can occur all in the same flower.
Leaves:	Heart-shaped, serrated edges, medium green.
Habit:	4″–8″ (10–20cm) tall. Low, mounded, spreading.
Culture:	Easy to grow. Prefers full sun to partial shade in well-drained, moist, humus-rich soil. Enjoys cool, sunny weather. Propagate by seeds.
Season of Bloom:	Spring to early winter.
Hardiness:	Zones 4–8.
Uses:	Popular to fill an island bed or ring a tree; a good edging plant in mixed beds or borders. May also be planted in window boxes.

European wild pansies are prolific reseeders, but since they bloom so early in the season it's impossible to have too many of them. 'Helen Mount' is prized for its deep purple and maroon coloring, giving it an appealing old-fashioned appearance.

Yucca
filamentosa

Common Name:	Yucca, Adam's-needle
Flowers:	Native to the United States. Nodding clusters of creamy white, bell-shaped flowers stud a giant stem.
Leaves:	Stiff, pointed, dark green, with needle-sharp tips; form evergreen rosettes. Some varieties are variegated green and yellow.
Habit:	3′–6′ (.9–1.8m) tall. Clump-forming.
Culture:	Easy to grow. Prefers full sun in well-drained, sandy or loam soil. Tolerates drought. Propagate by offsets.
Season of Bloom:	Early to midsummer.
Hardiness:	Zones 5–10.
Uses:	Dramatic accent in mixed beds or in rock gardens. Massed plantings on sloping banks can control erosion.

An important accent plant in the landscape, since the explosion of tough, sharply pointed leaves creates a textural quality in pleasing contrast to the softer, smoother forms of other perennial plants and shrubs. Several variegated varieties with gold striping are available as attractive foliage plants, with flowers as a bonus. The related species, *Y. glauca*, has narrower, more rigid leaves, creating a pincushion effect.

Bulbs

Acidanthera bicolor

Common Name:	Peacock orchid
Flowers:	Native to South Africa; related to gladiolus. Fragrant, creamy white flowers with purplish brown centers bloom in spikes. Up to 4″ (10cm) across.
Leaves:	Sword-shaped, irislike, bright green.
Habit:	24″–36″ (61–91cm) tall. Upright.
Culture:	Easy to grow. Prefers full sun in well-drained, humus-rich, sandy or loam soil. Propagate by corms and cormels. Needs two growing seasons to reach flowering size from cormlets. Mound up soil around plants to keep the stems erect.
Season of Bloom:	Late summer to autumn.
Hardiness:	Zones 7–10.
Uses:	Popular tall accent in mixed beds and borders. Sensational in cutting gardens.

Like gladiolus, if bulbs are planted a little deeper than recommended (4″–5″ [10–13cm], instead of 2″–3″ [5–7.5cm]), they are more likely to survive severe winters, and are less prone to fall over.

Agapanthus africanus, A. umbellatus

Common Name:	African lily, lily-of-the-Nile
Flowers:	Native to South Africa. Twelve to thirty gorgeous, bright blue, trumpet-shaped flowers borne in rounded clusters on tall, naked stems. White forms also available.
Leaves:	Straplike, green; arranged in a fountain.
Habit:	18″–36″ (46–91cm) tall. Upright, clump-forming.
Culture:	Prefers full sun or partial shade in moist but well-drained, humus-rich, sandy or loam soil. Propagate by root division.
Season of Bloom:	Summer.
Hardiness:	Zones 7–10. In zones 7–8, mulch with wood chips or salt hay to protect from cold weather.
Uses:	Beautiful in containers and on patios. Long-lasting cut flower. Possibly the most widely planted flowering bulb in mild coastal gardens.

'Headbourne Hybrids' is an especially good variety, hardier than most. 'Peter Pan' is a low-growing variety suitable for planting as a ground cover.

Allium
giganteum

Common Name:	Giant allium, giant onion
Flowers:	Native to Siberia. Large globes of purple, star-shaped flowers top tall, slender stems.
Leaves:	Flat, straplike, green; rosette-forming.
Habit:	4'–5' (1.2–1.5m) tall. Upright flower stems.
Culture:	Prefers full sun in well-drained, fertile, humus-rich, loam soil. Propagate by bulbs; if grown from seeds, wait two to three years for flowering.
Season of Bloom:	Late spring to midsummer.
Hardiness:	Zones 6–10.
Uses:	Makes an impressive show in perennial and shrub borders, planted in groups of at least six bulbs.

Many other purple-flowered alliums are popular as accents in perennial borders, especially *A. aflatunense,* which resembles *A. giganteum,* but is half the flower size and half the height.

Allium
moly

Common Name:	Lily leek
Flowers:	Native to Spain. Clusters of yellow star-shaped flowers borne on slender stalks.
Leaves:	Flat, pointed, green.
Habit:	12″ (31cm) tall. Clump-forming, fountainlike.
Culture:	Prefers full sun or partial shade in fertile, humus-rich, loam soil. Propagate by bulbs or seeds. If grown from seeds, wait two to three years for flowering.
Season of Bloom:	Spring.
Hardiness:	Zones 4–7.
Uses:	A wonderful edging. Good choice for planting in drifts in rock gardens.

Another good low-growing allium is *A. senescens*. With its rounded purple flower heads, it resembles clumps of chives. It flowers spectacularly in midsummer.

Allium
schoenoprasum

Common Name:	Chive
Flowers:	Native to Siberia. Grown primarily for the onion flavor of its hollow leaves. The rounded flowers are pink or purple and attract bees.
Leaves:	Perennial, long, slender, circular, green.
Habit:	12″–18″ (31–46cm) tall. Clump-forming.
Culture:	Prefers full sun. Enjoys high humidity and well-drained, fertile, sandy or loam soil. Propagate by seeds or root division.
Season of Bloom:	Late spring.
Hardiness:	Zones 4–8.
Uses:	Attractive edging. Popular accent in mixed perennial borders.

Chives make a beautiful ribbon of color to define herb gardens and vegetable gardens. Plants are often used as a culinary flavoring, chopped fine and sprinkled on salads, soups, and egg dishes.

Allium
tuberosum

Common Name:	Chinese chive, garlic chive
Flowers:	Native to China. Attractive clusters of white flowers stand erect on stiff stems.
Leaves:	Slender, pointed, green, with a light garlic taste.
Habit:	Up to 24″ (61cm) tall. Clump-forming.
Culture:	Prefers full sun in well-drained, humus-rich soil. After bloom remove flower heads and cut back leaves to their base. Propagate by seeds or root division. Divide clumps every three to four years.
Season of Bloom:	Late spring.
Hardiness:	Zones 5–9.
Uses:	Pretty ground cover or accent in a vegetable or herb garden. The dried seed heads are added whole to vinegars. Leaves are delicious in soups and salads.

Good component of all-white flower gardens. Excellent as a highlight in mixed perennial borders. Attractive to butterflies. Popular for old-fashioned cottage gardens.

Alstroemeria aurantiaca

Amaryllis belladonna

Common Name: Belladona lily, naked-lady lily

.h America. Large clusters of as flowers. Colors include orange

rdlike, green, resembling

1–91cm) tall. Upright, mounded, iing.

Culture: Prefers full sun or partial shade in well-drained, fertile, sandy or loam soil. Propagate by root division in early spring or autumn.

Season of Bloom: Early to midsummer.

Hardiness: Zones 6–10. In zone 6, plant next to a protected, sunny wall and mulch with wood chips or salt hay.

Uses: Attractive massed in mixed beds and borders. Prized cut flower in the floral industry.

The 'Ligtu' and other hybrids are especially colorful mixtures, and include a range of colors: white, yellow, orange, pink, and red.

Flowers: Native to South Africa. Sweetly fragrant flowers in clusters of six to twelve. Colors include pink, rose, and white.

Leaves: Flat, straplike, green, dying down by early summer before flowering occurs.

Habit: 24″ (61cm) tall. Upright, clump- and colony-forming.

Culture: Prefers full sun in well-drained, sandy, garden soil. Propagate by seeds or bulbs. Does not like to be disturbed.

Season of Bloom: Mid- to late summer, for six to eight weeks.

Hardiness: Zones 7–10. Mulch for winter protection.

Uses: Excellent for naturalizing in coastal meadows. Attractive in mixed shrub or perennial borders.

Often confused with the *Hippeastrum* species (also known as *Amaryllis*). The true *Amaryllis* comes from South Africa, while *Hippeastrum* comes from South America. Another look-alike is *Lycoris squamigera*, native to Japan and hardy to zone 5.

Anemone blanda

Common Name:	Grecian windflower
Flowers:	Native to Greece. Colorful, daisylike blossoms of white, rose, and blue flowers, which close at night and in cloudy weather.
Leaves:	Feathery, green.
Habit:	2″–8″ (5–20cm) tall. Low, colony-forming.
Culture:	Prefers full sun or partial shade in well-drained, humus-rich, garden soil. Propagate by dividing tubers in late autumn.
Season of Bloom:	Early spring.
Hardiness:	Zones 4–8.
Uses:	Beautiful naturalized as drifts in meadows and rock gardens. Attractive ground cover for slopes and for edging woodland paths. Readily self-seeds to form large colonies.

Many varieties are available as separate colors, including 'Blue Star', 'Pink Star', and 'Bridesmaid' (white). Very similar in appearance to *A. apennina*, mostly seen in blue or white.

Anemone coronaria

Common Name:	French anemone, poppy anemone
Flowers:	Native to the Mediterranean region. Large, bright, poppylike flowers with contrasting black centers. Colors include white, red, blue, and bicolors.
Leaves:	Feathery, deeply indented, green.
Habit:	9″–18″ (23–46cm) tall. Upright, sparse foilage.
Culture:	Prefers full sun or partial shade in well-drained, humus-rich, sandy or loam soil. Propagate by seeds or tuber division in late summer and autumn.
Season of Bloom:	Spring.
Hardiness:	Zones 7–9. In zone 6, plant in early spring, dig out of ground in the summer, and store in dry peat moss over winter.
Uses:	Attractive massed in perennial beds and borders. Good for coastal locations.

'Anemone De Caen' (single-flowered) and 'Anemone St. Brigid' (double-flowered) are the principal varieties. Both are very popular with florists as cut flowers.

Babiana
stricta

Common
Name: Baboon flower

Flowers: Native to South Africa. Sweetly scented,
delicate, freesialike flowers blanket long
stems. Colors include white, pink, violet,
and red.

Leaves: Sword-shaped, hairy, green, turning an
attractive russet-brown in late summer.

Habit: 6″–12″ (15–31cm) tall. Spreading, clump-
forming.

Culture: Easy to grow. Prefers full sun in well-drained,
manure-rich soil. Propagate by corms in
autumn; plant 3″ (7.5cm) deep and 3″ apart.

Season
of Bloom: Late spring.

Hardiness: Zones 8–10. In zone 7, mulch heavily in
autumn; in zone 6, dig up and store in dry peat
moss over winter.

Uses: Popular in rock gardens and flower borders,
massed as a ground cover.

Called baboon flower because in its native South Africa,
the bulb is a favorite food of baboons.

Begonia ×
tuberhybrida

Common
Name: Tuberous begonia

Flowers: Hybrid of species native to South America.
Waxy, showy flowers are available in all colors
except blue and green. The world record for
flower size is 13″ (33cm) across.

Leaves: Pointed, hairy, lobed, green.

Habit: 8″–18″ (20–46cm) tall. Upright, hanging, and
trailing varieties are available.

Culture: Prefers light to medium shade in moist but
well-drained, humus-rich soil. Propagate by
tubers or by taking cuttings from shoots that
appear on tubers in early spring.

Season
of Bloom: All summer to frost.

Hardiness: Zones 9–10. In areas with frost, dig up in
autumn and store in dry peat moss over
winter.

Uses: A fabulous flowering shade plant. Exquisite in
mixed beds and borders. May also be grown
in window boxes, containers, and hanging
baskets.

'Pacific Giant' hybrids, developed along the shores of
Monterey Bay, California, and 'New Belgian' hybrids,
developed by breeders in Belgium, are two extremely
large-flowered strains.

Belamcanda chinensis

Common Name: Blackberry lily

Flowers: Native to China. Clusters of orange flowers are marked with red dots up and down their petals. Attractive seed pods follow flowering. Pods split open as they mature, revealing shiny, black, pea-size seeds that resemble blackberries.

Leaves: Slender, grasslike, green.

Habit: 30"–36" (76–91cm) tall. Clump-forming, splayed like a fan.

Culture: Easy to grow. Prefers full sun or light shade in well-drained, sandy or loam soil. Propagate by root division in autumn, or by seeds. If grown from seeds, plants will produce blossoms in two years.

Season of Bloom: Midsummer.

Hardiness: Zones 6–10. In zones 5–6, mulch with wood chips or salt hay to protect from cold weather.

Uses: Beautiful in mixed perennial beds and borders. Tuberous root is used medicinally in India, as an antidote to cobra bites.

Plants are good to include in cutting gardens. The flowers are used in fresh arrangements, the seed pods in dried arrangements.

Bletilla striata

Common Name: Chinese orchid

Flowers: Native to China. Tall floral spikes bear clusters of pink, purple, and occasionally white flowers on pseudobulbs (tuberlike underground stems).

Leaves: Wide, pointed, prominently dark green.

Habit: 12"–24" (31–61cm) tall. Upright, clump-forming.

Culture: Easy to grow. Prefers partial shade in moist, fertile, humus-rich, loam soil. Propagate by clump division in autumn or spring.

Season of Bloom: Early summer.

Hardiness: Zones 5–10. In zones 6–7, provide a thick winter mulch.

Uses: Attractive in shady wildflower or perennial gardens. Good potted flowering plant. Long-lasting cut flower.

Generally sold as lavender flowered and white flowered, the flowers are perfect miniatures of the familiar florist orchid *(Cattleyas).*

Camassia species

Common Name: Camass

Flowers: Native mostly to North America. Lovely clusters of creamy white, and light to dark blue flowers on upright, naked spikes.

Leaves: Narrow, slender, green.

Habit: 18″–36″ (46–91cm) tall, depending on variety. Upright, spirelike.

Culture: Prefers full sun in well-drained, humus-rich soil. Propagate by seeds or bulbs. Flowers develop in four years from seed.

Season of Bloom: Spring.

Hardiness: Zones 4–7.

Uses: Perfect for naturalizing in woodland and meadows. Also pretty massed in mixed beds and borders.

C. cusickii is the tallest species and grows 30″–36″ (76–91cm) tall; *C. leichtlinii,* the most attractive and common to the Pacific Northwest, is 24″–36″ (61–91cm) tall; *C. quamash,* also native to the Pacific Northwest is 24″–36″ (61–91cm) tall; *C. scilloides,* the Atlantic camass, is 18″–24″ (46–61cm) tall.

Canna × generalis

Common Name: Canna, Indian shot

Flowers: Native to South America. Old-fashioned favorite. Colorful spikes of gladioluslike flowers in white, yellow, orange, pink, and red. Some colors are exotically spotted.

Leaves: Broad, deeply ribbed, green or bronze; resemble banana foliage.

Habit: 1½′–5′ (.5–1.5m) tall. Upright, spirelike.

Culture: Prefers full sun in well-drained, humus-rich, loam soil. Thrives in hot weather. Propagate by rhizome division in spring. Divide every three years.

Season of Bloom: Throughout the summer.

Hardiness: Zones 8–10. In colder zones, store roots indoors over winter.

Uses: Plant in masses of single colors near evergreen trees or shrubs and against walls. Attractive near pools and in containers.

'The President', a scarlet-red variety, is the most widely planted canna from rhizomes. The variety 'Tropical Rose', an All-America award winner, will bloom within three months from seed if started indoors and transplanted after there is no longer a danger of frost.

Cardiocrinum giganteum

Common Name: Giant Himalayan lily

Flowers: Native to western China. Pendant, white, trumpet-shaped blooms resemble Easter lilies, but have maroon stripes inside the throat. Borne on an immense flower spike.

Leaves: Large, heart-shaped, glossy, light green; form a rosette.

Habit: Up to 10′ (3m) tall. Spirelike.

Culture: The best plants are raised from bulbs produced from seeds, though it takes at least four years to produce flowers. Demands light shade in cool, well-drained, moist, humus-rich, acid soil.

Season of Bloom: Early summer.

Hardiness: Zones 6–8.

Uses: Most often a tall accent between azaleas and rhododendrons in woodland gardens.

Plants die after flowering but produce offsets so that a colony is established.

Chionodoxa luciliae

Common Name: Glory-of-the-snow

Flowers: Native to Asia Minor. Delicate blue or pink star-shaped flowers have contrasting white centers.

Leaves: Narrow, pointed, green.

Habit: 4″–6″ (10–15cm) tall. Low, mounded, fountainlike.

Culture: Easy to grow. Prefers full sun or partial shade in well-drained soil with compost applied to soil in autumn. Propagate by bulbs planted in autumn.

Season of Bloom: Early spring.

Hardiness: Zones 3–8.

Uses: Attractive in masses under deciduous trees, in front of shrubs, and as drifts in rock gardens. Long-lasting, dainty cut flower.

'Alba' (white) and 'Pink Giant' (a light pink) are available, but blue varieties are by far the most popular.

Clivia
miniata

**Common
Name:**   Kaffir lily

Flowers: Native to South Africa. Clusters of tubular
flowers borne on stout stems. Colors include
yellow, orange, and orange-red.

Leaves: Graceful, arching, straplike, dark green.

Habit: 12″–24″ (31–61cm) tall. Low, clump-forming.

Culture: Prefers partial shade in well-drained, moist,
humus-rich soil. Enjoys being crowded.
Propagate by bulbs planted in autumn.

**Season
of Bloom:**   Early spring.

Hardiness: Zones 9–10.

Uses: Attractive in pots, which can be brought indoors
for winter interest in areas with winter frosts.
Suitable for massing in mixed beds and borders.

Being pot-bound—or having the roots restricted by
stones—encourages spectacular flowering. A favorite
component of shade gardens in frost-free areas. Looks
especially attractive planted under tree ferns.

Colchicum
autumnale

**Common
Name:**   Autumn crocus

Flowers: Native to the Mediterranean region. Bright,
single or double, crocuslike flowers appear
before leaves emerge. Colors are white and pale
rose to lavender.

Leaves: Slender, straplike, green; appear in the spring
and die back by early summer.

Habit: 6″–8″ (15–20cm) tall. Low, clump-forming.

Culture: Prefers full sun or partial shade in well-
drained, moist, fertile, humus-rich soil. Does
not like to be disturbed. Propagate by corms
planted in early summer.

**Season
of Bloom:**   Autumn.

Hardiness: Zones 4–9.

Uses: Spectacular massed on verdant slopes or in
rock gardens. In smaller gardens, plant at the
edge of lawn and between shrubs along the
house foundation.

A related species, *C. speciosum,* has flowers that
resemble tropical water lilies. (The above photograph
shows colchicums flowering through turf at Claude
Monet's garden, Giverny, France.)

Convallaria majalis

Common Name: Lily-of-the-valley

Flowers: Native to Europe. Old-fashioned favorite. Sweetly fragrant, dainty, nodding, white or pink bells hang five to eight on an arching stem.

Leaves: Broad, pointed, bright green.

Habit: 6″–8″ (15–20cm) tall. Low. Spreads rapidly to form colonies.

Culture: Easy to grow. Prefers sun or partial shade in moist, acid soil. Mulch lightly in autumn with well-rotted cow manure for abundant blooms. Propagate by dividing the pips (the underground rootstalks) in autumn.

Season of Bloom: Late spring.

Hardiness: Zones 3–7.

Uses: An attractive ground cover for hard-to-plant places. Good massed under deciduous trees and as an edging. Popular in bouquets.

There is an unusual pale pink form *(C.m. rosea)* that can look enchanting mixed with the pure white.

Crocosmia × crocosmiiflora

Common Name: Montebretia

Flowers: Native to South Africa. Fiery orange-red, freesialike flowers borne along arching stems.

Leaves: Spear-shaped, arching, bright green.

Habit: 24″–48″ (61–122cm) tall. Upright, clump-forming.

Culture: Prefers full sun or partial shade in well-drained, fertile, humus-rich garden soil. Propagate by corms planted in spring or from seeds, which may take three years to flower.

Season of Bloom: Late summer to autumn.

Hardiness: Zones 6–10. In zones 6–7, provide a mulch for winter protection.

Uses: Attractive massed in mixed beds and borders. Sprays make long-lasting cut flowers.

'Jenny Bloom' is a beautiful golden yellow variety; 'Lucifer', a richly colored flame red. Popular in coastal gardens.

Crocus
tomasinianus

**Common
Name:** Crocus, snow crocus

Flowers: Native to Yugoslavia. Clusters of pretty purple flowers with bright golden stamens protrude from the ground, casting their petals wide open in bright sunny weather.

Leaves: Narrow, dark green, streaked with a white midrib.

Habit: 3″ (7.5cm) tall. Low, clump-forming.

Culture: Prefers full sun or partial shade in well-drained, humus-rich, sandy or loam soil. Self-seeder. Propagate by corms planted in autumn.

**Season
of Bloom:** Early spring.

Hardiness: Zones 3–7.

Uses: Thrives in rock gardens; naturalizes in woodland, lawns, and meadows.

Especially beautiful in combination with snowdrops and winter aconites, since all three bloom at about the same time; will naturalize freely in leaf mold under deciduous trees.

Crocus
vernus

**Common
Name:** Dutch crocus

Flowers: Native to Europe. Low clumps of bright white, lilac, purple, and multicolored striped flowers grow skyward.

Leaves: Narrow, dark green; white midribs appear the same time flowering occurs.

Habit: 4″ (10cm) tall. Low, clump-forming.

Culture: Easy to grow. Prefers full sun in well-drained, sandy or loam soil. Propagate by corms planted in autumn.

**Season
of Bloom:** Early spring.

Hardiness: Zones 3–7.

Uses: Popular for edging walkways and borders. Attractive naturalized in lawns. Suitable for containers.

This is the most widely cultivated type. Popular varieties include 'Pickwick' (purple-and-white-striped), 'Flower Record' (satinlike purple-mauve), and 'Remembrance' (huge deep blue-violet, considered the best for indoor forcing).

Cyclamen persicum

Common Name:	Florist's cyclamen
Flowers:	Native to Greece. Nodding white, pink, red, or lavender flowers bloom profusely on stiff, slender stems.
Leaves:	Heart-shaped, mottled, dark green and silver with a metallic sheen.
Habit:	6″–8″ (15–20cm) tall. Upright, clump-forming.
Culture:	Prefers partial shade in moist, humus-rich, loam soil. Propagate by seeds or corms planted in spring.
Season of Bloom:	Autumn to winter.
Hardiness:	Zones 8–9.
Uses:	Popular indoor houseplant for winter flowering. Suitable for shade gardens near patios and for bedding, massed in one color or in mixtures of color.

Smaller-flowered species, such as *C. hederifolium* are hardy to zone 6 and suitable for massing or edging along woodland paths. 'Giganteum' has the largest flowers for indoor enjoyment. 'Fast Track' hybrids are easiest to grow from seed, blooming in just seven months.

Dahlia pinnata hybrids

Common Name:	Dahlia
Flowers:	Native to Mexico. Dahlias come in all shapes and sizes, including rounded, double flowers as well as "quilled," or cactus-flowered types. Flower size ranges from 2″–14″ (5–36cm). Colors include white, yellow, orange, red, pink, purple, and bicolors.
Leaves:	Spear-shaped, serrated, bright green. Some varieties have lustrous bronze foliage.
Habit:	Up to 6′ (1.8m) tall. Upright, bushy, branching.
Culture:	Prefers full sun in well-drained, fertile, humus-rich, sandy or loam soil. Tall varieties require staking. Pinch off top of stems to grow bushier plants. Propagate by root division or stem cuttings. After flowering, dig up roots in autumn and store them in dry peat moss or vermiculite in a cold area.
Season of Bloom:	Midsummer to autumn.
Hardiness:	Zones 8–10.
Uses:	Most popular as a tall accent in mixed beds and borders or in a display garden. Excellent cut flower.

The *Dahlia pinnata* hybrids include the so-called dinnerplate dahlias, displaying massive blooms up to 14″ (36cm) across. Bedding dahlias easily grown from seed include such varieties as 'Rigoletto' (green foliage) and 'Redskin' (brown foliage).

Endymion
hispanicus

**Common
Name:**   Spanish bluebell

Flowers: Native to Europe. Showy, sweet-smelling, nodding, bell-shaped flowers delicately clustered on fleshy, arching stems. Colors are light blue, white, or pink.

Leaves: Cascading, spear-shaped, green.

Habit: 15″ (38cm) tall. Upright, arching, clump-forming.

Culture: Prefers partial shade in moist, fertile, humus-rich soil. Propagate by bulbs planted in autumn.

**Season
of Bloom:**   Spring.

Hardiness: Zones 6–10.

Uses: Makes lovely drifts in woodland gardens. Attractive in mixed beds and borders, and edging paths.

Similar in appearance to *E. non-scriptus* (English bluebells), but more adaptable to extremes of climate and more showy. Good companion to ferns. Sometimes listed as *Hyacinthoides.*

Endymion
non-scriptus

**Common
Name:**   English bluebell

Flowers: Native to England and France. Clusters of nodding, highly fragrant, ½″ (13mm), bell-shaped flowers on arching flower stems. Not as showy as Spanish bluebells, but more fragrant.

Leaves: Slender, straplike, green.

Habit: 12″ (31cm) tall. Clump-forming; plants form colonies, especially in woodlands.

Culture: Prefers light shade in moist, humus-rich soil. Propagate by bulbs planted in autumn.

**Season
of Bloom:**   Spring.

Hardiness: Zones 6–8.

Uses: Good for massing in woodland gardens along paths and in mixed beds and borders.

Though not as showy or as widely adaptable as the closely related Spanish bluebell, the English bluebell is intensely fragrant and looks sensational planted near rhododendrons.

Eranthis hyemalis

Common Name:	Winter aconite
Flowers:	Native to southern Europe. Glistening, sweet-scented, yellow, buttercup flowers open at ground level.
Leaves:	Deeply indented, bright green; encircle each flower.
Habit:	2″–4″ (5–10cm) tall. Low, mounded, clump-forming.
Culture:	Prefers full sun or partial shade in well-drained, humus-rich soil. Propagate by seeds in spring and tubers any time after flowering.
Season of Bloom:	Early spring, oftentimes blooming through melting snow.
Hardiness:	Zones 4–7.
Uses:	Excellent for naturalizing along woodland paths or edging mixed beds and borders.

Perfect companion to snowdrops and snow crocus, which bloom about the same time. Aconites will naturalize freely in leaf mold under deciduous trees to form large colonies.

Eremurus elwesii

Common Name:	Foxtail lily
Flowers:	Native to deserts of Asia. Towering flower stalks are massed with white florets that bloom from the bottom to the top of the floral spike.
Leaves:	Spear-shaped, green; form a rosette.
Habit:	6′–10′ (1.8–3m) tall. Upright, spirelike.
Culture:	Prefers full sun in well-drained, rich, sandy or loam soil. Doesn't like to be disturbed. Propagate by root division. Plant tuberous roots in autumn.
Season of Bloom:	Late spring to summer.
Hardiness:	Zones 5–8.
Uses:	Wonderful framed against dark evergreen shrubs, such as a tall hedge. Beautiful background accent in perennial borders.

Spectacular tall accents for early-flowering perennial borders. 'Shelford' hybrids are dwarf forms, just 4′–5′ (1.2–1.5m) tall. They include pink and yellow in their color range, though are not reliably hardy beyond zone 8.

Erythronium 'Pagoda'

Common Name:	Dogtooth violet
Flowers:	A hybrid of species native to the Pacific Northwest. Lovely, nodding, dainty, yellow flowers with recurved petals borne erect on naked stems.
Leaves:	Broad, pointed, green.
Habit:	10″ (25cm) tall. Upright, clump-forming.
Culture:	Prefers full sun or partial shade in well-drained, humus-rich soil. Propagate by bulbs planted in autumn.
Season of Bloom:	Early spring.
Hardiness:	Zones 4–8.
Uses:	A sensational woodland plant. Beautiful in rock gardens and planted around the margin of a small ornamental pond.

Erythronium is a genus consisting of about fifteen species mostly native to North America. Though 'Pagoda' is the best for garden display, 'White Beauty', 'Lilac Wonder', and 'Purple King' are also good varieties. Common in connoisseur gardens, they deserve to be much more widely grown in home gardens wherever a winter freeze can condition the bulbs.

Eucharis grandiflora

Common Name:	Amazon lily
Flowers:	Native to South America. Clusters of fragrant, small, white, daffodil-like flowers borne in clusters on slender stems.
Leaves:	Evergreen, broad, pointed, shiny, green.
Habit:	12″–24″ (31–61cm) tall. Upright, clump-forming.
Culture:	Prefers partial shade in well-drained, moist, humus-rich soil. Propagate by bulbs, allowing the pointed tops to show through the soil.
Season of Bloom:	Late winter indoors; early spring outdoors.
Hardiness:	Zones 9–10.
Uses:	Popular among florists. Can be grown as a houseplant in a warm greenhouse or sunny room. In mild areas, it makes a wonderful addition to a shady perennial bed or border.

Mostly grown as a flowering pot plant to bloom in late winter or early spring. The flowers are sensational in fresh arrangements.

Eucomis comosa

Common Name:	Pineapple flower
Flowers:	Native to South Africa. Interesting dense clusters of white to greenish white starlike flowers stud upright spikes capped with a topknot of green leaves resembling a pineapple.
Leaves:	Spear-shaped, dark green; form rosettes.
Habit:	12″–24″ (31–61cm) tall. Upright, clump-forming.
Culture:	Easy to grow. Prefers full sun in moist but well-drained, rich, sandy soil. Propagate by bulbs planted in spring.
Season of Bloom:	Midsummer.
Hardiness:	Zones 7–10. In zone 7, plant next to a sunny wall and mulch heavily with wood chips or salt hay to protect from cold weather.
Uses:	Unusual accent in mixed beds or borders, or grown in pots to decorate a patio.

Deserves to be much more widely grown. Though a familiar sight in botanical gardens, they are rarely a feature of home gardens.

Freesia × hybrida

Common Name:	Freesia
Flowers:	Native to South Africa. Clusters of fragrant, trumpet-shaped flowers grow along arching, wiry stems. Colors include white, yellow, orange, purple, red, and pink.
Leaves:	Narrow, sword-shaped, bright green.
Habit:	18″–24″ (46–61cm) tall. Clump-forming.
Culture:	Prefers full sun in well-drained, sandy or loam soil. The flower stems usually need staking to keep them erect. Propagate by corms. Plant so tip is just below the soil surface, in autumn.
Season of Bloom:	Early spring to summer.
Hardiness:	Zones 9–10.
Uses:	Plant in mixed beds or borders in mild winter areas. More frequently seen in large pots as a houseplant. Long-lasting cut flower.

'Super Giants Mixed' is a mixture of large-flowered freesias that will bloom in nine to twelve months from seed. Separate colors are available by planting corms. Yellow is considered the most highly fragrant variety.

Fritillaria imperialis

Common Name: Crown-imperial

Flowers: Native to Iran. Large clusters of orange, reddish orange, or yellow flowers nod below green leafy tufts that crown the flowering stems.

Leaves: Lilylike, green; emit a musky odor, similar to a skunk, when broken or bruised.

Habit: 30″–48″ (76–122cm) tall. Upright.

Culture: Prefers light shade in well-drained, fertile, humus-rich soil. Propagate by bulbs planted in autumn.

Season of Bloom: Spring.

Hardiness: Zones 3–8.

Uses: Attractive in woodland settings. Tall accent in mixed beds and borders. Combines especially well with tulips.

Though orange is the most popular color, yellow and orange planted together is a spectacular combination. A variegated form has white and green striping along the leaves, but since it is a weak plant that sometimes does not flower, it is grown mostly for foliage effect. Pink and white forms have been reported in the mountains of Iran, but these have not been brought into cultivation yet.

Fritillaria meleagris

Common Name: Checkered lily

Flowers: Native to Europe. White or purple nodding bells with mottled bicolor streaks on their petals.

Leaves: Narrow, grasslike, green.

Habit: 8″–12″ (20–31cm) tall. Upright, colony-forming.

Culture: Easy to grow. Prefers sun or light shade in well-drained, sandy or loam soil. Propagate by bulbs planted in autumn.

Season of Bloom: Spring.

Hardiness: Zones 3–7.

Uses: Attractive in naturalized woodland settings or wildflower meadows. Suitable for rock gardens. Will reseed to form colonies.

The genus *Fritillaria* consists of numerous species. They occur frequently in botanical collections. The only other species of landscape value is *F. persica*, producing handsome 36″ (91cm) spikes of nodding, maroon, bell-shaped flowers.

Galanthus elwesii

Common Name: Giant snowdrop

Flowers: Native to Europe. Tiny single or double, teardrop-shaped, nodding, white flowers, some petals tinged with green on their tips.

Leaves: Slender, green; leaves wither away by late spring.

Habit: 4″–6″ (10–15cm) tall. Low, clump-forming.

Culture: Prefers light shade in well-drained, fertile, humus-rich soil. Propagate by seeds and bulbs planted any time after flowering.

Season of Bloom: Early spring; one of the earliest-blooming spring bulbs.

Hardiness: Zones 3–7.

Uses: Pretty naturalized in woodland along trails and around the bases of trees. Popular for edging walkways, beds, and borders.

'Flore Pleno' is a double-flowered snowdrop that should be much more widely planted in home gardens. Snowdrops are spectacular in combination with *Eranthis hyemalis* (aconite); they will reseed freely in leaf mold and form beautiful large colonies.

Gladiolus × hortulanus

Common Name: Gladiolus

Flowers: Native to South Africa. Tall spikes of open-throated blooms cover the stems. Colors include green, cream, yellow, buff, orange, salmon, scarlet, pink, red, rose, lavender, purple, blue, tan, and bicolors.

Leaves: Graceful, swordlike, green.

Habit: 36″–48″ (91–122cm) tall. Upright, spirelike.

Culture: Prefers full sun in well-drained, fertile, loam or sandy soil. Store corms in the vegetable bin of a refrigerator and propagate by planting them in late spring for autumn bloom.

Season of Bloom: Summer. Stagger plantings to prolong flowering period.

Hardiness: Zones 7–10.

Uses: Excellent background plant. Popular in mixed beds and borders. Prized in the floral industry as a cut flower for its clear colors and ruffled blooms.

To prevent the flower from falling over, mound earth up against the plants or plant a hedge of marigolds on either side for support. By planting gladiolus 6″ (15cm) deep in areas where the ground freezes, it is sometimes possible to have them come back the following year. Many outstanding varieties are available, including 'Green Woodpecker' (green-flowered), 'Daybreak' (pink with cream throat), and 'Storm Clouds' (lavender-blue).

Hippeastrum hybrids

Common Name:	Amaryllis
Flowers:	Native to South America. Clusters of giant trumpet-shaped flowers borne upright on long, hollow, fleshy stalks. Usually sends up a second flower stalk after the first one begins to fade. Colors include white, pink, orange, red, and bicolors.
Leaves:	Arching, straplike, green.
Habit:	12″–24″ (31–61cm) tall. Upright stems, clump-forming.
Culture:	Prefers light shade in moist, fertile, humus-rich, sandy soil. Propagate by bulbs planted in autumn. Plant so pointed end is just visible above soil line.
Season of Bloom:	Winter to spring.
Hardiness:	Zones 9–10.
Uses:	A spectacular winter-flowering indoor houseplant; plant outside in southern areas. Good cut flower in frost-free areas.

Amaryllis described as "Christmas" hybrids will bloom by Christmas since they are generally imported from Africa where seasons are reversed. Other amaryllis, described as Dutch hybrids, generally bloom in March.

Hyacinthus orientalis

Common Name:	Dutch hyacinth
Flowers:	Native to the Mediterranean region. Highly fragrant and ornamental. Dense clusters of star-shaped flowers borne erect on stiff, fleshy stalks. Colors include white, pink, red, purple, blue, and yellow.
Leaves:	Straplike, fleshy, green.
Habit:	8″–10″ (20–25cm) tall. Upright.
Culture:	Prefers full sun in well-drained, fertile, humus-rich soil. Propagate by bulbs planted in autumn. After blooming, bulbs split in two, producing smaller flowers the second year. For large blooms, dig up old bulbs and replant area with new bulbs.
Season of Bloom:	Spring.
Hardiness:	Zones 3–8. In zones 4–7, mulch with wood chips or salt hay to protect from cold weather.
Uses:	Beautiful in masses or drifts in beds and borders, in window boxes, or in rock gardens.

Though there are one hundred varieties known to cultivation, only about twenty-five of them are featured in catalogs. Blue is the most popular color, represented by 'King of the Blues' (deep blue), 'Blue Magic' (a deep violet-blue with a white eye), and 'Perle Brillante' (a bright blue). 'Jan Bos' is the best of the reds (shown above with 'Pink Pearl').

Incarvillea delavayi

Common Name:	Hardy gloxinia
Flowers:	Native to China. Pretty clusters of tubular, pink or rose flowers with yellow throats, borne upright on sturdy stems.
Leaves:	Deeply divided, lustrous, veined, dark green; rosette-forming.
Habit:	12″ (31cm) tall. Low.
Culture:	Prefers full sun or partial shade in well-drained, fertile, humus-rich soil. Propagate by division of tuberous roots planted in autumn.
Season of Bloom:	Spring.
Hardiness:	Zones 5–7.
Uses:	Suitable for rock gardens and edging mixed beds and borders.

Incredibly, this compact, showy plant is not related to gloxinias, but to trumpet creepers native to North America and China. Makes an attractive flowering pot plant for greenhouses and sunrooms.

Ipheion uniflorum

Common Name:	Spring starflower
Flowers:	Native to Argentina. Mostly blue and white, 1″ (2.5cm) across, star-shaped.
Leaves:	Grasslike, light green.
Habit:	Up to 5″ (13cm) tall. Mounded, clump-forming.
Culture:	Prefers full sun in well-drained, sandy or loam soil. Propagate by bulb division in autumn.
Season of Bloom:	Spring.
Hardiness:	Zones 5–10.
Uses:	Spectacular edging to perennial borders. Suitable for rock gardens, planted in drifts to cascade over a rock ledge.

Sometimes listed in bulb catalogs as *Tritelia uniflora*. Readily forms attractive colonies. Combines well with *Phlox subulata* (creeping phlox).

Iris
cristata

Common Name: Dwarf crested iris

Flowers: Native to North America. White, blue, or purplish 2″ (5cm) flowers with a yellow crest borne upright on short stems near ground level.

Leaves: Arching, sword-shaped, light green; colony-forming.

Habit: 6″–12″ (15–31cm) tall. Low, spreading.

Culture: Prefers partial shade to almost full sun in well-drained, humus-rich, acid soil. Propagate by rhizome division after flowering.

Season of Bloom: Spring.

Hardiness: Zones 4–8.

Uses: Superb flowering ground cover, especially along woodland paths. Good in rock gardens or as an edging to sunny beds and borders.

'Alba' is a white variety, 'Caerulea' a blue. Will naturalize freely in leaf mold under light shade. Combines well with ferns.

Iris ×
hollandica

Common Name: Dutch iris

Flowers: A hybrid of species native to Europe. Bright, perky, 4″ (10cm) wide flowers are borne erect on stiff stems. Colors include white, yellow, orange, bronze, blue, purple, and bicolors.

Leaves: Spear-shaped, light green.

Habit: 24″–36″ (61–91cm) tall. Upright.

Culture: Prefers full sun or partial shade in well-drained, moist, fertile, humus-rich soil. Propagate by bulbs planted in autumn.

Season of Bloom: Mid-spring to early summer.

Hardiness: Zones 7–10. In zone 7, provide a protective mulch.

Uses: Sensational massed in beds and borders or naturalized in meadows. A popular component of cut-flower gardens.

'Wedgwood' is a clear blue, 'Polarice' a clear white with a blue flush, 'Golden Harvest', a golden yellow. Plants are grown commercially on a large scale to supply florists with cut flowers.

Iris
reticulata

**Common
Name:** Dwarf blue iris

Flowers: Native to the Caucasus mountains. These short, low-growing irises are the first to appear. Colors include blue, purple, and a rare white.

Leaves: Slender, pointed, green.

Habit: 4″–8″ (10–20cm) tall. Low, clump-forming.

Culture: Prefers full sun in well-drained, fertile, humus-rich soil. Propagate by bulbs planted in autumn.

**Season
of Bloom:** Early spring, before the last snowfalls of winter.

Hardiness: Zones 3–7.

Uses: Stunning planted in rock gardens and along pathways. May be forced for indoor blooms. Feeding with a high-phosphorus fertilizer in autumn encourages plants to form colonies.

'Harmony' is a beautiful deep blue, exquisite when seen in the morning against a background of frost or light sprinkling of snow. Combines well with *I. danfordiae,* a golden yellow dwarf iris from Asia Minor that blooms at the same time.

Ixia
maculata

**Common
Name:** Corn lily

Flowers: Native to South Africa. Clasping, cup-shaped flowers surround wiry stems. This species is white with a red eye, but hybrids resulting from crosses with other species include cream, yellow, red, and purple in their color range.

Leaves: Slender, spear-shaped, green.

Habit: 15″–18″ (38–46cm) tall. Upright, spreading.

Culture: Prefers full sun in well-drained, fertile, humus-rich, sandy or loam soil. Propagate by corms planted in autumn.

**Season
of Bloom:** Late spring to summer.

Hardiness: Zones 6–9.

Uses: Good accent for rock gardens and massed beds and borders.

Good companion to babianas, which bloom at the same time and require similar conditions. *I. paniculata* is a distinct eye-catching species displaying straw-colored, star-shaped flowers on long tubes in dense clusters.

Leucojum
aestivum

Common Name: Summer snowflake

Flowers: Native to Europe. Clusters of pendulous white bells resembling snowdrops grow on tall, stiff, arching stems.

Leaves: Narrow, straplike, green.

Habit: 24″ (61cm) tall. Upright, clump-forming.

Culture: Prefers partial shade in moist but well-drained, fertile, humus-rich soil. Propagate by bulbs planted in autumn.

Season of Bloom: Late spring.

Hardiness: Zones 3–9.

Uses: Attractive in perennial borders and lightly shaded beds. Good for cutting.

The variety 'Graveyte Giant' has the largest flowers, and grows to 36″ (91cm) tall. Just one clump can be eye-catching, especially when planted between azaleas and rhododendrons.

Lilium
Asiatic hybrids

Common Name: Asiatic hybrid lilies

Flowers: Developed from species native to Asia, Asiatic hybrid lilies consist of three subdivisions: 'Mid-Century' hybrids, with upright flowers (pictured above); a catch-all group, with outward-facing and pendant-shaped flowers with recurved petals; and Turk's-cap, with pendant-shaped flowers. Colors include white, yellow, orange, pink, red, lavender, and mahogany.

Leaves: Lance-shaped, green; run the length of each stem.

Habit: 2′–5′ (.6–1.5m) tall. Upright.

Culture: Prefers partial shade in moist, fertile, humus-rich soil. Demands excellent drainage. Propagate by bulbs planted in autumn or early spring.

Season of Bloom: Summer.

Hardiness: Zones 4–8.

Uses: Striking massed or planted in small groups along a picket fence or low hedge.

The variety 'Enchantment' is an especially carefree deep orange suitable for containers. 'Connecticut King' is similar, but bright yellow. Plants will form colonies in woodland.

Lilium candidum

Common Name:	Madonna lily
Flowers:	Native to Asia. Fragrant, trumpet-shaped blooms up to 8″ (20cm) long are pure white and arranged in a spike. Powdery yellow stamens in the throat of each flower are a conspicuous highlight.
Leaves:	Lance-shaped, dark green; run the entire length of each stem.
Habit:	5′–6′ (1.5–1.8m) tall. Upright.
Culture:	Prefers full sun or partial shade in well-drained, humus-rich soil. Propagate by bulbs planted in autumn or early spring.
Season of Bloom:	Summer.
Hardiness:	Zones 5–9.
Uses:	Spectacular massed in mixed beds and borders. Good cut flower.

Plant baby's breath around the base of madonna lilies to hide their long stems, which can look bare in dry summers. Madonna lilies are sensational combined with red shrub roses.

Lilium longiflorum

Common Name:	White trumpet lily
Flowers:	Native to China. Graceful clusters of fragrant, white, trumpet-shaped flowers are held erect on stiff stems. A hybrid form is grown as the popular Easter lily.
Leaves:	Lance-shaped, green; run the length of each stem.
Habit:	36″–48″ (91–122cm) tall. Upright.
Culture:	Prefers full sun in well-drained, humus-rich, sandy or loam soil. Propagate by bulbs planted in autumn for indoor flowering, early spring for outdoor flowering in the north.
Season of Bloom:	Summer.
Hardiness:	Zones 8–10.
Uses:	Suitable for mass plantings in mixed beds and borders. Wonderful cut flower.

The variety 'White Swan' can be raised from seed to flower the first year. Start early indoors and transplant to the garden in spring after there is no longer a danger of frost. 'Ace' is a good forcing variety to grow from bulbs under glass as Easter lilies.

Lycoris
squamigera

**Common
Name:** Magic lily, naked ladies

Flowers: Native to Japan. Clusters of fragrant, pink, trumpet-shaped flowers bloom on top of leafless fleshy, purple stems.

Leaves: Long, straplike, green; die back in early summer.

Habit: Up to 24″ (61cm) tall. Clump-forming.

Culture: Prefers full sun in well-drained, humus-rich, sandy soil. Propagate by bulbs planted in autumn or spring.

**Season
of Bloom:** Summer.

Hardiness: Zones 5–9.

Uses: An accent in mixed beds and borders especially near patios or walkways. Plants will form colonies in fertile soil. Especially attractive in coastal gardens.

A related species, *L. radiata* (red spider lily), is not so hardy, but popular for naturalizing in areas with mild climates.

Muscari
armeniacum

**Common
Name:** Grape hyacinth

Flowers: Native to Asia Minor. Lively, small, blue, bell-shaped flowers are arranged on upright spikes.

Leaves: Slender, pointed, green.

Habit: 6″–9″ (15–23cm) tall. Low, clump-forming.

Culture: Prefers full sun or partial shade in well-drained soil. Propagate by bulbs planted in autumn.

**Season
of Bloom:** Spring.

Hardiness: Zones 3–8.

Uses: Lovely naturalized around the edge of lawns or grown in masses under trees and shrubs. Looks good planted as drifts in rock gardens. Makes perfect miniature bouquets.

'Blue Spike' has double flowers, is more conspicuous in the landscape, and is a lighter blue. The famous "blue river" of flowers planted between shrubs in Keukenhof Gardens, Lisse, Holland (pictured above), is composed of grape hyacinths.

Narcissus minimus, N. asturiensis

Common Name: Miniature daffodil

Flowers: Native to Spain. Small, bright yellow, trumpet-shaped flowers bloom profusely on upright stems.

Leaves: Upright, slender, green.

Habit: Up to 6″ (15cm) tall. Upright, clump-forming.

Culture: Easy to grow. Prefers full sun or partial shade in well-drained, loam soil. Propagate by bulbs planted in autumn.

Season of Bloom: Spring.

Hardiness: Zones 4–8.

Uses: Lovely little miniatures of the larger trumpet daffodil, these look elegant planted in drifts under trees, in mixed beds and borders, or grown indoors in pots.

Sometimes listed in catalogs as *N. asturiensis*. Another good miniature species is the *N. bulbocodium* (hoop-petticoat daffodil), suitable for rock gardens and trough gardens. These plants readily form colonies if fed with a high-phosphorus fertilizer in autumn.

Narcissus tazetta

Common Name: Paper-white

Flowers: Native to the Mediterranean region. Clusters of highly fragrant, 1″ (2.5cm), white or yellow flowers with small cups atop erect stems.

Leaves: Slender, smooth, light green.

Habit: Up to 16″ (41cm) tall. Clump-forming.

Culture: Mostly grown indoors as a winter-flowering pot plant, usually with the bulb suspended over plain water or on top of moist gravel. Otherwise, plants prefer full sun in well-drained, sandy soil. Propagate by bulbs planted in autumn.

Season of Bloom: Winter indoors; early spring outdoors.

Hardiness: Tender bulb; overwinters outdoors only in zone 8 south.

Uses: Millions sold each year as a fragrant gift plant for Christmas.

The above photograph shows white-flowering paper-whites growing with early tulips in a shrub border.

Narcissus, Trumpet-division

Common Name: Trumpet daffodil

Flowers: A hybrid of species native to Europe. The trumpet or cup part of the flower is as long as or slightly longer than the petals. Colors include white, yellow, orange, buff, and bicolors.

Leaves: Upright, slender, green.

Habit: Up to 20″ (51cm) tall. Upright, clump-forming.

Culture: Easy to grow. Prefers full sun or partial shade in well-drained, fertile, loam soil. Propagate by bulbs planted in autumn.

Season of Bloom: Spring.

Hardiness: Zones 3–8.

Uses: Perfect for mass plantings in meadows, lawns, slopes, and banks. Plant as clumps in mixed beds and borders. Good cut flower. Suitable for forced indoor winter blooms.

'Unsurpassable' is a show-quality golden yellow; 'Mount Hood' a show-quality white. The variety 'Spellbinder' (lemon yellow trumpet and canary yellow petals) is exquisite for naturalizing.

Nerine bowdenii

Common Name: Nerine

Flowers: Native to South Africa. Clusters of gleaming magenta, silvery pink, rosy pink, scarlet, red, or white funnel-shaped flowers.

Leaves: Long, slender, straplike, green.

Habit: Up to 12″ (31cm) tall. Upright.

Culture: Easy to grow in frost-free areas. Prefers full sun or partial shade in well-drained, rich, loam or sandy soil. Propagate by bulbs planted in spring. Plant so bulb tip is at the soil surface.

Season of Bloom: Autumn.

Hardiness: Zones 8–10. Can be grown further north if planted in containers and brought indoors for the winter.

Uses: An attractive rock garden plant, also worth planting in containers on decks and patios. Excellent, long-lasting cut flower.

Valued for its autumn flowering, when it will outshine everything else in the garden in frost-free climates.

Ornithogalum umbellatum

Common Name:	Star-of-Bethlehem
Flowers:	Native to northern Africa. Pretty, fragrant, star flowers borne in flat-top clusters in groups of twelve to twenty. A greenish coloration appears on the petal undersides.
Leaves:	Narrow, pointed, grasslike, bright green; die back after blooming.
Habit:	9″–12″ (23–31cm) tall. Low, clump-forming.
Culture:	Easy to grow, even in impoverished soil. Prefers full sun or partial shade in well-drained, sandy, garden soil. Propagate by bulbs planted in autumn.
Season of Bloom:	Spring.
Hardiness:	Zones 6–10.
Uses:	Good for edging paths or drifts in rock gardens.

Plants reseed freely, creating large naturalized colonies. Also, healthy clumps will produce dozens of bulblets.

Polianthes tuberosa

Common Name:	Tuberose
Flowers:	Native to Mexico. Intense, sweet-smelling, creamy white to pinkish flower spikes grow two to five stalks per clump.
Leaves:	Long, sword-shaped, dark green; resemble gladiolus.
Habit:	24″–36″ (61–91cm) tall. Upright, spirelike.
Culture:	Prefers full sun in well-drained, fertile, humus-rich, loam soil. Propagate by bulbs planted in spring.
Season of Bloom:	Late summer to autumn.
Hardiness:	Zones 8–10.
Uses:	Grow in small groups in mixed beds and borders. Sensational cut flower. Popular for planting near patios and entrances, where its wonderful fragrance can be fully appreciated.

Basically, there is a choice of single-flowered and double-flowered. Single-flowered kinds are the most fragrant, but the doubles are more appealing in floral arrangements. Grow both! In northern areas where plants may not overwinter, gardeners plant bulbs each year in spring. Since flowering-size bulbs immediately split up into nonflowering bulblets, it is best to buy new bulbs fresh each season.

Puschkinia scilloides

Common Name:	Stripe squill, Lebanon squill
Flowers:	Native to Asia Minor. Creamy white or blue-striped white blossoms are borne on short, fleshy spikes. A close relative of *Scilla*.
Leaves:	Lancelike, bright green.
Habit:	4″–8″ (10–20cm) tall. Upright, clump-forming.
Culture:	Prefers full sun or partial shade in well-drained, sandy or loam soil. Enjoys cool climates. Propagate by bulbs planted in autumn.
Season of Bloom:	Early spring.
Hardiness:	Zones 3–7.
Uses:	Attractive naturalized at the edge of lawns and in rock gardens.

Combines well with *Scilla siberica,* to which it is closely related.

Ranunculus asiaticus

Common Name:	Persian buttercup
Flowers:	Native to eastern Mediterranean countries. Showy double flowers up to 3½″ (9cm) across have petals that resemble crepe paper. Blooms in almost every color except green and blue, but is available primarily in shades of orange, pink, red, yellow, and white.
Leaves:	Fernlike, green; die back soon after flowering.
Habit:	12″–18″ (31–46cm) tall. Upright, branching.
Culture:	Prefers full sun in well-drained, humus-rich, sandy or loam soil. Propagate by dividing tubers after foliage has withered. Some greenhouse varieties are best grown from seeds (see below).
Season of Bloom:	Early spring flower that lasts over several months. May be brought indoors for winter blooms.
Hardiness:	Zones 7–9.
Uses:	Suitable for mixed beds and borders and containers. Makes beautiful floral arrangements.

'Tecolote' hybrids are generally the best for garden display, with individual flowers up to 3″ (7.5cm) across. The 'Bloomingdale' series are hybrids grown from seeds, especially for forcing and sale as flowering pot plants. These produce extra-large flowers up to 3½″ (9cm) across.

Scilla
peruviana

**Common
Name:** Peruvian hyacinth, Cuban lily

Flowers: Native to South America. Spiky clusters of around one hundred 1″ (2.5cm), starlike flowers grow in cone-shaped clusters on slender stems. Blue is the primary color, but white is also available.

Leaves: Straplike, bright green; add a decorative backdrop to the blooming flowers.

Habit: 6″–12″ (15–31cm) tall. Clump-forming.

Culture: Easy to grow, even in impoverished soil. Prefers full sun or partial shade in well-drained, sandy or loam soil. Propagate by bulbs planted in autumn.

**Season
of Bloom:** Spring. Indoor plants bloom during winter months.

Hardiness: Zones 8–10.

Uses: Popular in rock gardens. Suitable for mass planting under trees and shrubs. Attractive grown indoors as a pot plant. Suitable for cutting.

In relatively frost-free areas, where this plant will overwinter, it creates a good ground cover for hard-to-plant slopes.

Scilla
siberica

**Common
Name:** Siberian squill

Flowers: Native to the Caucasus mountains. Clusters of pendulous bell-shaped flowers are borne on short, upright spikes. Colors include blue, pink, and white.

Leaves: Ribbonlike, green; die back soon after flowering.

Habit: 5″–6″ (13–15cm) tall. Upright, clump-forming.

Culture: Prefers full sun or partial shade in well-drained, sandy or loam soil. Propagate by bulbs planted in autumn.

**Season
of Bloom:** Spring.

Hardiness: Zones 3–7.

Uses: Eye-catching planted in drifts in rock gardens. Good for edging lawns and woodland paths.

'Spring Beauty' is the largest-flowered variety. A related species, *S. tubergeniana*, produces masses of white starlike flowers with a blue tint.

Sparaxis
tricolor

Common Name:	Wandflower, harlequin flower
Flowers:	Native to South Africa. Short spikes of bicolored or tricolored flowers in pastel shades of yellow, purple, and rose. Characteristic golden yellow throats are outlined in dark brown at the petal center.
Leaves:	Sword-shaped, green.
Habit:	8″–10″ (20–25cm) tall. Upright, clump-forming.
Culture:	Prefers full sun in well-drained, humus-rich, sandy soil. Propagate by corms planted in autumn.
Season of Bloom:	Spring.
Hardiness:	Zones 8–10.
Uses:	Good in rock gardens or mixed borders, planted in clumps. Suitable for floral arrangements.

'Tecolote' hybrids are the largest-flowered mixture, sometimes grown as flowering pot plants under glass, like freesias.

Sternbergia
lutea

Common Name:	Winter daffodil
Flowers:	Native to Asia Minor. Waxy yellow flowers resembling autumn crocus are borne on slender stems.
Leaves:	Grasslike, green.
Habit:	6″–12″ (15–31cm) tall. Low, clump-forming.
Culture:	Prefers full sun in well-drained, fertile, humus-rich, loam soil. Propagate by bulbs planted in spring.
Season of Bloom:	Late summer to early autumn.
Hardiness:	Zones 6–10.
Uses:	Attractive naturalized in lawns. Eye-catching clustered in rock gardens. Good for edging beds and borders.

A good companion to *Colchicum,* which flower at the same time. Spectacular when planted beneath *Caryopteris* × *clandonensis* (blue-mist shrub), which blooms about the same time.

Tigridia pavonia

Common Name: Tiger flower

Flowers: Native to Mexico. Unusual three-petaled flowers are mottled inside with red freckles. Colors include white, yellow, orange, pink, red, purple, and bicolors.

Leaves: Lancelike, green; resemble iris.

Habit: 18″–30″ (46–76cm) tall. Upright.

Culture: Easy to grow, even in poor soil. Prefers full sun in well-drained, fertile, sandy or loam soil. Propagate by bulbs planted in spring or from seeds started indoors eight weeks before outdoor planting.

Season of Bloom: Summer.

Hardiness: Zones 7–10.

Uses: Popular planted near stream banks and pond margins. Attractive clumped in mixed beds and borders.

Deserves to be much more widely grown. Seed is an inexpensive way of raising a large number of plants to create a spectacular massed display.

Tulipa, 'Darwin' hybrids

Common Name: 'Darwin' hybrid tulips

Flowers: A hybrid of species native to Asia. A large-flowered class, with blossoms and height among the largest of tulips. Colors include white, red, orange, pink, yellow, and bicolors.

Leaves: Broad, pointed, green.

Habit: 22″–30″ (56–75cm) tall. Upright.

Culture: Easy to grow. Prefers full sun in well-drained, fertile, humus-rich, loam soil. Propagate by bulbs planted in autumn.

Season of Bloom: Mid- to late spring; one of the mid-season tulips.

Hardiness: Zones 3–8.

Uses: Shimmering blooms make this an excellent choice for massing in a border. Good cut flower.

'Gudoshnick' is a spectacular yellow-and-red bicolor. Floral display of the 'Darwin' hybrids is not as long-lasting as regular 'Darwin' tulips, but are more spectacular.

Tulipa 'Double Early'

Common Name: Double flowering tulip

Flowers: A hybrid of species native to Asia. Bright colorful flowers display large sizes and multiple layers of petals. Some varieties have a black base in the center of the petals. Colors include white, red, pink, purple, yellow, and bicolors.

Leaves: Broad, pointed, green.

Habit: 18″–20″ (46–51cm) tall. Upright.

Culture: Easy to grow. Prefers full sun in well-drained, fertile, humus-rich, loam soil. Propagate by bulbs planted in autumn.

Season of Bloom: Spring. Early-flowering tulip.

Hardiness: Zones 3–8.

Uses: Popular massed or as an accent in beds or borders. As few as fifteen bulbs will create a spectacular mass of color.

'Peach Blossom' (pictured above) is a spectacular rose-red-and-white bicolor. Good companions to single-flowered tulips, such as 'Purissima' (white) and 'Mary Ann', (also shown above).

Tulipa 'Fosteriana'

Common Name: Foster's tulip

Flowers: Native to southern Russia. One of the largest tulips, with blossoms that measure up to 10″ (25cm) across. A black zone at the center of the flower heightens the brilliancy of the petals. Colors include red, orange, pink, and yellow. Flowers remain closed in cloudy weather.

Leaves: Broad, pointed, green.

Habit: 8″–20″ (20–51cm) tall. Upright.

Culture: Easy to grow. Prefers full sun in well-drained, fertile, humus-rich, loam soil. To encourage blooms for the following year, feed with a high-phosphorus fertilizer in autumn. Propagate by bulbs planted in autumn.

Season of Bloom: Mid- to late spring; one of the earliest-flowering tulips.

Hardiness: Zones 3–8.

Uses: Attractive massed in beds and borders. Good in rock gardens.

One of the most successful tulips, 'Red Emperor', belongs to this class. Early-flowering, it has shimmering crimson-red petals. A good companion is 'Pink Emperor' (also known as 'Pinkeen'), reputed to be the largest-flowered of all tulips, with a flower diameter of 10″ (25cm) across.

Tulipa
Kaufmanniana

Common Name:	Water-lily tulip
Flowers:	Native to Asia. Brilliant yellow or white star-shaped flowers open wide on sunny days, resembling a water lily. Centers are usually zoned in red or yellow.
Leaves:	Slender, pointed, green.
Habit:	6″ (15cm) tall. Clump-forming.
Culture:	Easy to grow. Prefers full sun in any well-drained, loam soil. Easy to establish. Propagate by bulbs planted in autumn.
Season of Bloom:	Spring.
Hardiness:	Zones 3–8.
Uses:	Good for rock gardens, edgings, or mixed beds and borders.

Plants are capable of forming colonies. Picture shows the variety 'Sweetlink' planted with *Hyacinth* 'Gypsy Queen'.

Zantedeschia
aethiopica

Common Name:	Calla lily
Flowers:	Native to South Africa. Fragrant white flower spathes have powdery yellow pistils. Other species include yellow and pink.
Leaves:	Spear-shaped, wavy, glossy, green.
Habit:	24″–48″ (61–122cm) tall. Upright.
Culture:	Prefers partial shade at midday in moist, fertile, humus-rich soil. Tolerates swamplike conditions. Propagate by rhizome division in late autumn or early summer or by seeds. Seeds produce flowering autumn plants their second year.
Season of Bloom:	Spring to early summer.
Hardiness:	Zones 8–10.
Uses:	Smaller species make excellent houseplants. Plant in mixed beds or borders, or near streams and ponds. Long-lasting cut flower.

'Green Goddess' has a green petal tip. A related species, *Z. elliottiana,* is a golden yellow variety preferred for pot culture.

Shrubs

Brugmansia × 'Charles Grimaldi'

Common Name: Golden angel's-trumpet

Flowers: A hybrid of species native to South and Central America. Nodding, golden yellow, trumpet-shaped blooms measuring more than 12″ (31cm) long are honey-scented.

Leaves: Spear-shaped, attractively ribbed, scalloped, green.

Habit: Up to 12′ (3.7m) tall. Treelike.

Culture: Grows in sun or light shade; prefers well-drained, fertile loam soil. Best grown in containers so plants can be moved indoors for winter protection. Easily propagated by cuttings. This tender, vigorous shrub will flower the first year from rooted cuttings taken during winter.

Season of Bloom: Flowers prolifically in flushes several times a year.

Hardiness: Overwinters outdoors only in frost-free areas (zones 9 and 10).

Uses: Good accent along the house foundation. Suitable for containers.

Brugmansia used to be classified as *Datura*. There are numerous species and hybrids, including white and pink forms. All are considered poisonous.

Buddleia davidii

Common Name: Summer lilac, butterfly bush

Flowers: Native to China. Tight clusters of tiny lavender flowers with orange throats are borne on lilaclike spikes.

Leaves: Long, spear-shaped, dark green, with downy undersides; die back during the winter and reappear in the spring.

Habit: 3′–10′ (.9–3m) tall. Bushy, billowing.

Culture: Easy to grow and vigorous. Prefers full sun in well-drained, fertile, loam soil. Makes a good coastal plant. Propagate by cuttings.

Season of Bloom: Mid-July to frost.

Hardiness: Zones 5–9.

Uses: Popular as a lawn highlight and foundation plant or border shrub in perennial gardens. Attracts butterflies.

Of the many varieties available, 'Dubonnet' is one of the best, displaying large deep purple flowers.

Calluna
vulgaris

**Common
Name:** Scotch heather

Flowers: Native to Europe. Pendulous clusters of small, urn-shaped flowers blanket the erect, branching stems. Colors include white, pink, and purple. There are hundreds of varieties to choose from.

Leaves: Evergreen, needlelike, dark green, turning a bronze color in autumn.

Habit: 15"–30" (38–76cm) tall. Erect, bushy, low-spreading.

Culture: Prefers full sun or partial shade in well-drained, acid, sandy soil that is rich in organic material. Dislikes strong wind. To encourage new growth, prune plants in the spring. Propagate by seeds or cuttings.

**Season
of Bloom:** Midsummer to early autumn.

Hardiness: Zones 4–8.

Uses: Popular ground cover. Good for edging and mixed borders.

The genus *Erica* is closely related and contains over two hundred species, but plants generally are not as cold-hardy as *Calluna* species.

Camellia
japonica

**Common
Name:** Common camellia

Flowers: Native to China. Single or double, waxy, gardenia-shaped flowers are 2½"–4" (6.5–10cm) wide. Colors include white, light pink, deep red, and bicolors.

Leaves: Evergreen, oval, shiny, dark green. Perhaps the most beautiful leaves of any flowering shrub.

Habit: 15'–45' (4.6–13.8m) tall with a spread of 6'–15' (1.8–4.6m). Upright, bushy, eventually growing into a small tree.

Culture: Easy to grow. Prefers full sun or partial shade in well-drained, moist, acid, humus-rich soil. Does not like exposed conditions. Prune back to desired shape. Propagate by cuttings.

**Season
of Bloom:** Early spring.

Hardiness: Zones 7–9.

Uses: Popular as a specimen plant grown against walls. May be trained as an espalier. Can be pruned hard for a flowering hedge.

Revered by the Japanese as "living jade." Varieties of a related species, *C. sasanqua*, are generally early-flowering—October and November in relatively frost-free climates.

Campsis radicans

Common Name: Trumpet vine, trumpet creeper

Flowers: Native to North America. Large orange and scarlet trumpet flowers are borne in clusters on shrubby vines. The nectar attracts hummingbirds.

Leaves: Deciduous, dark green, turning a yellowish green color in autumn.

Habit: 30'–40' (9.4–12m) tall. Vigorous, vining, spreading.

Culture: Fast-growing. Prefers full sun or partial shade in well-drained, sandy or loam soil. Prune back in spring to keep within bounds. Propagate by seeds or cuttings.

Season of Bloom: Midsummer to early autumn.

Hardiness: Zones 4–9.

Uses: Excellent for screening. Attractive on trellises or arbors; plants will completely cover an arbor.

The variety 'Madame Galen' is a large-flowered hardy hybrid. 'Flava' is a rare yellow. Up to 10' (3m) of growth can be expected the first year.

Caryopteris × clandonensis

Common Name: Blue mist shrub, bluebeard

Flowers: A hybrid of species native to Asia. Whorls of airy, powdery blue flowers are borne upright on erect, stiff, new stems.

Leaves: Deciduous, lance-shaped, fragrant, grayish green.

Habit: Up to 48″ (122cm) tall with equal spread. Open, bushy.

Culture: Prefers full sun in well-drained, sandy or loam soil. Prune back in spring to encourage blooming on new shoots. Propagate by cuttings.

Season of Bloom: August to frost.

Hardiness: Zones 6–9.

Uses: Good accent for mixed perennial beds and shrub borders. Makes a lovely hedge. Good for cutting.

The species *C. incana* has bright violet-blue flowers and needs heavy pruning to keep it compact.

Ceanothus thyrsiflorus

Common Name: Blueblossom, California lilac

Flowers: Native to California. Tight clusters of attractive light to deep blue flowers cover the plant in spring.

Leaves: Evergreen, glossy, dark green.

Habit: 4'–20' (1.2–6m) tall. Bushy; some varieties are low and spreading.

Culture: Prefers full sun in well-drained, sandy or loam soil. Tolerates drought. Propagate by cuttings.

Season of Bloom: Early to mid-spring.

Hardiness: Zones 8–10.

Uses: Attractive accent against walls or fences, and cascading over boulders in rock gardens.

Many varieties are available, some spreading and useful as a ground cover. Many related species are also worth considering for ground-cover use, such as *C. griseus horizontalis* (Carmel creeper) and *C. gloriosus* (Point Reyes creeper).

Cercis chinensis

Common Name: Chinese redbud

Flowers: Native to central China. Attractive, $3/4''$ (19mm) purple or white pea-shaped flowers blanket leafless, branching stems.

Leaves: Deciduous, heart-shaped, shiny, dark green, turning yellow in autumn.

Habit: 4'–10' (1.2–3m) tall. Open, bushy.

Culture: Prefers full sun in well-drained, humus-rich, sandy or loam soil. Pruning is not generally recommended except to remove dead branches. Propagate by cuttings.

Season of Bloom: Early to mid-spring.

Hardiness: Zones 5–9.

Uses: Excellent accent shrub. Combines well in woodland settings with dogwood trees.

A related species, *C. canadensis,* native to North America, grows into a small tree. *C. siliquastrum,* native to the Mediterranean, is a little more free-flowering than *C. canadensis,* but is more tender, surviving only in zones 7–9.

Chaenomeles speciosa

Common Name: Flowering quince, Japanese quince

Flowers: Native to eastern Asia. Gorgeous, single or double, white, pink, or red, 2″ (5cm) flowers are oftentimes forced indoors for early spring display. The flowers may be followed by fragrant, yellow, rounded fruits that add interest to the autumn landscape.

Leaves: Deciduous, narrow, pointed, glossy, green; on thorny branches.

Habit: 6′–10′ (1.8–3m) tall with a spread of 8′–12′ (2.4–3.7m). Bushy.

Culture: Prefers full sun in moist but well-drained, humus-rich, acid soil. Prune to desired shape throughout the year. Propagate by cuttings.

Season of Bloom: Early to mid-spring.

Hardiness: Zones 4–8.

Uses: Excellent showy specimen shrub with all-season interest. Creates an excellent dense hedge.

Especially beautiful planted near yellow forsythia and white *Magnolia stellata* (as pictured above). A related species, *C. japonica*, is similar but not so ornamental. There are many good hybrids between the two.

Clematis species and hybrids

Common Name: Clematis

Flowers: Developed from species native to China and Europe. Extraordinary star-shaped flowers, 3″–7″ (7.5–18cm) wide grow on light, airy vines. Colors include white, pink, red, purple, blue, and bicolors.

Leaves: Deciduous, attractive, light green; grow on a twining vine with tendrils.

Habit: 5′–18′ (1.5–5.5m) tall. Grows vigorously—as much as 5′–10′ (1.5–3m) a year; vining.

Culture: Prefers full sun or partial shade in well-drained, fertile, aerated soils. Plant roots in shady spot. Prune according to variety; generally, flowering occurs in spring or summer on old growth. Propagate by cuttings.

Season of Bloom: Spring, summer, and autumn, depending on the variety.

Hardiness: Zones 3–9.

Uses: Spectacular screening plant on trellises, posts, walls, and fences.

The variety 'Nelly Moser' is a spectacular pink and white bicolor. 'Ernest Markham' is a good red. 'Jackmani' is a popular dark blue.

Corylopsis
glabrescens

Common Name: Fragrant winter hazel

Flowers: Native to Japan. Clusters of pendulous, bell-shaped, yellow flowers bloom profusely on naked branches.

Leaves: Deciduous, oval, dark green, turning yellow in autumn.

Habit: Up to 5′ tall (1.5m) with equal spread. Bushy.

Culture: Prefers partial shade in well-drained, moist, acid, loam soil. Does not usually need pruning. Propagate by softwood cuttings in the spring and semihardwood cuttings in the summer.

Season of Bloom: Early spring; one of the earliest flowering shrubs.

Hardiness: Zones 5–8.

Uses: Popular in woodland settings and as a foundation shrub. The branches make interesting spring flower arrangements.

C. spicata (pictured above) is a taller species, to 12′ (3.7m). A good companion to *Hamamelis* species (witch hazels) and early-flowering rhododendrons such as *Rhododendron mucronulatum.*

Cytisus
scoparius

Common Name: Scotch broom

Flowers: Native to Europe. Abundant, golden yellow, pea-shaped blooms appear singly or in pairs at the axils of long, arching stems.

Leaves: Deciduous, medium green; on thorny branches.

Habit: 4′–6′ (1.2–1.8m) tall with equal or greater spread. Bushy, spreading.

Culture: Fast-growing. Prefers full sun in well-drained, sandy or loam soil. Tolerates drought. May be invasive. Annual pruning will encourage blooming. Prune stems back by two-thirds after blooms have faded. Propagate by seeds and softwood cuttings.

Season of Bloom: Late spring to early summer.

Hardiness: Zones 5–8.

Uses: Interesting shrub that will grow in even the poorest soil. Makes an excellent windbreaker. Plant as an accent in rock gardens, along sunny embankments, or in groups to form a hedge.

C. × praecox (Warminster broom) is a hybrid broom that is incredibly free-flowering, dominating the landscape with sulphur yellow flowers. 'Andreanus' (pictured above) is a beautiful orange variety.

Daphne × burkwoodii

Common Name: Burkwood daphne

Flowers: A hybrid of wild species native to China. Grown primarily for its fragrance. Pinkish white flowers are borne in clusters and are followed by poisonous, bright red berries.

Leaves: Semievergreen, pointed, leathery, dark green, with a yellowish white edge in some varieties.

Habit: 36″–48″ (91–122cm) tall. Upright, bushy.

Culture: Prefers full sun in cooler climates and light shade in hotter areas in well-drained, moist, loam soil. May be slow-growing. Propagate by cuttings.

Season of Bloom: Spring throughout May.

Hardiness: Zones 4–8.

Uses: Popular next to entryways where fragrance can be enjoyed. Looks good in mixed shrub borders. Good cut flower.

The variety 'Carol Mackie' is an especially beautiful compact flowering shrub producing masses of pale pink flowers and variegated leaves that are green edged with gold.

Deutzia gracilis

Common Name: Slender deutzia

Flowers: Native to China. Delicate clusters of white, fragrant, star-shaped blossoms stand upright on sweeping branches and are so profuse as to bend the branches in a weeping habit.

Leaves: Deciduous, slender, light green, turning a bronze color in autumn.

Habit: 24″–48″ (61–122cm) tall with equal spread. Erect, bushy.

Culture: Easy to grow. Prefers full sun or light shade in well-drained, fertile, loam soil. Propagate by cuttings.

Season of Bloom: Late spring to early summer. First of the deutzias to flower.

Hardiness: Zones 4–8.

Uses: Attractive in the front of mixed borders or as a specimen plant. May be grown as an unclipped hedge.

D. gracilis has been used to hybridize a beautiful pink form, *D.* × *rosea*.

Enkianthus campanulatus

Common Name: Redvein enkianthus

Flowers: Native to Japan. Graceful clusters of delicate, bell-shaped flowers, yellow with streaks of red, appear in the spring before the leaves.

Leaves: Deciduous, small, pointed, dark green, turning a showy orange and red in autumn; arranged in whorls.

Habit: 8'–15' (2.4–4.6m) tall. Erect, bushy.

Culture: Prefers full sun or partial shade in humus-rich, acid soil. Propagate by seeds or cuttings.

Season of Bloom: Late spring.

Hardiness: Zones 4–7.

Uses: Grown for its attractive display of flowers and autumn leaf color. Use as a foundation planting with rhododendrons and azaleas. May also be grown as a container or bonsai plant.

'Albiflorus' is a white-flowered variety. *E. perulatus* is a white-flowered species. All have a beautiful wintry silhouette.

Forsythia × intermedia

Common Name: Forsythia

Flowers: A hybrid of species mostly native to Europe and Asia. A herald of spring. Popular for its rich burst of golden yellow flowers, each 1″ (2.5cm) wide, in early spring.

Leaves: Slender, medium green, turning yellow in autumn.

Habit: 7'–10' (2.1–3m) tall with equal spread. Bushy, branching.

Culture: Prefers full sun or light shade in well-drained, sandy or loam soil. Tolerates neglect. Propagate by seeds and cuttings.

Season of Bloom: Early to mid-spring.

Hardiness: Zones 5–9.

Uses: Excellent informal hedge. The open, spreading habit of this plant should be left alone and not heavily pruned to conform to a formal hedge. An attractive accent plant. The flowers are especially attractive when forced to bloom in winter arrangements.

'Spectabilis' is a free-flowering golden yellow variety that is extremely popular. 'Lynwood Gold', a branch mutation discovered in Ireland, is an improvement over it. Weeping and ground-cover forms of forsythia are also available. Forsythias look sensational planted near weeping pink cherries (as pictured above).

Fothergilla gardenii

Common Name:	Dwarf fothergilla, witch alder
Flowers:	Native to the northeastern United States. Grown for its all-round seasonal interest. In spring, fuzzy white flowers are borne on stark brown, twiggy branches.
Leaves:	Leathery, dark green, turning bright yellow, orange, and red in autumn.
Habit:	Up to 48″ (122cm) tall with equal or greater spread. Erect, twiggy.
Culture:	Prefers full sun or partial shade in well-drained, light, acid, sandy soil. Propagate by cuttings.
Season of Bloom:	Mid- to late spring.
Hardiness:	Zones 5–8.
Uses:	Attractive with azaleas and early rhododendrons. Makes a good foundation planting or border plant. Good in spring flower arrangements.

F. major (also called *F. monticola*) is a related species with taller growth habit and larger leaves, which are especially attractive when in full autumn color.

Fuchsia × hybrida

Common Name:	Lady's-eardrops
Flowers:	A hybrid of species native to South America. Pendulous sprays of nodding flowers are generally bicolored and come in shades of white, bluish violet, purple, pink, red, and orange.
Leaves:	Small, oval, pointed, medium green.
Habit:	3′–12′ (.9–3.7m) tall. Mostly upright, branching.
Culture:	Prefers partial shade in well-drained, moist, humus-rich soil. Wilts easily, so water frequently. Prune back tips to prevent legginess. Propagate by cuttings.
Season of Bloom:	Early summer to frost.
Hardiness:	Zones 6–10.
Uses:	A favorite in coastal gardens where summers are cool and winters mild. Popular as a hanging basket or border shrub. May be trained as an espalier or standard tree. Attracts hummingbirds.

Hundreds of varieties are available. 'Jack Shahan' is an extremely free-flowering rose-pink suitable for hanging baskets.

Gardenia jasminoides

Common Name:	Common gardenia
Flowers:	Native to China. Classic, creamy white, waxy flowers are redolent with fragrance.
Leaves:	Attractive, lancelike, shiny, leathery, dark green.
Habit:	3'–5' (.9–1.5m) tall with equal spread. Bushy.
Culture:	Prefers partial shade or full sun in well-drained, moist, fertile, acid soil. Heavy feeder. Prune to shape plants and to remove spent blooms. Propagate by cuttings.
Season of Bloom:	Late spring to late summer; can be flowered indoors during early spring.
Hardiness:	Zones 8–10.
Uses:	In warm climates, grow as a low hedge, screen, or lawn highlight. In colder climates, treat as a houseplant.

The variety 'Fortuniana' has double flowers up to 4" (10cm) across. Plants need pampering to keep them healthy indoors. Bright, indirect light, a regular feeding and watering schedule (plus pest control) are necessary to ensure worthwhile flowering.

Gelsemium sempervirens

Common Name:	Evening trumpet flower, Carolina jasmine
Flowers:	Native to the southern United States. Fragrant, yellow, trumpet flowers are borne on a vigorous, twining vine.
Leaves:	Evergreen, lancelike, glossy, medium green; grow on brittle vines.
Habit:	10'–20' (3–6m) tall. Vining.
Culture:	Prefers full sun or partial shade in well-drained, moist, humus-rich soil. May be pruned back to 36" (91cm) in order to control excessive rambling. Propagate by seeds or cuttings.
Season of Bloom:	Late winter to early spring, and occasionally, in autumn.
Hardiness:	Zones 6–9.
Uses:	Suitable for covering trellises, fences, and stone walls and as a ground cover. Caution: this plant is poisonous.

Often confused with *Jasminum nudiflorum* (winter jasmine), which is hardy into zone 6. A good plant to cover chain-link fences. Also grown as a houseplant.

Hamamelis mollis

Common Name:	Chinese witch hazel
Flowers:	Native to China. Unusual "spidery" flowers and an extra-early flowering period make this a good plant for winter gardens.
Leaves:	Deciduous, round, pointed, medium green, turning yellow and red in autumn.
Habit:	10'–15' (3–4.6m) tall with equal spread. Open.
Culture:	Prefers full sun or partial shade in well-drained, moist, acid soil. Tolerates pollution. Propagate by seeds or cuttings.
Season of Bloom:	Winter to early spring.
Hardiness:	Zones 5–8.
Uses:	Wonderful lawn accent, especially against a background of needle evergreens. Cut flowering twigs make very interesting winter floral arrangements.

Hybrids between *H. mollis* (Chinese witch hazel) and *H. japonica* (Japanese witch hazel) have produced some spectacular free-flowering varieties such as 'Arnold's Promise' (bright yellow) and 'Jelena' (copper).

Hibiscus syriacus

Common Name:	Rose-of-Sharon, shrub althea
Flowers:	Native to China. Cheery single or double, hibiscuslike flowers are white, purple, red, or blue with a dark crimson eye. Flowers last about a day, but a succession of blooms will occur until frost.
Leaves:	Oval, pointed, dark green. One of the last shrubs to leaf out in spring.
Habit:	6'–20' (1.8–6m) tall with half the spread. Bushy.
Culture:	Prefers full sun in moist but well-drained, humus-rich soil. Tolerates pollution. Prune to control size. Propagate by seeds or cuttings.
Season of Bloom:	Late summer to early autumn; preferred for its late blooming cycle.
Hardiness:	Zones 5–9.
Uses:	Excellent for coastal gardens. Attractive as a small lawn accent. Makes a good screen or hedge.

Still sometimes listed under its old botanical name, *Althea*. 'Blue Bird' is a beautiful blue with contrasting dark centers. 'Helena' is a huge white with red centers. There are numerous double forms, but these are not nearly as attractive as the singles.

Hydrangea macrophylla

Common Name: French hydrangea

Flowers: Native to Japan. Old-fashioned favorite due to its lacy clusters of giant snowball flowers. Colors include white, red, pink, and blue.

Leaves: Heart-shaped, pointed, crinkled, bright green.

Habit: 5'–8' (1.5–2.4m) tall with a spread that is a little wider than its height. Rounded, bushy.

Culture: Prefers full sun or light shade in well-drained, sandy or loam soil. Blue or pink flower color depends upon the soil's pH factor: acid soil produces blue flowers; neutral or alkaline soil produces pink or red flowers. Propagate by softwood cuttings.

Season of Bloom: Summer to early autumn.

Hardiness: Zones 6–9.

Uses: Attractive lawn accent or hedge plant. Hydrangeas also look pretty in fresh flower arrangements.

Numerous varieties exist, divided between the groups hortensias (rounded flower clusters) and lacecaps (flattened flower clusters). 'All Summer Beauty' is a free-flowering hortensia; 'Blue Wave' is a rich blue lacecap. Hydrangeas make good companions to shrub roses.

Hydrangea quercifolia

Common Name: Oak-leaf hydrangea

Flowers: Native to the southeastern United States. Large, cone-shaped flower clusters are white, fading to pink.

Leaves: Deeply lobed, like an oak leaf; green, turning russet colors in autumn.

Habit: Up to 6' (1.8m) tall. Mounded, bushy.

Culture: Grows in sun or light shade, prefers well-drained, fertile, loam soil. May need heavy pruning in autumn to maintain a tidy, compact shape. Propagate by cuttings.

Season of Bloom: Summer.

Hardiness: Zones 5–9.

Uses: Good accent in mixed beds and borders. Suitable for containers.

The variety 'Snow Queen' is exceptionally free-flowering with flower clusters often exceeding 10" (25cm) in length.

Hypericum calycinum

Common Name:	Creeping St.-John's-wort
Flowers:	Native to southeastern Europe. The showy flowers are large and yellow with prominent stamens protruding from their centers. Primarily grown for its strong early-summer bloom display and its ability to thrive in shady conditions.
Leaves:	Semievergreen, oblong, bright green, with netted veins.
Habit:	Up to 24″ (61cm) tall. Low, compact.
Culture:	Prefers full sun or partial shade in well-drained, moist, loam soil. A fast grower that can be invasive. Tolerates drought. Rarely needs pruning, but dead wood may be cut back in the spring. Propagate by division or cuttings.
Season of Bloom:	Mid- to late summer.
Hardiness:	Zones 5–8.
Uses:	A perfect ground cover. Use on slopes to prevent erosion. Looks good edging driveways.

Numerous other species are grown in gardens, notably *H. patulum* from China, and *H. frondosum* from the northeastern United States. All are good companions to needle evergreens.

Kalmia latifolia

Common Name:	Mountain laurel
Flowers:	Native to eastern North America. Valued for its pretty clusters of hexagon-shaped flowers. Flowers consist of large, showy clusters with purplish cinnamon bands marking the centers. Colors include white, pink, red, and purple.
Leaves:	Evergreen, lancelike, dark green; form whorls.
Habit:	4′–8′ (1.2–2.4m) tall. Upright, spreading; tends to become more open with age.
Culture:	Prefers full sun or partial shade in cool, well-drained, moist, acid soil. One of the best flowering shrubs that can be situated in shady areas. Mulch for winter protection. Propagate by cuttings.
Season of Bloom:	Early summer.
Hardiness:	Zones 4–9.
Uses:	There is nothing quite so spectacular as a woodland planting of mountain laurel massed under giant pine and fir trees. Needless to say, this is an excellent choice in a naturalized setting. It is also effective planted near the house as an accent or in a shrub border along with other broadleaf evergreens, such as azaleas and rhododendrons.

Numerous varieties are available, notably 'Otsbo Red', which has deep red flowers in bud, and 'Pink Charm'. They are good companions to ferns and hostas, planted along stream banks and pond margins.

Kerria
japonica

Common Name:	Japanese rose
Flowers:	Native to Japan. Golden yellow, five-petaled, 1½″ (4cm) flowers last about two weeks.
Leaves:	Slender, pointed, serrated; bright green for most of the year, poor autumn color.
Habit:	Up to 6′ (1.8m) tall with a spread of 8′ (2.4m). Upright, spreading, twiggy.
Culture:	Prefers partial shade in well-drained, moist, fertile, loam soil. Tolerates heavy pruning. Propagate by cuttings.
Season of Bloom:	Spring.
Hardiness:	Zones 4–9.
Uses:	Striking lawn accent. Effective background in spring-flowering bulb and perennial borders.

'Pleniflora' has double flowers; 'Picta' is a variegated variety with attractive white-edged leaves. Combines well with dogwoods and azaleas.

Kolkwitzia
amabilis

Common Name:	Beautybush
Flowers:	Native to China. Beautiful, arching clusters of yellow-throated pink flowers appear in late spring. Groupings of small downy seed heads follow the flowering cycle.
Leaves:	Deciduous, narrow, lancelike, dark green, turning a dull red in autumn. The brown trunk gives a shaggy appearance as it sheds large strips from its bark and stems.
Habit:	7′–15′ (2.1–4.6m) tall with almost equal spread. Dense, bushy.
Culture:	Easy to grow. Prefers full sun or partial shade in well-drained, loam soil. Propagate by cuttings.
Season of Bloom:	Late spring to early summer.
Hardiness:	Zones 4–8.
Uses:	Excellent specimen shrub planted near the house. Can be effective in mixed borders.

'Pink Cloud' and 'Rosea' are beautiful pink varieties that originated in Europe. Effective planted with *Laburnum* × *vossii* (golden chain tree).

Lonicera japonica 'Halliana'

Common Name: Hall's Japanese honeysuckle

Flowers: Native to Japan. Creamy white flower cluster composed of trumpet-shaped florets fades to yellow throughout the summer. The flowers are powerfully scented with a pleasant aroma.

Leaves: Semievergreen, oval, green, with downy undersides; cover vigorous, trailing, vining stems in pairs.

Habit: Up to 15′ (4.6m) tall. Vining.

Culture: Prefers full sun in any well-drained, garden soil. Grown for its ability to adapt to almost any difficult planting situation. A rapid grower as well as a low-maintenance plant that rarely has insect or disease problems. Plant can be invasive and even suffocate young trees. Propagate by seeds or cuttings.

Season of Bloom: Late spring and early summer.

Hardiness: Zones 4–8.

Uses: Excellent quick ground cover. Effective covering for screens and fences.

Two other good vining honeysuckles are *L. sempervirens,* a native American variety displaying red flowers, and *L.* × *heckrottii,* a hybrid red and yellow bicolor. These two are not nearly as invasive as the Japanese honeysuckle.

Magnolia stellata

Common Name: Star magnolia

Flowers: Native to Japan. A multistemmed, shrub variety of *Magnolia.* The attractive pubescent buds unfold into beautiful masses of snowy white, star-shaped blossoms that cover the naked branches in early spring. Flowers are fragrant, generally free of insects, and followed by knobby conelike fruit.

Leaves: Oval, dark green, turning yellow to bronze in autumn.

Habit: 15′–20′ (4.6–6m) tall with a 15′ (4.6m) spread. Low-branched, shrubby.

Culture: Prefers full sun or light shade in well-drained, fertile, humus-rich soil. Plant in protected areas to minimize damage to the flowers by late spring frosts. Propagate by softwood cuttings in June or July.

Season of Bloom: Early to mid-spring.

Hardiness: Zones 3–8.

Uses: All-season interest because of its beautiful wintry silhouette. Perfect in foundation plantings or as a specimen plant.

The variety 'Waterlily' is pink in bud but opens white. Plants are mounded, bushy, and extremely free-flowering. Good companions are forsythia, flowering quince, and *Rhododendron mucronulatum.*

Mandevilla × amabilis 'Alice Du Pont'

Common Name: Mandevilla vine

Flowers: Discovered in Jamaica. Beautiful rose-pink, hibiscuslike flowers, up to 5″ (13cm) across, bloom nonstop all summer.

Leaves: Oblong, pointed, lustrous, dark green.

Habit: Up to 15′ (4.6m) tall. Vigorous, vining.

Culture: Prefers full sun and good drainage in humus-rich, loam soil. Best grown in a pot so it can be moved indoors for protection during cold winters. Propagate by cuttings.

Season of Bloom: Summer to autumn frost.

Hardiness: Zone 10. Killed by frost.

Uses: Sensational for covering trellises and arbors, especially where summers are hot.

Deserves to be much more widely grown on sun porches and patios, and in conservatories.

Nerium oleander

Common Name: Common oleander

Flowers: Native to the Mediterranean region. Fragrant, single or double, white, pink, or red flowers are borne in clusters.

Leaves: Evergreen, narrow, lancelike, glossy, tough, dark green.

Habit: 6′–20′ (1.8–6m) tall with equal spread. Upright, rounded, branching.

Culture: Prefers full sun or partial shade in well-drained, sandy or loam soil. A quick-growing shrub that is primarily valued for its tolerance to hot, intense weather. Tolerates pollution and coastal conditions. Grows as a pot plant indoors. Propagate by cuttings.

Season of Bloom: Spring to autumn.

Hardiness: Zones 8–10.

Uses: Attractive in background plantings, as a hedge or screen, or massed in borders. In areas with frost, grow in containers. Caution: all parts of the plant are poisonous.

'Petite Salmon' is an especially free-flowering variety suitable for containers and low hedging. Effective in floral arrangements. Good companion to tropical hibiscus and lavender.

Paeonia suffruticosa

Common Name: Tree peony

Flowers: Native to China and Japan. Beautiful single, double, and semidouble flowers, up to 10″ (25cm) across, are borne singly on stiff, erect stems. Clusters of yellow stamens contrast brightly with the white, yellow, pink, red, or purple petals.

Leaves: Deciduous, graceful, divided, gray-green; die back in autumn.

Habit: 3′–6′ (.9–2.7m) tall, with twice the spread. Rounded.

Culture: Prefers partial shade in well-drained, fertile, humus-rich soil. Enjoys having its head in the sun if its roots can stay cool. Propagate by cuttings.

Season of Bloom: Late spring to early summer.

Hardiness: Zones 3–8.

Uses: Popular accent in mixed borders and in foundation plantings. One of the most popular floral subjects in Oriental paintings. Widely used in Chinese- and Japanese-style gardens.

Hundreds of varieties are available, though 'Joseph Rock', a semidouble white with maroon petal markings, is perhaps the most highly prized. Good companions to *Laburnum*, as pictured here with *P. suffruticosa* 'Thunderbolt' (dark red) and 'Amber Moon' (yellow).

Passiflora caerulea

Common Name: Blue passion flower

Flowers: Native to Central America and the southern United States. Fragrant, 3½″ (9cm) flowers resemble a water lily. A purplish blue crown of filaments overlap white petals, giving the flower a bluish appearance.

Leaves: Ivylike, three-lobed, smooth, dark green.

Habit: Up to 15′ (4.6m) tall. Vigorous, vining.

Culture: Prefers a well-drained, fertile, loam soil and a strong trellis upon which to climb. Grows in sun or light shade. Propagate by seeds or cuttings.

Season of Bloom: Summer to autumn frost.

Hardiness: Zones 8–10; will grow further north with protection from wind and severe freezes.

Uses: Excellent fence or screen cover. One of the best flowering pot plants to grow indoors on a sunny windowsill, in a sunroom, or in a conservatory.

A hybrid, *P. × alatocaerulea,* has a deeper blue coloring than the species. The flowers are beautiful floating in a shallow dish of water, as a table centerpiece.

Philadelphus coronarius

Common Name: Sweet mock orange

Flowers: Native to southeastern Europe. Grown for its sensational, sweet, fruity fragrance. The small, open, white flowers dangle in clusters with centers of protruding yellow stamens.

Leaves: Oval, pointed, deeply veined, dull green; supported by hairy stems.

Habit: 7'–10' (2.1–3m) tall with equal spread. Rounded, garlandlike.

Culture: Prefers full sun or partial shade in well-drained, fertile soil. Tolerates dry soil. Vigorous grower that tends toward legginess if not pruned. Propagate by seeds or cuttings.

Season of Bloom: Late spring to early summer.

Hardiness: Zones 4–8.

Uses: Attractive as an informal screen or windbreak, especially close to a porch or sitting area where the scent can drift by. Also good as a foundation planting and as an informal lawn accent.

There are numerous good hybrids, including 'Belle Etoile', which has the largest flowers, and 'Minnesota Snowflake', a fragrant double white. Good companion to roses.

Pieris japonica

Common Name: Lily-of-the-valley bush, Japanese andromeda

Flowers: Native to Japan. Drooping clusters of creamy white, urn-shaped flowers are highly fragrant and quite showy. Of added interest are the attractive flower buds in winter.

Leaves: Evergreen; leaf tips open to a copper color and turn leathery, glossy, and dark green as they mature. Set in whorls.

Habit: 9'–12' (2.7–3.7m) tall with a spread of 6'–8' (1.8–2.4m). Upright, thick.

Culture: Prefers full sun or partial shade in well-drained, moist, acid, sandy soil. Prune to encourage bushiness. Propagate by cuttings.

Season of Bloom: Early to mid-spring.

Hardiness: Zones 5–8.

Uses: Good in mixed borders with other broadleaf evergreen plantings, such as azaleas and rhododendrons. Also good as a foundation planting and as a lawn accent.

There are numerous varieties, including dwarf kinds suitable for use as ground cover and some with pink flowers. These plants can be enhanced with an underplanting of *Helleborus orientalis* (Lenten rose) and heather.

Pittosporum tobira

Common Name: Japanese pittosporum

Flowers: Native to Japan. Fragrant clusters of greenish white to yellow flowers cover the plant in the spring. Flowers resemble orange blossoms.

Leaves: Evergreen, lancelike, leathery, glossy, dark green; set in whorls. Produce a disagreeable odor when crushed.

Habit: 6'–12' (1.8–3.7m) tall with a spread of 4'–5' (1.2–1.5m). Dense, spreading.

Culture: Prefers full sun or partial shade in well-drained, sandy or loam soil. Prune to retain bushiness and to create desired shape. Propagate by cuttings.

Season of Bloom: Mid- to late spring.

Hardiness: Zones 8–10.

Uses: An all-purpose shrub suitable for almost any well-ventilated position. Makes an excellent foundation accent, hedge, screen, or barrier planting. Leaves are attractive additions to floral arrangements.

'Variegata' is an especially handsome shrub, with leaves edged in white. Popular for growing in containers to decorate courtyards, terraces, decks, and patios, especially in coastal locations where it displays good salt tolerance.

Poncirus trifoliata

Common Name: Hardy orange

Flowers: Native to northern China. Abundant, single, white flowers are similar to orange blossoms. Inedible, small, golden yellow oranges appear in autumn.

Leaves: Deciduous, lancelike, lustrous, dark green, turning yellow in autumn; arranged in sets of three. Thorns cover the trunk, which starts out green and becomes slightly furrowed as it ages.

Habit: An unusual-looking low-branching shrub or small tree. 10'–15' (3–4.6m) tall with a spread of 12'–15' (3.7–4.6m). Oval with sharp green thorns.

Culture: Prefers full sun in well-drained, acid, sandy or loam soil. Propagate by seeds or cuttings.

Season of Bloom: Mid- to late spring.

Hardiness: Zones 6–9.

Uses: Makes an excellent hedge or screen since the sharp thorns assure privacy. Good lawn accent.

Despite claims to the contrary, the fruits are not edible since they are extremely astringent (though they have a pleasant fragrance similar to lemon soap). Many books on woody plants describe the flowers as fragrant, but this is not so.

Potentilla fruticosa

Common Name: Shrubby cinquefoil

Flowers: Native to the Northern Hemisphere. This shrub bursts into bloom in late spring and continues to bloom intermittently throughout the summer. Flowers range in color from an occasional white to the more usual bright yellow single flowers.

Leaves: Deciduous, small, finely textured, bright green; consist of five oval leaflets.

Habit: 24″–48″ (61–122cm) tall with equal spread. Low-growing, bushy.

Culture: Prefers full sun or partial shade in well-drained, sandy or loam soil. Grown for its hardiness and ability to handle drought conditions. Propagate by cuttings.

Season of Bloom: Mid-spring to late summer.

Hardiness: Zones 2–8.

Uses: Excellent ground cover and accent in mixed beds and borders.

A large selection of varieties is available, including 'Primrose Beauty'—considered one of the best for cold climates. The variety 'Red Ace', from England, is a weak plant and has proven unsuitable for areas with hot summers.

Prunus glandulosa 'Alboplena'

Common Name: Flowering almond

Flowers: Native to Japan. An attractive spring-flowering shrub that is generally seen with double flowers. When in bloom, this shrub is completely covered with a gorgeous mass of white, pink, or red flowers.

Leaves: Deciduous, small, oval, light green. Ornamentally unimportant.

Habit: 3′–5′ (.9–1.5m) tall with equal spread. Upright.

Culture: Prefers full sun in well-drained, moist, fertile, loam soil. Propagate by cuttings.

Season of Bloom: Early spring.

Hardiness: Zones 4–8.

Uses: Popular accent in mixed borders. Combines well with spring bulbs and early perennials.

'Rosea Plena' is one of the best varieties, displaying double pink flowers. Good companion to fothergillas.

Pyracantha coccinea

Common Name: Firethorn

Flowers: Native to China. Pyracanthas are known for their dense bunches of orange to red berries that persist throughout the winter. However, the flowers are almost as interesting since they are white and bloom in profusion. Up close, the flowers have a disagreeable odor.

Leaves: Evergreen, narrow, pointed, thick, glossy, dark green.

Habit: Up to 6' (1.8m) tall with a spread of 10' (3m). Upright.

Culture: Prefers full sun or partial shade in well-drained, sandy or loam soil. May need some winter protection. Propagate by seeds or cuttings.

Season of Bloom: Mid-spring to early summer.

Hardiness: Zones 6–9.

Uses: Handsome as a hedge or espaliered against a wall. Attractive in mixed shrub borders and berry gardens.

Numerous varieties are available, offering yellow, orange, or red berries. 'Mohave', a hybrid developed by the United States National Arboretum, is especially free-flowering, bearing heavy clusters of orange-red berries that persist well into winter.

Raphiolepis indica

Common Name: Indian hawthorn

Flowers: Native to Japan and Korea. Produces a showy display of creamy white, pink, and almost red blooms that are followed by ornamental dark blue berries. Grown for its year-round interest.

Leaves: Pointed, leathery, shiny, dark green. Immature leaves have an attractive, coppery appearance.

Habit: 4'–5' (1.2–1.5m) tall with equal spread. Dense, bushy.

Culture: Prefers full sun in well-drained, sandy or loam soil. Tolerates light shade and drought. Prune to encourage compact growth. Propagate by seeds or cuttings.

Season of Bloom: Late autumn or midwinter to late spring.

Hardiness: Zones 7–10.

Uses: An excellent foundation planting. Also a good informal hedge, low divider, and ground cover.

Many good varieties are available, including 'Enchantress', a compact, low-growing form, and 'Majestic Beauty', which can reach treelike proportions.

Rhododendron (Azalea) species and hybrids

Common Name: Azalea

Flowers: Mostly native to China and North America. Azaleas and rhododendrons both belong to the same genus or flower group called *Rhododendron*. Azaleas, however, generally have a low, compact growth habit with smaller leaves and flowers. The funnel-shaped flowers range in colors that include white, yellow, orange, apricot, pink, red, crimson, and purple.

Leaves: Deciduous or evergreen; oval, leathery, medium green; set in whorls. May be hairy.

Habit: 2'–15' (.6–4.6m) tall and 3'–9' (.9–2.7m) wide. Upright, spreading.

Culture: Prefers full sun or partial shade in well-drained, fertile, humus-rich, acid soil. Intolerant of strong, cold winds. Tolerates air pollution. Prune after blossoms have fallen to shape plant. Propagate by seeds or cuttings.

Season of Bloom: Spring to early summer.

Hardiness: Zones 4–10.

Uses: A favorite plant for foundation and mass plantings. Excellent in mixed shrub borders and as an understory planting for tall pines.

Hundreds of species and hybrids are popular with home gardeners, especially the fragrant deciduous 'Exbury' varieties (pictured above). *R. indicum* (Indian azalea) is suitable for warm climate areas. Dramatic when planted in combination with flowering dogwood.

Rhododendron species and hybrids

Common Name: Rhododendron

Flowers: Native mostly to China and North America. Generally large, rounded flower clusters up to 10" (25cm) across, mostly in red, pink, white, yellow, and purple.

Leaves: Evergreen, large, oval, smooth, leathery, green; usually splayed out like a fan.

Habit: Dependent on individual specimen. Up to 20' (6m) tall. Billowing, with a widely variable spread.

Culture: Prefers light shade in moist but well-drained, fertile, humus-rich, loam soil. Propagate by cuttings.

Season of Bloom: Spring to early summer.

Hardiness: Zones 4–8.

Uses: Popular accent, especially as a foundation planting. Attractive in mixed shrub borders and rock gardens. Especially beautiful in deciduous woods with a high leaf canopy.

Thousands of varieties have been developed. The popular hybrid 'America', a cross between North American and Himalayan species, is a free-flowering red that is extra-hardy and large-flowered.

Romneya coulteri

Common Name: California tree poppy

Flowers: Native to California. Large, 10″ (25cm) crinkled, white, poppylike flowers have a conspicuous dome of powdery yellow stamens at the center.

Leaves: Oval, deeply indented, gray-green.

Habit: Up to 5′ (1.5m) tall. Shrubby.

Culture: Prefers full sun and good drainage in sandy soil. Plants are sometimes temperamental and dislike being transplanted, but once established can be invasive. Propagate by seeds or division.

Season of Bloom: Early summer.

Hardiness: Zones 8–10.

Uses: Good accent used sparingly in mixed borders.

The variety 'White Cloud' is an especially free-flowering hybrid developed by crossing *R. coulteri* and a similar species, *R. trichocalyx.*

Rosa 'American Pillar'

Common Name: Climbing rose group

Flowers: Hybridized by Van Fleet in 1902 and introduced by Conard & Jones in 1908. A cross between *R. wichuraiana* and *R. setigera* onto an unnamed, red hybrid perpetual. Single flowers, carmine pink with a white eye, up to 2½″ (6.5cm) across, are held in clusters. Prolific flowering, though no repeat bloom.

Leaves: Medium-size, leathery, medium green; on thorny canes.

Habit: Up to 20′ (6m) tall. Vigorous, disease-resistant, though subject to mildew in southern climates.

Culture: Prefers full sun and good drainage in fertile, loam soil. Needs strong support. Propagate by cuttings.

Season of Bloom: Spring.

Hardiness: Zones 5–8.

Uses: Excellent for covering arbors and gazebos, and good for training along walls.

Suffers where summers are hot and humid, but spectacular during its heavy flush of early summer color.

Rosa banksiae 'Lutea', 'Lady Banks' Rose

Common Name:	Species rose group
Flowers:	Introduced from China. Yellow, 1″ (2.5cm) double flowers are borne in dense clusters. There is a white-flowered form that is slightly fragrant.
Leaves:	Small, light green.
Habit:	10′–20′ (3–6m) tall. Vigorous, long canes are almost thorn-free. Can be kept bushy by heavy pruning.
Culture:	Grows in sun or light shade; prefers good drainage and fertile, loam soil. It is grown mostly in mild-winter climates as a climber, since it is not reliably hardy in areas with freezing winters. Propagate by cuttings.
Season of Bloom:	Early spring.
Hardiness:	Zones 8–10.
Uses:	Train up trellises, over arbors, and on walls and fences. Combines well with azaleas and wisteria.

Probably the most heat-resistant of roses, this plant is popular in climates that have mild winters but hot, dry summers. A specimen in Tombstone, Arizona, is listed in *The Guinness Book of World Records*. It has a trunk diameter of over 12″ (31cm) and a canopy supported on a trellis, with a spread sufficient to shelter 150 people.

Rosa 'Betty Prior'

Common Name:	Floribunda group
Flowers:	Hybridized by a British rosarian in 1935. A cross between 'Kirsten Poulsen' and an unnamed seedling. Single flowers, carmine-pink with white centers, up to 3½″ (9cm) across, are borne profusely in clusters.
Leaves:	Medium-size, medium green; on thorny canes.
Habit:	Up to 48″ (122cm) tall. Vigorous, bushy, disease-resistant.
Culture:	Prefers full sun and good drainage in fertile, loam soil. Propagate by cuttings.
Season of Bloom:	Mostly spring-flowering.
Hardiness:	Zones 5–9.
Uses:	Good accent plant used alone or when combined with perennials. Makes an attractive flowering hedge.

'Betty Prior' is a highly rated rose variety in Great Britain and North America.

Rosa
'Cardinal de Richelieu'

Common Name: Old garden rose group

Flowers: Classified a Gallica hybrid, introduced by Laffay (France) in 1840, though its true origin may be Holland. Possibly a cross between a Gallica and China rose. Flowers are purple with a white button center, double with cupped petals, slightly fragrant, up to 2″ (5cm) across, borne in clusters.

Leaves: Small, glossy, dark green.

Habit: Up to 48″ (122cm) tall. Compact, bushy, smooth, with disease-resistant canes.

Culture: Prefers full sun and good drainage in fertile, loam soil. Propagate by cuttings.

Season of Bloom: Late spring.

Hardiness: Zones 5–8.

Uses: Good accent in informal, cottage-style gardens.

An unusual color for roses. Floral arrangements composed of 'La Reine Victoria' and 'Cardinal de Richelieu' are sensational for their old-fashioned, romantic appearance.

Rosa
'Constance Spry'

Common Name: Shrub rose group

Flowers: Developed by David Austin (England) in 1961. A cross between 'Belle Isle' and 'Dainty Maid.' Flowers are pink, double, with an old-fashioned garden rose form and myrrhlike fragrance, up to 5″ (13cm) across.

Leaves: Glossy, dark green; on thorny canes.

Habit: 6′–10′ (1.8–3m) tall. Upright, bushy, arching, disease-resistant.

Culture: Prefers full sun and good drainage in fertile, loam soil. Best if given a strong support to climb. Propagate by cuttings.

Season of Bloom: Late spring.

Hardiness: Zones 5–8.

Uses: Use as an accent in mixed beds and borders. Train along fences. Popular with floral arrangers.

This rose honors a famous British flower arranger. Trained to a wall or trellis, the plants will climb.

Rosa
'Dortmund'

Common Name: Shrub rose group

Flowers: Hybridized by the House of Kordes (Germany) and introduced in 1955. A cross between an unnamed seedling and *R. kordesii*. Classified as Kordesii. Red with white eyes, up to 3½" (9cm) across, single, borne in large clusters. The lightly fragrant flowers bloom heavily with some repeat bloom, followed by decorative red hips in autumn.

Leaves: Glossy, dark green.

Habit: Up to 12' (3.7m) tall. Vigorous, disease-free.

Culture: Prefers full sun and good drainage in fertile, loam soil. Best if given a strong support to climb. Propagate by cuttings.

Season of Bloom: Spring.

Hardiness: Zones 5–8.

Uses: Excellent for training along walls and up trellises and arbors.

A good companion to mixed pastel colors of clematis. Stands out like a stoplight in the garden.

Rosa
'Graham Thomas'

Common Name: Shrub rose group

Flowers: Hybridized by David Austin (Great Britain) and introduced in 1983. A cross between an unnamed seedling and 'Charles Austin' onto an 'Iceberg' seedling. Flowers are rich, deep yellow, up to 4" (10cm) across, highly fragrant, fully double, cupped like old-fashioned shrub roses, but bloom recurrently.

Leaves: Small, glossy, dark green.

Habit: Up to 5' (1.5m) tall. Upright, bushy, arching.

Culture: Prefers full sun and good drainage in fertile, loam soil. Propagate by cuttings.

Season of Bloom: Early summer to late autumn.

Hardiness: Zones 5–8.

Uses: Good accent for mixed beds and borders. Suitable for informal hedges.

Probably the most popular of a series of new roses known as English old rose hybrids. Superb planted with a rich pink like 'Gertrude Jekyll'.

Rosa hugonis, 'Father Hugo's Rose'

Common Name: Species rose group

Flowers: Cultivated since 1899, when it was introduced from China. Bright yellow, single, up to 2″ (5cm) across. Extremely free-flowering, though not fragrant.

Leaves: Medium-size, lustrous, green; on thorny canes.

Habit: Up to 6′ (1.8m) tall. Bushy, arching.

Culture: Prefers full sun and good drainage in fertile, loam soil. Propagate by cuttings.

Season of Bloom: Spring.

Hardiness: Zones 5–9.

Uses: Good accent in mixed perennial and shrub borders. Suitable for rock gardens.

This vigorous plant has elegant arching canes that look especially beautiful planted on a terrace. When the canes drape down, they create a curtain of dazzling blossoms that seem to grab all the sunlight and reflect it right back to you.

Rosa 'Iceberg'

Common Name: Floribunda group

Flowers: Hybridized by the House of Kordes (Germany) and introduced in 1958. A cross between 'Robin Hood' and 'Virgo.' Pure white, double, fragrant, cup-shaped flowers measure up to 3″ (7.5cm) across, borne in dense clusters.

Leaves: Glossy, light green.

Habit: Up to 8′ (2.4m) tall; climbing 'Iceberg' grows to 12′ (3.7m) tall. Vigorous, upright, bushy; susceptible to black spot.

Culture: Prefers full sun and good drainage in fertile, loam soil. Best if given something to climb. Propagate by cuttings.

Season of Bloom: Early summer to late autumn.

Hardiness: Zones 5–9. Hardy.

Uses: Probably the most widely planted white rose in England and America. Especially popular trained up a trellis where it produces an avalanche of flowers in spring and good repeat bloom.

It is tough to decide whether to favor 'Iceberg' or the beautiful shrub rose, 'Nevada', when there is room for only one white rose in a garden. 'Nevada', a huge, single-flowered hybrid developed by a Spanish rosarian, needs space to spread—it's 12′ (3.7m) wide and high—and favors some kind of support. In large gardens or plantings with an all-white theme, use both.

Rosa
'La Reine Victoria'

Common Name:	Old garden rose group
Flowers:	Developed by J. Schwartz in 1872. Classified as a Bourbon rose, derived from crosses between China roses and Damask roses. Shell-pink, cupped, double 3″ (7.5cm) flowers resembling a poppy or ranunculus, have a wonderful apple fragrance. Prolific-flowering.
Leaves:	Semiglossy, light green.
Habit:	Up to 6′ (1.8m) tall. Upright, spreading. Thorny, disease-resistant canes.
Culture:	Prefers full sun in well-drained, fertile, loam soil. Best if given some support to climb. Propagate by cuttings.
Season of Bloom:	Late spring.
Hardiness:	Zones 5–8.
Uses:	Probably the most popular of all old garden roses. Spectacular trained on a wide trellis or high fence with the canes splayed out like a fan. A true, old-fashioned look and old-fashioned aroma highly prized by floral arrangers.

Since the introduction from England of David Austin's "English garden roses" with their "everblooming" quality, demand for some of the true antique garden roses may decline. It is doubtful, however, that the daintiness and heavy exhilarating aroma of 'La Reine Victoria' will ever be matched.

Rosa
'Peace'

Common Name:	Hybrid tea group
Flowers:	Hybridized by the house of Meilland (France) and introduced by Conard-Pyle Company (Pennsylvania) in 1945. A complicated cross involving 'Margaret McGredy' as one parent and a seedling from numerous crosses as the other parent. Light yellow with a blush of pink at the petal edges, up to 6″ (15cm) across, double, and slightly fragrant.
Leaves:	Glossy, dark green.
Habit:	Up to 6′ (1.8m) tall; climbing 'Peace' grows taller. Vigorous, erect, branching, disease-resistant.
Culture:	Prefers full sun and good drainage in fertile, loam soil. Propagate by cuttings.
Season of Bloom:	All summer to autumn frost.
Hardiness:	Zones 5–9.
Uses:	One of the world's most popular roses. Good garden accent in beds and borders, and also good for massing.

The flowers are exhibition-quality and prized for cutting. Plants were released for evaluation at the outbreak of World War II and could not be named or introduced to gardens until after peace was declared.

Rosa rugosa, Rugosa Rose, Turkestan Rose

Common Name: Species rose group

Flowers: Introduced in 1845 from northeastern Asia. Usually mauve, single, up to 3½″ (9cm) across, heavily fragrant, but there are double forms and a pure white. Produces large, decorative scarlet hips, the skins of which are edible and rich in vitamin C.

Leaves: Large, textured, glossy, dark green.

Habit: 4′–5′ (1.2–1.5m) tall. Dense, bushy, spreading.

Culture: Prefers full sun. Tolerates impoverished soil that provides drainage. Propagate by cuttings.

Season of Bloom: Continuous from late spring to autumn.

Hardiness: Zones 4–9.

Uses: Hedge, windbreak, and ground cover. Will grow on sand dunes and control soil erosion.

At home throughout North America, especially in coastal gardens. Numerous good hybrids of *R. rugosa* are offered by rosarians. The variety 'Hansa' is a large, fragrant, double form.

Skimmia japonica

Common Name: Japanese skimmia

Flowers: Native to Japan. Plant at least one male plant for every twelve female plants to produce a crop of attractive, bright red berries that appear in October. The beautiful flowers buds are rosy purple and open to fragrant, creamy white or pink-tinted blossoms.

Leaves: Evergreen, oblong, light green with lighter undersides. Larger and broader on the female plants.

Habit: 1′–5′ (.3–1.5m) tall with equal spread.

Culture: Prefers partial shade in well-drained, moist, humus-rich, acid soil. Propagate by seeds or cuttings.

Season of Bloom: Early to mid-spring.

Hardiness: Zones 6–9.

Uses: Extremely attractive in mixed foundation plantings, especially when combined with azaleas and rhododendrons. Good as a ground cover and in rock gardens.

Though valued for its flowers, female plants produce spectacular red berry displays in autumn.

Spiraea ×
vanhouttei

Common Name:	Bridal-wreath
Flowers:	A hybrid of species native to Japan. One of the best-flowering of the spiraeas. Tiny, flat clusters of white flowers bloom in profusion on arching branches.
Leaves:	Deciduous, dull green, turning from orange to red in autumn.
Habit:	6'–8' (1.8–2.4m) tall with a spread of 8'–10' (2.4–3m). Arching.
Culture:	Easy to grow. Prefers full sun in well-drained, fertile, loam soil. Propagate by cuttings.
Season of Bloom:	Mid- to late spring.
Hardiness:	Zones 5–10.
Uses:	Popular foundation accent and hedge.

Several other species of *Spiraea* are popular in home gardens. One of the best is *S. nipponica*, especially the variety 'Snowmound', producing a dazzling quantity of snow-white flowers on compact plants.

Syringa
vulgaris

Common Name:	Common lilac
Flowers:	Native to southern Europe. A beloved favorite for the heavenly scent of its flowers. White, lavender-blue, purple, or red flowers are borne upright in graceful clusters.
Leaves:	Deciduous, heart-shaped, semiglossy, bluish green.
Habit:	8'–15' (2.4–4.6m) tall with a spread of 6'–12' (1.8–3.7m). Erect, billowing.
Culture:	Prefers full sun in well-drained, humus-rich, sandy or loam soil. Prune after flowering to revitalize or shape plants. Propagate by cuttings.
Season of Bloom:	Late spring.
Hardiness:	Zones 3–7.
Uses:	Popular lawn accent. Suitable for foundation plantings. Flowers make attractive floral arrangements. Effective as a tall hedge.

Many other species are popular in home gardens. However, the most spectacular ornamental varieties are hybrids of *S. vulgaris,* especially varieties classified as French hybrids.

Tamarix ramosissima

Common Name: Five-stamen tamarisk

Flowers: Native to eastern Europe and Asia. Unusual, dense, fluffy clusters of pink flowers.

Leaves: Deciduous, lancelike, bright green; borne along arching branches that appear light and airy.

Habit: 10′–15′ (3–4.6m) tall. Upright, weeping.

Culture: Prefers full sun in well-drained, acid, sandy or loam soil. A hardy shrub adaptable to most environments including coastal areas. Easy to grow. Propagate by seeds or cuttings.

Season of Bloom: Late spring to midsummer.

Hardiness: Zones 2–10.

Uses: Attractive when cascading over walls or fences. Good in mixed shrub borders.

Frequently listed as *T. pentandra*, this is the hardiest of many species, some of which are highly drought-tolerant. Good companion to lilacs.

Trachelospermum jasminoides

Common Name: Star jasmine, confederate jasmine

Flowers: Native to China. Strong, sweet fragrance bursts forth from delicate, creamy white flowers arranged in small clusters.

Leaves: Evergreen, oval, pointed, glossy, dark green; hang from a trailing vine.

Habit: Up to 20′ (6m) tall. Vining.

Culture: Prefers full sun or partial shade in well-drained, moist, garden soil. Fast grower. Prune back to no more than one-third its size for shaping and revitalization. Propagate by cuttings.

Season of Bloom: Late spring to midsummer.

Hardiness: Zones 7–9.

Uses: Popular near entryways where fragrance can be enjoyed. Train on fences, poles, walls, and trellises. Combines well with trumpet creeper. Widely used in areas with mild winters as a ground cover, especially in shade.

In areas with freezing winters, this is a popular plant for growing indoors, especially trained up a wire cylinder in a greenhouse or sunroom.

Viburnum opulus 'Sterile'

Common Name: European snowball bush

Flowers: Native mostly to the Mediterranean region. Showy clusters of white flowers are occasionally tinged with pink as they mature. Makes a spectacular "snowball" flower display.

Leaves: Deciduous, maplelike, lustrous, light green; provide autumn interest of yellow, red, and purple colors.

Habit: 8'–12' (2.4–3.7m) tall with a spread of 10'–15' (3–4.6m). Upright, bushy.

Culture: Prefers full sun or partial shade in well-drained, garden soil. Propagate by seeds or cuttings.

Season of Bloom: Late spring.

Hardiness: Zones 3–8.

Uses: Attractive lawn accent. Good in mixed shrub borders. May also be grown as a screen; especially attractive planted against walls and fences so the flower sprays can sprawl over the edges. A beautiful companion to late-flowering azaleas, as pictured above.

The hardiest of the viburnums. There are many other *Viburnum* species and hybrids popular in home gardens, some of which produce bright red berry displays in the autumn. *V. dilatatum* and *V. trilobum* are two of the best berry bearers.

Vinca minor

Common Name: Common periwinkle, myrtle

Flowers: Native to Europe. Masses of showy, lilac-blue star flowers bloom continuously and are long-lasting. A hardy vine that is one of the best sellers in the nursery trade.

Leaves: Evergreen, oval, lustrous, dark green with prominent veins; on a twining, vining stem.

Habit: 3"–4" (7.5–10cm) tall with a spread of at least 36" (91cm). Vining.

Culture: Prefers full sun or partial shade in well-drained, moist, acid soil. Propagate by cuttings or division.

Season of Bloom: Early spring to early summer.

Hardiness: Zones 3–8.

Uses: A fabulous ground cover that will grow in areas where most plants have given up. Popular in containers and window boxes, to trail over the side.

A related species, *V. major*, is preferred in warm summer climates since it is slightly larger-flowered; it is not reliably hardy above zone 7. Both of these vincas have escaped into the wild and naturalized freely in woodland throughout North America.

Weigela
florida

**Common
Name:**   Weigela

Flowers: Native to Japan. The spectacular masses of
lovely white, purplish pink, or red trumpet-
shaped flowers make this shrub a show-
stopper.

Leaves: Deciduous, oval, coarse, light green; on
weeping branches. Prune branches back after
flowering to revitalize each year.

Habit: 6′–9′ (1.8–2.7m) tall with a spread of 9′–12′
(2.7–3.7m). Upright, bushy.

Culture: Prefers full sun or partial shade in well-
drained, sandy or loam soil. Propagate by
softwood cuttings in summer.

**Season
of Bloom:**   Mid- to late spring.

Hardiness: Zones 5–8.

Uses: Good background for perennial borders.
Effective accent in mixed borders.

Many varieties and hybrids are available. 'Bristol
Ruby' is a dark ruby-red; 'Dropmore Pink' is a good
deep pink form; 'Variegata' is a lovely rose-pink with
attractive ivory white edging to the leaves.

Wisteria
floribunda

**Common
Name:**   Japanese wisteria

Flowers: Native to Japan. Fragrant flowers are violet-
blue or white and are borne on hanging
clusters.

Leaves: Deciduous, long, oval, light green; divided into
leaflets. Prune and train plant to desired size
and shape by cutting back to the main stems.

Habit: Up to 30″ (9.4m) tall. Vining. This plant is so
versatile that it can be treated as a tree, shrub,
or vine.

Culture: Prefers full sun in well-drained, humus-rich,
garden soil. Propagate by seeds.

**Season
of Bloom:**   Spring.

Hardiness: Zones 5–10.

Uses: Attractive when allowed to sprawl on walls,
arbors, and trellises.

W. sinensis (Chinese wisteria) is similar but generally
not as spectacular. Either is sensational when
combined with flowering dogwoods and azaleas.

Trees

Aesculus ×
carnea

**Common
Name:** Red horse chestnut

Flowers: Developed from species native to North
America. One of the smaller horse chestnuts
that are adaptable to confined spaces. It offers
a good winter silhouette, upright clusters of
pink to rosy red flowers in spring. The dark
brown fruit has a prickly round casing.

Leaves: Palm-shaped, coarsely toothed. Lustrous, dark
green, turning bright orange in fall. The gray
bark is fissured.

Habit: 30'–40' (9.4–12m) tall with equal spread.
Pyramidal when young, becoming rounded
with age.

Culture: Prefers full sun or light shade in moist, deep,
fertile soil. Leaf scorch occurs if soil dries out.
Propagate by grafting or budding.

**Season
of Bloom:** Mid-spring.

Hardiness: Zones 4–8.

Uses: Excellent lawn or street tree where space is
limited. Caution: leaves and fruit are
poisonous.

Similar to *A. pavia* (red buckeye) from which it was
hybridized.

Albizia
julibrissin

**Common
Name:** Silk tree

Flowers: Native to China. Silky, pink flower plumes
resembling a powderpuff are borne in clusters,
followed by beanlike brown pods.

Leaves: Feathery, fernlike, resembling mimosa; light to
mid-green. Each board leaf is composed of
multiple overlapping leaflets.

Habit: Up to 40' (12m) tall with a spreading mounded
canopy that casts light shade, enabling grass to
grow up to the trunk.

Culture: Prefers full sun, good drainage. Tolerates hot,
dry summers, poor sandy soil. Propagate by
seeds.

**Season
of Bloom:** Summer.

Hardiness: Zones 6–10.

Uses: Good lawn highlight for areas with hot, dry
summers. Creates a tropical effect. Excellent
for shading a patio.

The varieties 'Rosea' (bright pink) and 'Charlotte' (deep
pink) are especially good.

Amelanchier
arborea

Common Name:	Serviceberry
Flowers:	Native to North America. Grown for its early spring–flowering and all-season interest. Attractive, star-shaped, white flowers are followed by sweet, edible, blueberrylike purple berries that are hidden beneath leaves and much loved by birds.
Leaves:	Immature leaves are purplish and downy, turn smooth and green when they mature, and yellow, orange, or red in autumn. The gray bark is covered with interesting longitudinal fissures.
Habit:	15'–25' (4.6–7.6m) tall with equal spread. Fine-textured, twiggy; grows more rounded with age.
Culture:	Prefers full sun or partial shade in well-drained, moist, sandy or loam soil. Propagate by seeds.
Season of Bloom:	Mid-spring.
Hardiness:	Zones 4–9.
Uses:	Beautiful set against dark evergreens. Effective as an understory planting beneath larger trees or at the edge of a woodland.

Good companion to flowering pink quince and yellow forsythia, which bloom at the same time.

Cercis
canadensis

Common Name:	Redbud
Flowers:	Native to North America. Beautiful, rosy-pink, pealike blooms stud the bare branches in spring, followed by beanlike pods that persist through winter.
Leaves:	Heart-shaped, green, turning yellow in autumn. The tree bark is smooth, dark brown.
Habit:	20'–30' (6–9.4m) tall with a spread of 25'–35' (7.6–10.7m). Flat-topped, somewhat spreading.
Culture:	Prefers light shade in either acid or alkaline soil. Can handle full sun if not in stressful conditions. Propagate by seeds.
Season of Bloom:	Mid-spring.
Hardiness:	Zones 5–9.
Uses:	Perfect for understory or woodland plantings. Combines well with other native plants including dogwoods. Effective planted in groves.

'Alba' is a white-flowered form; 'Forest pansy' has decorative purple leaves and pink flowers.

Chionanthus virginicus

Common Name:	Old-man's-beard, fringe tree
Flowers:	Native to eastern North America. Masses of white, straplike petals are borne in clusters.
Leaves:	Oval, bright green.
Habit:	Up to 40' (12m) tall. Mounded crown, shrublike when young, growing into a handsome tree. Billowing appearance when in bloom.
Culture:	Prefers full sun, good drainage, and fertile soil. Propagate by seeds and cuttings.
Season of Bloom:	Spring.
Hardiness:	Zones 6–8.
Uses:	Good lawn highlight.

A related species, *C. retusus* (Chinese fringe tree) is also a beautiful small tree, a good companion to azaleas and early-flowering rhododendrons.

Cornus florida

Common Name:	Flowering dogwood
Flowers:	Native to the eastern United States, this dogwood is smaller and easier to grow than its Pacific Northwest counterpart, *C. nuttallii*. The buttonlike buds that appear near the end of the stems open into showy, butterflylike white bracts. The true flowers are greenish white to yellow and have little ornamental value. As they ripen in August and September, clusters of glossy red berries are eaten by birds.
Leaves:	Dark green, with six to seven pairs of prominent veins. Leaves turn an attractive red to reddish purple in autumn.
Habit:	20'–25' (6–7.6m) tall with a spread of 25'–30' (7.6–9.4m). Low-layered, horizontal branching.
Culture:	Prefers light shade in well-drained, moist, humus-rich, acid soil. Intolerant of drought and high winds. Propagate by seeds and softwood cuttings.
Season of Bloom:	Mid-spring.
Hardiness:	Zones 6–9.
Uses:	Lovely in a shady, wooded area or in the garden as an accent plant. Sensational near the edges of woods, protected by the shade of taller trees.

'Pluribracteata' is a sensational double-flowered variety; 'Cherokee Chief' a rich ruby red; and 'Fragrant Cloud' a slightly fragrant white.

Cornus
kousa

**Common
Name:**   Kousa, Japanese flowering dogwood

Flowers: Native to Japan. Blooms later and longer than other dogwoods and has a pleasing winter effect. The showy white bracts are pointed and stand erect above the leaves. In late August through October, red, edible stone fruit hangs from the branches.

Leaves: Sharply pointed, glossy, medium green, with wavy leaf margins. Turn a yellow and scarlet in autumn. Bark exfoliates with age, producing patches of gray, tan, and brown.

Habit: 25'–30' (7.6–9.4m) tall with equal spread. Upright, rounded shape when young, spreading horizontally with age.

Culture: Prefers full sun in well-drained, acid soil. Prune to shape. Propagate by seeds.

**Season
of Bloom:**   Mid- to late spring.

Hardiness: Zones 5–8.

Uses: Beautiful as a small accent tree or multi-stemmed shrub.

'Milky Way' is an extremely free-flowering variety. This tree does not have the disease problems of *C. florida*. Though not as early-flowering, the floral display can be equally spectacular.

Cornus
mas

**Common
Name:**   Cornelian cherry

Flowers: Native to Europe and Asia. Profuse clusters of yellow blossoms cover the naked branches in early spring. Bright red berries follow in September.

Leaves: Deciduous, spear-shaped, green. Bark is shaggy, revealing patches of gray and brown.

Habit: Up to 15' (4.6m) tall with a spread of 15'–20' (4.6–6m). Rounded, low-branching.

Culture: Prefers partial shade in well-drained, moist, acid soil. Tolerates alkaline soil. Propagate by seeds.

**Season
of Bloom:**   Late winter to early spring. One of the earliest dogwoods to bloom.

Hardiness: Zones 4–8.

Uses: Low-branching, multistemmed shrub that can be pruned into a small tree. Attractive lawn accent.

A related species, *C. officinalis*, blooms earlier and is more free-flowering, but specimens are hard to find.

Cotinus coggygria

Common Name: Smoke tree

Flowers: Native to southern Europe and Asia. Grown for its cloak of unusual clusters of fluffy cream, pink, or purple flower stems that give the appearance of smoke when viewed from a distance. The small, purplish red fruit is not very ornamental.

Leaves: Oval, bluish green, turning brilliant orange-red in autumn. Mature brown or purplish bark with small fissures is beautiful.

Habit: 10'–15' (3–4.6m) tall with a spread of 10'–20' (3–6m). Upright, spreading, billowing.

Culture: Prefers full sun and good drainage in sandy or loam soil. Propagate by seeds and softwood cuttings.

Season of Bloom: Flowers bloom early summer, but the main showy puffs of "smoke" appear midsummer to early autumn.

Hardiness: Zones 5–8.

Uses: Attractive accent tree. Use as a background screen.

'Royal Purple' has rich maroon-purple leaves and deep purple flowers.

Crataegus oxyacantha, C. laevigata

Common Name: English hawthorn

Flowers: Native to Europe. Although this is one of the loveliest of hawthorns, grown for its crimson flowers and attractive red fruit in autumn, *C. laevigata* cultivars are generally the ones planted. Try 'Paul's Scarlet' for double red flowers or 'Crimson Cloud' for single, bright red blooms with a white, star-shaped center.

Leaves: Dark green on thorny branches. No autumn color. Brown bark.

Habit: 15'–20' (4.6–6m) tall with a spread of 12'–20' (5.7–6m). Rounded, with ascending branches.

Culture: Prefers full sun in well-drained, slightly acid soil. Tolerates drought, cold spells, and pollution. Propagate by seeds or root cuttings.

Season of Bloom: Mid- to late spring.

Hardiness: Zones 4–7.

Uses: Colorful lawn or street tree. Use to shade a patio.

The Washington hawthorn (*C. phaenopyrum*) is a beautiful round-headed tree from the Pacific Northwest, with white flowers and an attractive berry display.

Davidia
involucrata

**Common
Name:** Dove tree

Flowers: Native to China. Grown for its exotic blooms, which are actually white flower bracts that measure 3″–4″ (7.5–10cm) at the top and 6 inches (15cm) long. When bracts flower, they resemble a flock of doves resting among the bright green leaves. Closely related to dogwoods.

Leaves: Clean-looking, heart-shaped, bright green; strongly veined and toothed, silky undersides. No autumn color. Attractive, coarse, reddish brown bark exfoliates with age.

Habit: Up to 30′ (9.4m) tall with a spread of 20′–30′ (6–9.4m). Broad, pyramidal.

Culture: Prefers light shade in well-drained, moist, humus-rich soil. Propagate by seeds.

**Season
of Bloom:** Mid-spring.

Hardiness: Zones 6–8.

Uses: A good understory tree that contrasts dramatically against a backdrop of dark conifer trees. Use as a lawn highlight.

Not widely offered by garden centers; the best sources are large tree nurseries and botanical gardens, which often make specimens available during plant sales.

Franklinia
alatamaha

**Common
Name:** Franklin tree

Flowers: Native to Georgia (U.S.A.). One of the few late summer-flowering trees; blooms sometimes compete with autumn foliage color. Tight, rounded buds open into cup-shaped, white flowers with a center of yellow stamens.

Leaves: Oblong, dark green, turning orange-red in autumn. The gray bark is striped with reddish brown fissures.

Habit: 20′–25′ (6–7.6m) tall with a spread of 15′ (4.6m). Upright, spreading, with some multiple stems.

Culture: Prefers full sun in well-drained, moist, acid soil. Needs partial shade in hot climates. Propagate by seeds and softwood cuttings.

**Season
of Bloom:** Late summer to early autumn.

Hardiness: Zones 5–8.

Uses: Interesting lawn or patio tree, but thrives only where summers are usually warm and sunny.

Attempts are being made to select for larger flowers and a more free-flowering characteristic. The tree is extinct in the wild, believed to have disappeared when a root disease (introduced by planting cotton in the southern United States) killed off the native stands.

Koelreuteria paniculata

Common Name:	Varnish tree, golden-rain tree
Flowers:	Native to China. Profuse yellow flower clusters bloom in early summer when few other trees are in bloom. Attractive, papery seed pods follow.
Leaves:	Toothed, bright green, turning a dull yellow in autumn. Light brown bark becomes ridged in older trees.
Habit:	30'–35' (9.4–10.7m) tall with equal spread. Rounded, billowing.
Culture:	Fast-growing. Prefers full sun in well-drained, sandy or loam soil. Tolerates drought, wind, and pollution. Propagate by seeds and cuttings.
Season of Bloom:	Early to midsummer.
Hardiness:	Zones 5–9.
Uses:	Valued as a street or lawn tree in difficult soils and conditions.

A related species, *K. bipinnata,* is similar but prefers a Mediterranean climate. Its decorative seed pods turn an attractive pink rather than russet-brown.

Laburnum × watereri

Common Name:	Golden-chain tree
Flowers:	Native to Europe. Bright, dangling, yellow chains of flowers provide a sunny relief from the dreary reminder of winter. Pods follow in October.
Leaves:	Cloverlike, light green. No autumn color. Olive-green bark.
Habit:	15' (4.6m) tall with a spread of 5'–8' (1.5–2.4m). Upright, columnar.
Culture:	Easy to grow. Prefers light shade in well-drained, moist soil, but will grow in most soils as long as they are not waterlogged. Avoid crowding and direct late-afternoon sun. Prune after flowering. Propagate by seeds.
Season of Bloom:	Late spring.
Hardiness:	Zones 5–7.
Uses:	A great specimen tree or multistemmed shrub. Magnificent planted with purple irises or among peonies. Caution: all parts are poisonous.

The variety 'Vossii' is an extremely free-flowering form. This is the preferred form for creating a *Laburnum* tunnel, whereby trees are planted close together in parallel lines so their branches knit together and produce a flowering canopy.

Lagerstroemia indica

Common Name: Crape myrtle

Flowers: Native to India. Popular in areas with warm, sunny summers. Admired for its profuse, crinkled, white, pink, or lavender flowers.

Leaves: Immature leaves are reddish, turning yellow, orange, or red in autumn. Bark is gray with some exfoliation revealing fresh white patches.

Habit: 12'–20' (3.7–6m) tall with a spread of 8'–12' (2.4–3.7m). Branching.

Culture: Prefers full sun in sandy or loam soil that is rich in peat moss or leaf mold. Tolerates strong heat and drought. Prune to shape as a shrub or small tree. Propagate by cuttings.

Season of Bloom: Mid- to late summer.

Hardiness: Zones 7–10.

Uses: Good lawn accent and informal screen or hedge. Also a good container plant.

A series of hybrids with names of Indian tribes has been introduced by the United States National Arboretum. They are hardy into zone 6. They may winter-kill to the roots in severe winters but will produce vigorous new flowering shoots in spring. These hybrids generally flower the first year, even from rooted cuttings.

Magnolia × soulangiana

Common Name: Saucer magnolia

Flowers: Native to China. Valued for its giant, showy, creamy white, pink, or purple, saucer-shaped flowers. Rough, conelike fruit follows bloom.

Leaves: Oblong, pointed, green, turning brown in autumn. Bark is smooth and silvery gray.

Habit: Up to 30' (9.4m) tall with a spread of 30'–35' (9.4–10.7m). Low branching, spreading.

Culture: Prefers full sun in moist, but well-drained, deep, slightly acid soil. Tolerates heat and air pollution. Propagate by softwood cuttings in mid-June.

Season of Bloom: Mid- to late spring and intermittently throughout the summer.

Hardiness: Zones 4–9.

Uses: Beautiful lawn accent.

A series of hybrids from the United States National Arboretum—all with girls' names—are extremely free-flowering in a bold range of colors, including a creamy yellow ('Ann') and a glowing deep pink ('Susan').

Magnolia
virginiana

**Common
Name:**   Sweet bay

Flowers: Native to North America. Flowers in late
spring when most trees have finished
blooming. The white lemon-scented flowers
resemble small saucer magnolias. Beautiful
dark red fruit follows, splitting in August to
reveal bright red seeds.

Leaves: Deciduous to semievergreen. Dark green with
silvery undersides grow on green twigs, turn
crimson in autumn. Older bark is gray.

Habit: 20'–35' (6–10.7m) tall with a spread of 10'–20'
(3–6m). Upright, pyramidal, multistemmed.

Culture: Prefers full sun in moist soil. Tolerates shade.
Intolerant of drought. Propagate by softwood
cuttings.

**Season
of Bloom:**   Summer.

Hardiness: Zones 5–9.

Uses: Gorgeous patio or garden tree. Spectacular
next to a pool or inside an enclosed atrium.

Attempts are being made to develop a true evergreen
variety. The flowers are exquisite in floral arrangements.
Prized for small-space gardens.

Malus
floribunda

**Common
Name:**   Showy crab apple

Flowers: Native to Japan. Bred to enhance their
flowering ability, the round minature apples
now serve mostly for ornamental purposes. An
outstanding characteristic of *M. floribunda* is
its pleasing winter silhouette. Another fine
feature includes the show of dark pinkish red
buds opening into fragrant light pink flowers
that slowly fade to white.

Leaves: Lancelike, bright green. Poor autumn color.

Habit: 25'–30' (7.6–9.5m) tall, with a spread of 35'
(10.7m). Rounded, wide-spreading, densely
branched.

Culture: Crab apples are the hardiest and easiest to
grow of all the small flowering trees. Prefers
full sun in well-drained, moist, acid soil. Needs
room and space. Prune young trees in early
spring or winter to maintain a pleasing shape.
Propagate by seeds.

**Season
of Bloom:**   Mid-spring.

Hardiness: Zones 4–8.

Uses: A heavy bloomer that holds its fruit well into
October. Makes a fine lawn accent.

In addition to species like *M. floribunda,* there are
many hybrid crab apples, some with deep pink and
ruby-red flowers. A small grove of trees composed of
white, pink, and red flowering kinds is especially
attractive.

Malus 'Red Jade'

Common Name: Weeping crab apple

Flowers: A mutation discovered at the New York Botanical Garden. Strikingly attractive. Profuse, deep pink flowers are followed by ruby-red fruits.

Leaves: Deep green. No autumn color.

Habit: 15′ (4.6m) tall with equal spread. Weeping.

Culture: Prefers full sun in well-drained, moist, acid soil. Susceptible to fire blight. Propagate by cuttings.

Season of Bloom: Mid- to late spring, with red fruits ripening in September and October.

Hardiness: Zones 4–8.

Uses: Good lawn accent. Grow in rows to line driveways or walkways. Beautiful as the focal point in a bulb garden.

Contrasts well with 'Dorothea', a yellow-fruited crab apple that can be planted as a background. 'Red Jade' is suitable for growing in containers.

Prunus × yedoensis

Common Name: Yoshino cherry

Flowers: Native to Japan. Popular for its spectacular early-spring flower display. These are the famous cherry trees surrounding the Tidal Basin in Washington, D.C. Sumptuous, slightly fragrant, single, white to pink flowers cover the tree like a billowing cloud.

Leaves: Oval, toothed, green, turning yellow in autumn. Bark is metallic gray with horizontal darker markings called lenticels.

Habit: 30′–35′ (9.4–10.7m) tall with equal spread. Flat-topped, spreading, good horizontal branch structure.

Culture: Prefers full sun in well-drained, moist, humus-rich soil. Propagate by seeds or softwood cuttings.

Season of Bloom: Early to mid-spring.

Hardiness: Zones 6–8.

Uses: A lovely cherry tree that has fewer problems with insects and diseases than most other varieties. Plant alone as a lawn accent or in parallel lines to create an avenue.

There is a weeping form, 'Shidare', and a pink form, 'Shell Pink', though the regular white is the most widely available.

Pyrus
calleryana

Common Name:	Callery pear
Flowers:	Native to northern China. Gorgeous bursts of heavy white flowers, resembling crab apple blossoms, blanket this tree in spring.
Leaves:	Oval, serrated, glossy, dark green, turning to a lustrous, scarlet to purple color in autumn. Clusters of small, round, brown fruits sometimes develop in autumn.
Habit:	30'–40' (9.4–12m) tall, spread of 20'–30' (6–9.4m). Pyramidal form begins spreading as the tree ages.
Culture:	Prefers full sun in well-drained, sandy or loam soil. Adaptable to most soil conditions. Propagate by softwood cuttings.
Season of Bloom:	Mid- to late spring.
Hardiness:	Zones 4–8.
Uses:	Popular street tree since it tolerates polluted air. Attractive as a lawn accent.

The original 'Bradford Pear'—a popular variety of *P. calleryana*—is not long-lived on account of susceptibility to storm damage. Newer varieties such as 'Chanticleer' have a stronger branch structure less prone to damage.

Styrax
japonica

Common Name:	Japanese snowbell
Flowers:	Native to Japan. An attractively shaped tree to walk under as the pendulous chains of white bell flowers are best observed from directly underneath the tree. A grayish green stone fruit follows in August.
Leaves:	Small, lancelike, serrated, green. Poor autumn color. Handsome grayish brown bark is marked by fissures.
Habit:	Up to 30' (9.4m) tall with equal spread. Broad, spreading, horizontal.
Culture:	Prefers full sun or partial shade in moist but well-drained, humus-rich soil. Propagate by seeds or softwood cuttings.
Season of Bloom:	Late spring to early summer.
Hardiness:	Zones 5–9.
Uses:	Striking lawn accent.

'Pendula' is a beautiful weeping variety; 'Rosea' a pale pink. When the flowers fall, they carpet the ground like a galaxy of stars. In Japan the trees are planted on hummocks of moss so the fallen white blossoms are accentuated.

Hardiness Zones

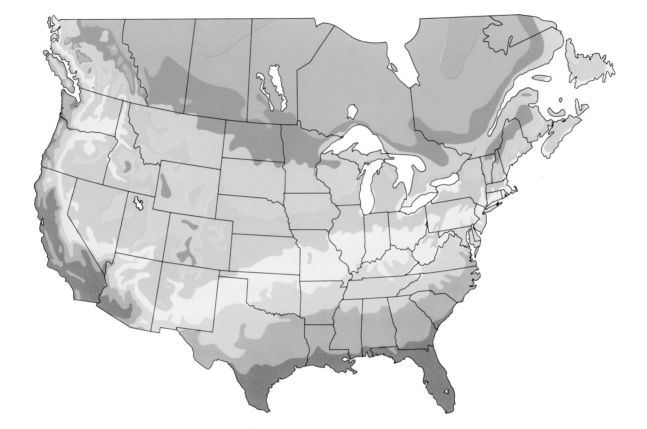

RANGE OF AVERAGE ANNUAL MINIMUM
TEMPERATURES FOR EACH ZONE

ZONE 1	BELOW –50° F	(–45° C)
ZONE 2	–50° TO –40°	(–45° to –40°)
ZONE 3	–40° TO –30°	(–40° to –34°)
ZONE 4	–30° TO –20°	(–34° to –28°)
ZONE 5	–20° TO –10°	(–28° to –23°)
ZONE 6	–10° TO 0°	(–23° to –17°)
ZONE 7	0° TO 10°	(–17° to –12°)
ZONE 8	10° TO 20°	(–12° to –6°)
ZONE 9	20° TO 30°	(–6° to –1°)
ZONE 10	30° TO 40°	(–1° to 4°)

Index